Around the World in 80 Years:

The Oldest Man to Sail Alone Around the World - Twice!

Harry L. Heckel, Jr.

With Florence Heckel Russell

Rambling Star

An Imprint of Blue Grande Publishing

Published by Rambling Star Publishing

Inscription

I cannot rest from travel; I will drink
Life to the lees. All times I have enjoy'd
Greatly, have suffer'd greatly, both with those
That loved me, and alone; on shore, and when
Thro' scudding drifts the rainy Hyades
Vext the dim sea.

-Alfred Lord Tennyson, *Ulysses*

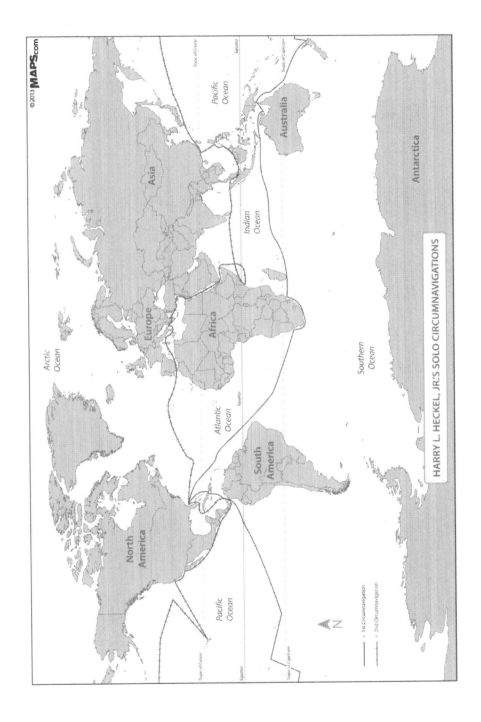

HARRY L. HECKEL, JR.'S SOLO CIRCUMNAVIGATIONS

—— = 1st Circumnavigation

---- = 2nd Circumnavigation

©2013 MAPS.com

Harry Heckel, Jr. aboard *Idle Queen*, c. 2000

Idle Queen, Kagoshima, Japan, 2001

Faith S. Heckel on *Idle Queen*

Table of Contents

Chapter 1: I Become a Solo Sailor 11
Chapter 2: Mission Accomplished 18
Chapter 3: I Lose My Boat 30
Chapter 4: A Stop in Galapagos 36
Chapter 5: Island Hopping across the Pacific 39
Chapter 6: I Build a Boat 50
Chapter 7: *Idle Queen's* Maiden Voyage, Part 1 57
Chapter 8: *Idle Queen's* Maiden Voyage, Part 2 67
Chapter 9: No Going Back...76
Chapter 10: Cruising Down Under 84
Chapter 11: The Wild Coast..92
Chapter 12: Medical Emergency 103
Chapter 13: I Set Out Again 108
Chapter 14: Wintering in Spain 112
Chapter 15: Sailing the Mediterranean 117
Chapter 16: Turkish Delight 124
Chapter 17: The Hostile and the Hospitable.......................................133
Chapter 18: Wild Pirates, Wild Animals, Mad Bombers 144
Chapter 19: Of Sails and Sailors 152
Chapter 20: Exploring Southeast Asia with Capt'n..............................157
Chapter 21: From Calming Waters to Killing Fields............................168
Chapter 22: The Scrutable East...173
Chapter 23: My Year in Japan...184
Chapter 24: Anatomy of a Rescue 198
Chapter 25: Older But No Wiser: Forging On....................................208
Epilogue 219
Afterword...221

Chapter 1

I Become a Solo Sailor

The ocean has always been a salve to my soul…
-Jimmy Buffet

I didn't plan to sail around the world. I merely planned to travel in retirement.

I took early retirement from Allied Chemical at the age of fifty-six. I started working for the company right after graduating from Berkeley with a Ph.D. in chemistry. I stayed with them my entire career. Upon retirement, Faido and I moved onto our 29-foot sailboat, the first *Idle Queen*. I named the boat from the poem *Ulysses* by Alfred Lord Tennyson. Ulysses was an idle king who sailed the seas. Faido and I planned to emulate him. I thought if there were an idle king there should be an idle queen. Faido was quick to point out, when explaining the name, that idle queen did not mean lazy wife.

Faido and I sailed our home down both U.S. coasts, into the Caribbean, through the Panama Canal, out into the Pacific. Our attempt to sail across the Atlantic to Europe was less successful. In Bermuda Faido found a lump in her breast. We immediately sailed back to the mainland for treatment. Afterward, we did make it to Europe, but this time we flew.

Within five years, Faido's cancer returned. Given six months to live, Faido lasted nine. For those final months, we left the boat in Florida and rented an apartment in Richmond, Virginia. We had raised our four children in Virginia. Two of them, and numerous friends, were still there. I thought the familiar surroundings would comfort Faido. I believe they made her final months more bearable for us both. Faido died at the age of sixty-nine, after forty-five years of marriage.

After her death, I returned to *Idle Queen*. I climbed aboard and stood several minutes in the cockpit, getting used to the idea, then walked below. Faido's presence filled the cabin: her books piled on the dinette, a quilt she'd made thrown over the bunk. In her wedding gown, she smiled at me from a picture on the bulkhead. After a moment, I stirred myself and started putting the boat in order.

The thirty-two foot boat now seemed too big for one person. I felt adrift, uninterested in sailing, yet unable to sit still. I threw myself into boat cleaning. I went through Faido's clothes and possessions and mementoes. I divided them among the four children, boxed them up, and mailed them off. Jack and Maggie Farrington drove me to the post office.

Jack and Maggie were docked near me at Green Cove Springs Marina. Jack, a POW in World War II, was a laid-back man, prone to practical jokes. Maggie was a cheerful buxom brunette who worked as a dental assistant. They kept an eye on me, had me over for dinner, and drove me on my errands. In February 1990, eight months after Faido's death, they took me out for my birthday. I turned seventy-four. My age and the realization that time was passing motivated me. I knew I had to keep moving or I would stop. I needed something to look forward to, some personal challenge. I decided to sail solo across an ocean.

I provisioned *Idle Queen*, threw off the lines, and headed north.

I stopped in Elizabeth City, North Carolina, one of Faido's and my favorite anchorages along the Intracoastal Waterway. The last time Faido and I docked here we were on our way to Bermuda in our failed attempt to sail across the Atlantic Ocean.

I thought I'd try that sail again, but I was in no hurry. I felt uneasy attempting it. What if I tried and failed? My future sails would be limited and uninspired, over territory I had traversed many times before. That future looked bleak, and I was afraid to face it.

One day, as I sat procrastinating, a young woman stopped by the boat. A slim blonde in her mid-thirties, Beth was a photographer for the local paper. She asked if I would take her out in *Idle Queen* so she could photograph Elizabeth City's skyline. I wasn't busy at the moment, so I did. That was the first of several outings. Then Beth asked if I would teach her to sail. I enjoyed those lessons. They made me feel youthful yet mature. During these lessons, Beth learned of my plans to sail to Bermuda. Sensing my reluctance, she volunteered to be my crew. She could use her vacation time and take pictures for the newspaper. My procrastination was over.

Bermuda lies approximately 600 miles off the Atlantic coast, about equidistant from points along the arc from New England to Hatteras. This British colony comprises many small, and a few large, islands, but only about twenty square miles in all. In spring and early summer, when sea winds are light and warm, the island becomes a goal for coastal yachtsmen who want to prove they are blue water sailors.

Beth and I had a fast, uneventful, and uneasy sail. Beth thought the trip would be like a relaxing cruise. I thought Beth would be like Faido, anticipating the wind and automatically adjusting the sails. We were both disappointed and relieved when we docked. We left Elizabeth City in mid-May. We reached St. Georges on 1 June, the one-year anniversary of Faido's death.

After we cleared Customs, we celebrated with a Yorkshire bitter at the seawall restaurant. St. Georges was filled with itinerant small boat sailors celebrating arrivals or departures. We spent the next week remarking on the British accents, Bermuda shorts, the gold-platers moored to buoys in Hamilton Harbor, and the relaxed attitude of natives and tourists alike.

One day a sailor stopped on the pier to admire *Idle Queen*. To Lee Werth, a bespectacled philosophy professor from Cleveland, she looked like his old Tahiti ketch. An amiable man, Lee joined us when Beth and I went out in the evenings. He introduced himself as Beth's father and me as her grandfather. We were too old to keep up with Beth, though. One night we left her in a bar teaching the natives the Electric Slide. A few days later, her vacation over, Beth flew home.

The following evening, over drinks, Lee asked my plans.

"To sail solo across the rest of the Atlantic," I said. I sipped my drink. "I don't know if I can," I added.

By last call, Lee, and the rum, convinced me to try. I decided to winter in Portugal. Faido had been particularly fond of Portugal.

At dawn on 30 June I gritted my teeth and set sail. It was like diving into ice water. The wind and rain were relentless. Salt spray found all the weak seams in my foul weather gear. After three days of being cold and wet, I wondered if I'd made a mistake setting out on this caper. I sat on the settee in wet clothes and mended a twelve-inch rip in a staysail panel. Piles of damp clothing lay about the cabin. One pile sat in the middle of my berth.

The low pressure system, scheduled to move southwest, had not done so. My sophisticated new autopilot, which keeps the boat on course when I'm not on watch, stopped working at random times. Forced to make my own autopilot, I ran lines from the jib to the tiller and bungee-corded the tiller to my desired course. This complicated sheet-to-tiller system of sails and control lines allows the boat to steer herself. With two crewmembers it works well enough and saves effort. With only one crew, it requires a daunting amount of attention.

On the fourth day, the sun appeared. The Navico autopilot once again operated. The wind was high and favorable in direction. As *Idle Queen* pounded along at great speed, I felt deep satisfaction, the previous days' frustrations forgotten. In mid-morning the Navico jammed. I couldn't fix it. I dug out my old and much-maligned First Mate autopilot. This unit always exhibited a mind of its own, frequently making course changes to fit its own view of the proper route. This phenomenon caused some scary times on inland waters. I thought it might do well enough at sea, and it did. Two days later, the First Mate stopped holding course. I took it apart, made adjustments to the feedback system, and it worked fine for the rest of the trip.

Through the first half of this passage I made fine progress: 855 miles in seven days. At one point, twelve-foot seas pushed me on. Later, I sailed in too close to the Azores high and ran out of wind. It took ten days for the first 1150 miles of the trip and ten days for the last 750 miles. I motored during daylight hours only, and not always then; my fuel supply is good for only a few hundred miles. On several occasions, I lay all night with the sails down.

Even windless, I never thought that I couldn't make it. The bad weather at the start of the trip seemed like an initiation into solo sailing. I had handled it. I could handle anything else that came, even the lulls.

My disappointing progress was offset by the endless enjoyment of observing wildlife. I found Bermuda tropic birds out of the tropics, as far north as thirty-seven and a half degrees. Near the islands, shearwaters and petrels abounded. One lonely pomarine skua investigated me, but found nothing edible. One morning I found a ten-inch flying fish on deck, the biggest I've ever seen, and a welcome change from breakfast cereal.

I saw only four ships. From one, the friendly tanker *Poncherie Coast*, I received position and weather reports. This was several years before I joined the greater sailing community and equipped the boat with a GPS. To find my position in the world, I took sextant sights of the sun and worked up the numbers on a chart. This exercise gave me a feeling of affinity with earlier sailors. I thought it might keep my mind sharp.

Eighteen days after leaving Bermuda I reached a point just south of Flores in the Azores, but not close enough for me to see the island.

I thought briefly about changing course to pay my respects to that old English seadog, Sir Richard Grenville and his amazing battle here with the Spanish, but I sailed on. That same day I heard a radio station broadcasting from Horta in the Azores. The completion of my longest ocean passage was in hearing, if not in sight.

On the evening of the nineteenth day I sighted the sharp peak of active volcano Ponta do Pico poking up well above the heat haze. I had reached the Azores! I was tired but elated. I had sailed across an ocean alone! That night I lay ahull offshore in a dead calm, and the next morning, with a rising feeling of excitement, I motored in.

The islands of Faial and Pico are as beautiful as any I've seen. The lower slopes along the southwest coast of high and mildly rugged Faial are covered with small green fields separated by hedgerows. Clusters of white houses with red roofs are punctuated by church spires. Joaquin Miller, the poet, had his color wrong: "Behind him lay the gray Azores." No gray here.

Horta (garden) was laid out before the day of the automobile, but the auto found Horta. The narrow brick-paved streets are a challenge to car and pedestrian. I thought it strange that there were no bicycles and few motor scooters; the hill roads must be too steep. The tessellated sidewalks are all laid in black and white one inch by two inch smooth rock blocks. Where do people find time to do this? The town is old, but its two- and three-story buildings are not architecturally interesting.

The people are pure Portuguese. The islands were uninhabited when discovered and settled by Portuguese explorers in the fifteenth century. The gloomy aspect attributed to the natives did not penetrate to the happy crowd around the marina.

The tourist group, such as it is, is dominated by the yachting set. The little municipal marina is low cost and prices in town meet U.S. standards. Eighty-odd boats from all over the world fill the docks. Americans are in the minority. Many acquaintances, eating and drinking buddies from Bermuda days, are here. The newly arrived often made themselves conspicuous in the bar. Portuguese beer has roughly twice the alcohol content of American beer. Those unaware of this difference provide entertainment for the locals.

Sandy and Mary, the young Canadian couple off *Keno*, whom I first met in Elizabeth City, showed me around the town. Sandy is a tall athletic man who played basketball in college and now teaches. Mary is a social worker, bright and good-natured. We took a taxi up into the hills where the view is panoramic and spectacular. I wished Faido were here to see it. With Sandy and Mary I attended fado concerts and enjoyed the large get-togethers at the marina restaurant. Associating with the couple, I felt less secluded.

The island of Pico lies just across the Canal do Faial from Horta. A half-hour ferry run got me to the port of Madalena. The island is quite different from Faial. In the eighteenth century volcanic eruptions left the area covered with chunks of frozen lava. The ground has since been cleared, at least on the flatter slopes, by piling these rocks into three-to-four foot high fences which separate little plots of ground into labyrinth-like sections. Wine grapes grow on the fences, which enclose cabbage and corn plots reminiscent of kitchen gardens. I was impressed that early Portuguese settlers took this harsh landscape and made something productive of it. A small whaling museum shows what whaling was like in bygone years, and how important it was to the local economy.

I spent two weeks in the Azores. I explored the peaks and pastures of Faial by foot and by bus, as I recharged my personal batteries. All the while, I reveled in the knowledge that I had sailed to these rocky islands on my own.

Traditionally, visiting yachtsmen leave a pictorial "Kilroy was here" notice on the walls near the marina. I was incapable of doing this, but it is bad luck, so sailors say, to ignore this tradition. Sandy insisted that he would do it for me with a proper artistic design. I saw it years later: *Idle Queen*, with her gold crown, was brilliantly memorialized.

On 17 July I said my good-byes, cleared my departure with Customs and Immigration authorities, and left for the 965 mile sail to Portugal. For the first few days I had moderate winds, misty rain, and a few lightning displays. I lay becalmed one night. I was awakened the next morning by sounds of banging and clanking. The autopilot had broken loose from the tiller. Parts of it dangled over the side of the boat, banging the hull with each rolling wave. I resigned myself to sheet-to-tiller steering for the rest of the passage. This arrangement meant less sleep.

The weather became overcast. I generally managed at least one sextant sun sight per day. I had none on the eighth day as I neared land. A sun sight is necessary only the day before making a landfall, but this did not ease my mind. On the tenth day, in low clouds and misty rain, I approached the heavy shipping lanes off the European coast. I hove-to for the day and awaited better visibility before I tackled the heavy ship traffic. In late afternoon, the skies began to clear. I got underway. At 2150, a glow in the sky showed the lights of Lisbon bearing almost due east. I felt like an excited child, faced with the best Christmas present ever.

Through the rest of the night and into daylight I slipped through the stream of south-, then north-bound ships. I kept in sight the powerful light on Cabo da Roca that guided me to the Rio Tejo entrance. As daylight broke, Cabo da Roca did not disappoint me. This huge bluff-like promontory, a bastion of strength, demarcated the westernmost point of continental Europe.

The afternoon of 28 July 1990, I tied-up, stern-to, to a protected bulkhead in Lisbon. I shut the engine off. I mixed a celebratory gin and tonic, raised my glass in a silent toast and grinned. I had sailed across an ocean by myself. Despite my seventy-four years, life looked brighter than it had a year earlier.

Chapter 2

Mission Accomplished

The world is a book, and those who do not travel read only one page.
-St. Augustine

Lisbon lies a few miles inland from the sea along the banks of the Tagus River. This capital city has a million people but only one real marina, filled with local boats. Several tie-ups, lacking marina facilities, exist. I was lucky to find a place in one at the foot of Old Lisbon's Alfama district, with the business district only a half mile away.

Lisbon may not be a beautiful city, but it is charmingly different. The Alfama district lies on the side of a San Francisco-type hill. The five- or six-story buildings rise up from streets that are only donkey-cart wide, but too steep for a donkey with a cart. People living in this area do not seem as poverty-stricken as sometimes portrayed. Prices are not low anywhere in the city, and the Alfama is full of thriving little mom-and-pop shops.

Not far away is the Avenida da Liberdade, one hundred yards wide and separated by tree and grass meridians into traffic lanes running down the center of town. The area was destroyed in one of history's major earthquakes in 1755, killing 30,000 people. The master plan to which the city was rebuilt is still admired today.

As everywhere, traffic is a problem. I used public transport—bus, streetcar and train—to explore the area. The climb to Castelle Sao Jorge at the top of a hill was almost too much for me. I caught my breath, as I looked at the outstanding view, stretching out over river and city. It's a view that stays with me. Vasco de Gama's tomb is in the Jeronimos Monastery. I stood awhile admiring the building and thinking of how bold those Portuguese navigators must have been who first showed the way around the Cape of Good Hope.

By 7 August I decided that the hot hazy weather was never going to clear. I set off for Vilamoura Marina in the Algarve region on the south coast of Portugal. The first day a northwest wind drove me easily south to Sines. Sines has a fine harbor with clear water in spite of the oil refinery with its large tankers.

An unexpected east wind came up during the night bringing with it a San Francisco-Maine type fog. In the morning I raised anchor and ventured out into the thick murk. I imagined the fast-moving oil tankers like ravenous rabid dogs pacing in the grayness, ready to attack if I crept in their way. Cautiously I advanced, figuratively biting my fingernails all the way, until mid-afternoon when the fog finally lifted.

I rounded the high cliffs of magnificent Cabo Sao Vicente, Europe's southwest corner, and went into the deep anchorage at Enseada Belixe. Above me lay the plateau of Sagres where Henry the Navigator taught the great explorers during Portugal's sea dominance.

I consulted a guide book, as I headed into Vilamoura. The dock master is headquartered on the inlet feeding into the marina. I tied up and cleared in. During the process, the dock master confiscated my 12-gauge sawed-off shotgun and its ammunition. I had never used the gun. Faido and I bought it from a retired police officer after intruders twice, in different ports, boarded *Idle Queen*. Fortunately, our yells had been enough to drive them off. Holding the shotgun, the Portuguese official stared at me, as he decided if I looked dangerous. After a moment, he handed back the ammunition. The shotgun he kept until I left Portugal.

The Vilamoura Marina is a fancy, south Florida type facility with hundreds of slips facing a five-star hotel. The majority of the boats were Portuguese, but many countries were represented. To my relief, spoken English is common. In the restricted parking area around the marina I saw two Rolls Royce Cornices, a Maserati, a Ferrari, a Lotus, many BMWs and Mercedes, a few Alfa Romeos, and very few Japanese cars. Draft beer on the waterfront was $2.45; gin and tonic, $4.

The passage across the ocean left me feeling like a punch-drunk fighter. I thought my arrival in Europe would find me excited and exuberant. I had crossed a whole wide ocean all by myself. I should be acting like a freshman in the rooting section after a football victory. I should be sending letters to all my friends as my way of shouting to them, "I made it!" Instead I felt weirdly depressed. It came into my mind that I was missing the thrill I felt when Faido and I had sighted Hiva Oa after our crossing into the South Pacific. Perhaps my trouble was, "Faido is not here." The thought lifted me; I had an explanation. The next day looked brighter, and I plunged with vigor into the challenges of exploring the new and the old Portugal. I took a bus to Faro, the city Faido and I enjoyed so much on our European trip.

Leisurely, I wandered the town, revisiting the sites I first saw with Faido and eating again in the restaurants where we dined. The sentimental journey restored my equilibrium.

Back at the marina, Sandy and Mary on *Keno* arrived from the Azores. I admire this couple for their dedication to sailing. Their boat was smaller than mine and they were both subject to seasickness. They ate nothing but crackers during their Atlantic crossing.

Whenever Sandy and Mary rented a car, they included me in their sightseeing. In the Alentejo hills we saw rural, non-touristy Portugal with its subsistence farming and cork oak gathering. The long-standing masonry houses are maintained in good repair. The countryside florae are reminiscent of southern California—too dry for anything but scrub trees. In the little village of Alte, situated on the sides of a small stream in a ravine, we imbibed a memorable wine-filled lunch.

Together we toured Silves. In 1985 Faido and I had lunch here. The town, probably founded by the Phoenicians, became the capital of Al-Gharb after the Moors took over in 711. The large Moorish fort of red sandstone, said to be the best example of Moorish fortifications in Portugal, sits atop the hill above the town and river. The views over the valley and down to the seaport at Portimao leave a good impression of this countryside, green from the fall rains. At one time the Rio Arade was navigable to Silves and was used by the Portuguese discoverers in their trips around Africa and to the Far East. Now it is silted to canoe depth. Old (not ancient) mooring rings are still ready for use on the stone wharf. The thirteenth century cathedral, built on the site of a mosque, sports Moorish arches. I gave a hundred escudos to support maintenance of this edifice because the elderly lady in the foyer, knowing no English, struggled to explain to us how the cathedral obviously spanned two building periods as a result of the 1755 earthquake.

We drove to Olhao, 9 km east of Faro. The town and harbor lie behind the barrier islands that make up the coast for thirty miles around Cabo de Santa Maria. This port must be one of the best protected in Portugal for vessels of no more than about eight-foot draft. It is strictly Old Portugal and old time commercial fishing. Yachts are not welcome and there are few tourists. We took a clue from the local clientele and enjoyed a great fish dinner at Club Nautico, one of the least prepossessing of establishments.

The town of Tavira lies at the eastern end of the thirty miles of lagoon. The little Rio Gilao passes through the town center, and small fishing boats tie up to the ancient masonry bulkheads a block from the main plaza. The "new" bridge spanning the Gilao rattles and shimmies violently whenever a car passes over. The abandoned Roman-arched bridge, one hundred meters upstream, looks considerably safer to walk on.

I spent an afternoon here bird-watching with Britishers Anne and Derek, a middle-aged, jovial couple from *Thursday's Child*. Around the mouth of the Gilao, the salt pan flats are covered with avocets and curlews. Black-headed and black-backed gulls flew overhead. A few snowy egrets stood like sentinels on the flats while we snapped picture after picture.

In Sao Bartolomeu de Messines, tucked away in a cirque surrounded by hills, the traveling semi-gypsies were in town. This group travels from town to town setting up temporary markets to supply the locals with bargain household goods. The prices were cheap. I bought socks, a hat, and a belt.

Back in the marina, as I relaxed on *Idle Queen*, I watched a young Belgian couple as they brought their boat in. Jan and Ann were on their way to the Caribbean. Ann sat at the helm and steered the boat; Jan, at the bow, fended off and secured a line ashore. I approved of this division of duties between captain and mate. So often the man sits lazily at the helm while the wife throws a line ashore or even manhandles the anchor. Ann and Jan demonstrated how it should be done.

At Christmas, my younger daughter, Faith, and her husband, Robo, flew in from the U.S. to explore the countryside with me. I was most excited by our visit to Sagres on the high plain behind the Cabo Sao Vicente light. Here, where Henry the Navigator taught marine navigation to his inchoate sailors, a mock compass is outlined by stones in a fifty-yard diameter circle. This compass is unlikely to be that used in the fifteenth century. Henry taught his students so well that they dominated sea exploration for a period.

We rented a car to make the day-long trip to see the wonders of Seville Cathedral in Spain. The quantity of gold inside this huge building is impressive, but in a depressive way: the gold was stolen from the Americas. On the drive back to Vilamoura in the dark I remember being startled each time the headlights illumined a Portuguese family driving along in a three-wheeled motorbike. These motorbikes had only a candle-sized taillight to ward off imminent tragedy. Robo's reflexes were given a work out that night.

Faith and Robo departed, as winter drew to an end. I reflected on my adventure. The experience of living for a year outside America was an enlivening prod to my spirit. I had not done much with language; too tough for me. I am convinced one must be native-born to understand spoken Portuguese. Most of my contacts were fluent in English.

I formed some opinions of the country and its people: The Portuguese are gloomy and reserved, as reputed, but only until they become acquainted with you. Then they open up. They are outstandingly honest; nowhere in the U.S. can one leave items lying about the way one can here. Many people have cars, but the general populace gets around on the good bus system or on motorized two- and three-wheel bikes. There are no obvious homeless people in the country, only homeless dogs.

The country suffers from lack of capital and initiative. So many things done by hand are done elsewhere by machinery. Wages are low and prices high; a poor country does not mean low prices. The government is slowly privatizing business, but much remains to be done.

As spring approached, I became anxious to cross the Atlantic to avoid hurricanes. When I broke the news to Danielo in the marina office that I was leaving the next morning, he seemed concerned.

"Have you looked at the weather chart for day after tomorrow? It shows force 6 (22 to 27 knots) between here and Madeira," he said.

"Yes, but it's a norther and I'm heading southwest. No problem." I forgot the adage about not leaving port if the weather is doubtful. I expressed appreciation for Danielo's advice, and we parted with regrets and a handshake.

Despite light rain showers in the night, and a few in the morning, *Idle Queen* and I motored off in calm conditions. I had lingered in the country perhaps longer than I should, but was equally reluctant to leave. The Atlantic Ocean challenged me again.

Early in the afternoon I raised sail in light wind, but remained with engine running to cope with the heavy ship traffic around Cabo Sao Vicente. Once I counted seven ships turning the corner at the cape. By 1600, my tensions eased as I cleared the last of the worrisome freighters. The wind picked up, and I sailed toward Madeira in good spirits.

By early evening, the wind was more than I needed. I dropped the jib and double-reefed the main. Before midnight, I ran off under staysail alone in a strong northeaster. Lightning lit the northern horizon. Before dawn, the wind increased to gale force. My autopilot died. To compensate, I tied off the tiller at a suitable angle. I sheeted the little staysail hard in. *Idle Queen* took care of herself in quartering seas on a course set by the wind. Fortunately, I was west of the usual ship traffic lanes for I had little control of course or speed. The high seas made it difficult for me to be seen by ships.

By late afternoon of the second day, the gale roared at force 8 (34 to 40 knots) with seas eighteen feet high. Foam and spray blew horizontally. Oftentimes, since her death, I say aloud, "Faido, I wish you were here." On this occasion I said aloud, "Faido, it's just as well you're not here; you would not like this."

A boarding sea broke on the deck and tore out part of the protective weather cloth around the cockpit. I maintained my cowardly watch below deck behind the Plexiglas washboard, concerned by the unceasing roar of wind and sea. By early next morning, the weather slackened. In late afternoon, I raised the main and got the autopilot to work. Alternating calms, increasing wind, and rain showers over the next three days brought me within sight of the peaks of Madeira's neighboring island of Porto Santo. The next morning I reached the harbor of Funchal in Madeira.

Madeira is a lovely green mountain jutting out of the sea. There are no beaches, only rocky cliffs and deep ravines. Funchal has an old colonial look. Windows on the sea-facing sides of buildings are outlined by shutters and carapaces. It is a town of parks, fountains, and statues. Henry the Navigator sits under his big hat facing the Atlantic and studying the navigational problems of the world. A short airport runway has been scraped out of a hillside, but the big jets have to land at Porto Santo, a two-hour ferry ride away.

The harbor is comfortable and protected, but small. The marina, with no room for expansion, is crowded even during the off season. When I arrived I was directed to raft alongside another boat because no slip was available. When a slip opened up a few hours later, a dockhand urged me to move into it quickly. A few moments later a German boat motored up. The captain howled at me and cursed, shouting that I had taken his just-assigned slip. I sat unmoved. The dockhand chuckled in the background. I deduced that Germans are not popular.

A local DJ, Tony, and his wife, Rita, lived on *Mistress*, docked near me. They described the delights of Madeira one evening while we downed samples of the island's most famous product: its wine.

Jose, the harbormaster, took it upon himself to place my overseas phone call through the Funchal exchange. Later, he offered to find a way to reduce my dockage charges when I came for a longer stay.

As I prepared to sail away, he said, "We're crowded here, but when you come back, I will personally find a place for you."

I waved my thanks. *Being old has it benefits,* I thought.

The route south from Madeira is an easy sail in the prevailing northeasterlies, but a shock awaited me after I cleared the Funchal breakwater. The autopilot, repaired while I was in Portugal and used only six days, refused to do anything but turn the boat in circles. Madeira seemed an unlikely place for repairs. I put IQ under sheet-to-tiller steering for the three-day run to the Canary Islands.

I was fortunate in my choice for a port-of-call in the Canaries. Las Palmas de Gran Canaria is a major shipping center rather than a tourist spot. No fewer than six ships were always at anchor in the roadstead awaiting dockage in the large inner harbor. Many hands helped me secure stern-to to the mole. A six-lane divided highway along the waterfront always appeared to be at rush hour. The high-rises are large and dirty, often with dusty, bare vacant land between them.

Pedro, jovial operator of the Texaco marine station, said, "When I'm in New York, I speak English. When you're in Las Palmas, you have to speak Spanish."

He changed his mind when he heard my few Spanish words, now corrupted by Portuguese. Pedro lost no time finding an electronic expert to repair the autopilot. The people at Etel, whose business is electronic repairs on big ships, ordered a fax of the autopilot's wiring diagram. Five days later, my temperamental autopilot operated again.

That Sunday, I watched the start of a regatta of fifteen unique racing boats, the Vales Latinas Canarias. These lateen-rigged, interior-ballasted twenty-footers carry a crew of about ten and are tacked by muscling the lateen yard from the bow around aft of the mast and back to the bow. This is the rig used by early Portuguese explorers.

I felt uneasy about the voyage's time schedule. I wanted to avoid at all costs a tangle with an early season hurricane. The days lost in Las Palmas convinced me to skip a stop in the Cape Verde Islands. I passed within 240 miles of the islands and, in retrospect, my decision was a poor one. If I had gone that far south earlier in the crossing, I would have had stronger winds and a shortened time at sea.

The preferred course for St. Lucia, 2700 miles away, is a big curve to the south before heading west. Heading west too early means heading into light variable winds or even calms. I headed west too early. Eight days out of Las Palmas, when I was in latitude 22°, instead of below 20°, I was forced to sit out two days of dead calm. I thought of going swimming, but settled for watching the small yellow and black banded fishes nibble at a Portuguese man-of-war jelly fish. Eventually I reached the trades. The wind returned mildly and, once south of 20°, I moved slowly but more consistently to the west.

Shearwaters—Manx, greaters, and sooty—swooped gracefully around IQ. Occasionally, a petrel showed. A pair of friendly Arctic terns spent several hours fishing in my wake, and flocks of least terns flew by. One morning I found a baby squid on deck. Sometimes at night flying fish knocked on the plastic windows on the dodger and landed aboard. Gazing at the night sky, I thought: *What better company for the solo sailor than Antares and the bejeweled grin of the scorpion's tail high overhead?*

During the hot and muggy daylight hours, I tried to check on ships every twenty minutes. At night my alarm clock roused me every hour. I saw no ships for weeks across the wide stretch of the Atlantic. The high point of the day was the noon sun sight which, when used in conjunction with the morning sight, fixed my position and allowed me to calculate the day's run and the distance still to go. My hot meal was at noon—canned meat and vegetables except for a few days of fresh vegetables after each port. Occasionally I baked cornbread, two boxes at a time. My set of new paperback books ran out halfway across, but I enjoyed rereading Morison's *The Southern Voyages: 1492-1616.*

As I approached St. Lucia, I proceeded cautiously. There is no navigation light on St. Lucia. The light on neighboring Martinique was unlit. Lights of villages on the southeast coast of Martinique showed me the general location before I ran afoul of the extensive reefs there. I turned south and after sunrise located Rodney Bay. Thirty-six days out of Las Palmas, I tied up to the Customs dock in Rodney Bay, St. Lucia. The marina facilities are modern and well run, with reasonable prices. Dock boys with eager hands, looking for a tip, often bother me. This time I welcomed Jackie and Byron to take lines and fend off as I came in. The boys were helpful, and next day I hired them to scrape the bottom.

St. Lucia is a volcanic island with a heavily-wooded mountainous interior. The French deposed the natives, but the British took over in 1814. Today it is an independent nation. English is the primary language.

The Caribbean scenery is lush. The poincianas were in brilliant orange bloom. Over the next two days I made trips into Castries to pick up provisions. Castries is a low-built, crowded, rabbit warren of a town with no laudable architectural features. The minibuses roar up and down the two-lane highway into town on the English side of the road. They stop at any point for passengers, and toot at friends along the way.

The natives were kind and helpful. There are few white faces; perhaps there's a connection. I bought $8.65 worth of stamps at the post office. Getting out all my small change I came up with $8.60. I reached for a ten dollar bill. The lady who had been ahead of me in line was stamping envelopes at the counter. She immediately pulled out five cents and insisted on adding it to my pile.

"You are the most friendly people," I said.

"That's what life is all about, isn't it?" she replied.

The weather pattern shifted toward the wet season. Every day in St. Lucia it showered, sometimes twice, with the temperature always in the nineties. After spending four days ashore, I raised sail, moved on, and headed for the British Virgins. I sailed close along Martinique but did not stop to visit Josephine's old home. The second night out of St. Lucia, around midnight, I startled a hitchhiking white-capped noddy (and he me) when I came up the companionway steps. He flew off, but soon came back and spent the rest of the night perched on the dodger, adding his decorations. The flashlight full in his face did not bother him.

The 334 mile trip to Road Town, in the British Virgin Islands, took less than three days. I approached Road Town at night and in a solid overcast. I reduced sail to the small staysail alone early on to decrease speed so that I landed in daylight. I counted on the glow of city lights from Christiansted, St. Thomas, and Road Town to provide rough bearings. Two 14-mile lights on the southern British Virgins should provide good fixes. When I was within a few miles of the islands, according to the chart, I could see no lights. As I slowly jogged on, I could not see the lighted navigational aids. Daylight broke. To my surprise, nothing showed on the horizon.

The sun glowed through the overcast but did not present a clear disk. There is never fog in the Virgins. Rough sextant sights indicated I must be on the general longitude of Virgin Gorda, easternmost of the Virgins. Northeast of Virgin Gorda, the sea is a rock garden strewn with wrecks. I stood puzzled and concerned. By happenstance, I looked over the side of the boat and was startled to see rocks immediately beneath me. I executed a panic-stricken 180 degrees. When I was in deeper water I studied the murky atmosphere to the west. I spotted the dim outline of the rugged bulk of Virgin Gorda three miles away. Unknown and unvisualized by me, I was traveling in, as the radio later explained it, a thick pall of dust blown in from the drought-stricken Sahara. The visibility remained less than five miles all through my four-day stay in the Virgins and until I was a day's run north of the islands. I was converted: on my next trip, this atavist will travel with a space-age, push-button, electronic position finder. I will also need a new type of autopilot. As I came into Road Harbor, the deservedly much-maligned instrument broke down once more. I stowed it in the bilge.

Road Town Harbor is almost circular with hills rising abruptly from the water. At night, lights glow around the periphery and up the hillsides where houses are peppered in widely scattered fashion on contour roads. Streetlights, with yellow or green tints, mark these house clusters and give nighttime charm to a daytime dull town. Here I stood up for British naval tradition and drank a tot of Pusser's rum in the pub of the same name. Walls of this old establishment are covered with pictures of naval scenes: *Victory* at Trafalgar and *Formidable* at Les Saintes, but nothing of *Bon Homme Richard* or even *Serapis* at Flamborough Head.

The Virgin Islands aren't the thick tropical jungle I expected. Vegetation is green, but sparse and stunted. Virgin Gorda looks almost barren. The area must be unbeatable for pure sailing. The winds are moderate and unidirectional, and the circle of islands leaves the inner sea of Drake Channel remarkably smooth. Another anchorage is never more than a few miles away.

Eager to get home, I stayed in port only a few days, refueling and re-provisioning for the final lap. For the first few days after leaving Road Town, *Idle Queen* pranced along handsomely: 534 miles in four days. Then I fell into a black hole. In the next nine days I progressed only 422 miles. This was a wretched period of sailing with little wind except in thunderstorms. Tidal currents pushed me either on or off the Bahama banks. Ship traffic was a constant menace. I anchored behind Great Stirrup Cay in the Bahamas to rest and to await better conditions. By the third day the weather cleared, the trades reasserted themselves, and it took but twenty-six hours to cross the Gulf Stream to Lake Worth Inlet and Palm Beach. I motored the 300 miles of Intracoastal Waterway north to Green Cove Springs. Jack and Maggie Farrington and sailors at the marina congratulated me on my successful voyage.

In turns I felt exhausted, as if I had climbed Mt. Everest, and exhilarated, for I had sailed across an ocean alone. And, perhaps, a bit clairvoyant. I knew I could do it again. After I rested.

The world was mine to explore.

VOYAGE I

1991 - 1994

Chapter 3

I Lose My Boat

Two roads diverged in a wood and I –
I took the one less traveled by.
And that has made all the difference.
-Robert Frost

Two years after losing Faido I still lived in the past in many ways. I replayed in my mind our many trips together. In our maiden voyage in *Idle Queen*, we had sailed to the South Sea Islands in the Pacific Ocean. I decided to repeat that trip, to make a commemorative voyage. Starting from Florida I would head south, transit the Panama Canal, and sail west into the Pacific. One morning in December 1991, at the age of seventy-five, I set out from Green Cove Springs Marina.

As I traveled, I sniffed the wind and sea like an old dog hanging his head out a car window, salivating at the world. I felt the thrill of adventure. I felt as my father must have felt, the summer he crewed on a cattle freighter to Europe. He worked on fishing boats as he made his way along the English coastline. Perhaps I inherited my adventurous spirit from him. When I was growing up, we were always off somewhere on summer vacations. Before super highways, we drove from Los Angeles to the Grand Canyon or Death Valley or some other part of the country.

We never owned a boat. My love of the sea came from a more prosaic source, the written word. In school I was captivated by Robert Southey's *Life of Lord Nelson*. In 1928, when I was twelve, the *National Geographic* had an engrossing article by Harry Pidgeon, who had built a wooden 34' sailboat, the *Islander*, and singlehanded her around the world. He visited the South Sea Islands on the way. Later, seeing the *Islander* tied up to a wharf in San Pedro harbor, I became as excited as if I'd seen a rock star. I wouldn't have a boat until decades later, but on reflection, the seeds of Faido's and my maiden voyage in *Idle Queen* had been planted those many years earlier. I was happy repeating the trip.

My happy feeling soon turned to frustration. I was forty miles off the Florida coast, motoring in light winds, but my speed was only two knots. I had to make five knots to transit the Panama Canal. I sat at the tiller and ran through possible causes for the problem. I might be dragging a crab pot or have a plastic bag wound around the propeller. I leaned over the side; the clear water and calm sea showed both these premises to be false. I went below, grabbed the engine owner's manual, and flipped pages as I searched for an answer. A U.S. naval vessel, lurking to seaward, radioed to ask if I needed assistance. I told them I was fine, for I didn't see how they could help. Finally, I diagnosed the problem as a slipping clutch. I couldn't fix this at sea. Reluctantly, I headed back to shore. The next afternoon I docked at Camachee Cove Yacht Harbor in St. Augustine. By land, I was twenty miles from my starting point. My voyage had not started auspiciously.

Six weeks passed before my mechanic fixed the problem. As soon as the clutch was installed, I left St. Augustine in a rush, in too much of a hurry to get a weather report. Twenty-four hours later, after crossing the Gulf Stream, I hove-to in southerly winds of twenty-five to thirty-five knots. I remained so for thirty-six hours, riding out the wind and occasionally berating myself for my stupidity. At last the gale moderated and the wind shifted northwest. I entered Green Turtle Cay in the Abaco chain of the Bahamas.

Locating Green Turtle from the eastern side of the featureless chain of Abaco Cays was a triumph for my new hand-held GPS. The boat was not equipped with radar, a chart plotter, autopilot, watermaker, television, ham radio or an anchor windlass. But the GPS was a necessity.

The town of New Plymouth on Green Turtle is a neat, old-fashioned place of narrow streets and well-kept small houses. A tiny formal park is dedicated to the Loyalists who fled the rebel colonies in the late 1700s. Situated on six-foot pedestals, about twenty busts represent the heroes and heroines, whites and blacks, of that migration. Faido and I visited here in 1974.

The harbor at New Plymouth is not well protected and I motored the twenty miles south to the more comfortable anchorage of Marsh Harbour. I was pleasantly surprised to discover the familiar shape of another Dreadnought, IQ's sister ship, the *L'il Dolly*, riding at anchor.

"Ahoy, Dreadnought!" I yelled as I came in. I maneuvered close to the boat.

Jean Gendreau, the old San Francisco friend who influenced me to get a Dreadnought, came up on deck. He shouted, astounded to see me. Jean, also singlehanding, was encamped in the harbor for the winter. He pitched in enthusiastically to help me realign the shaft which had gone awry. I stayed in the harbor long enough to help Jean celebrate his birthday. He complained about Bahamian music, the only kind available. I gave him the tape of Tommy Dorsey's "Marie," as a present. He was ecstatic.

I planned to reach Panama by sailing east of the Bahamas, past San Salvador, through the Crooked Island and Windward Passages, and into the Caribbean around the eastern end of Cuba. Soon after setting out from the Abaco Islands, I was reminded by the ships around me that this is also the route taken by sea traffic headed to and from the canal and South America. It is not the best route for a singlehander. For the next five days and four nights, I was mostly awake and dodging ship traffic. I intended to stop and rest at San Salvador, but the anchorage was open to the west. A rare westerly gale was blowing. Sleep-deprived as I was, I sailed on.

I found a much-needed refuge in Little Harbour, on the southeast end of Long Island. There are no facilities or houses here, but the harbor is all-weather, more than deep enough, and easy to enter. One outboard skiff with friendly fishermen worked the area, and they led me in. After I anchored, I promptly went to bed.

This south end of Long Island is almost solid rock, with impenetrable brush set off occasionally by palmettos and pipe stem cactus. Reputedly, the settlement called Roses is about three miles away across the island. The trail hacked out through the undergrowth must have been a long-term project. Faido and I tramped the higher hills of the island's more populated north end seventeen years earlier.

I shared the refuge with two other yachts, a Swiss catamaran and a big steel German ketch. While I watched, a man on the ketch rowed out a second anchor he planned to put down. The anchor was huge, taking up much of the dinghy, and looked heavy.

"Do you need help?" I called over.

"No," he shouted back, "it's a Fortress anchor, made of aluminum." He held the anchor aloft with one hand.

Fortress anchors, I thought, *would be ideal for the older sailor.*

I waited a week in this peaceful pond for the weather to change before I set off for the Crooked Island and Windward Island passages. A passing U.S. Coast Guard cutter checked my identity by radio. The officer concluded by saying, "Keep a sharp lookout. There are a lot of Haitian refugee boats in this area."

Certainly, I thought, *and get a good night's sleep as well.*

The weather deteriorated again, as I approached the Cuban coast. A squall line developed into a four-hour blow with sixty knot winds and heavy rain. My 230-square foot staysail was up but not reefed. The wind tore out a panel. I crawled along a forty-five degree canted deck to claw down the sail, but not until it was badly ripped. I didn't need to worry about the boat rolling without a sail: wind pressure on the mast as I lay ahull held IQ steadily heeled at a sharp angle. That evening the weather bureau in Miami spoke of a "storm center forming" off central Cuba, but nothing further developed.

Fortunately, I had saved an old, but still usable, staysail, and the next morning I raised it for the three-day run through the Windward Passage and on to Jamaica. Unlit lights were characteristic of my landfalls, and Port Antonio was no exception. I hove-to offshore one night and entered in the morning. The harbor is a splendid spot for anchoring, well protected with a good hard mud bottom.

After clearing in, I tied up to the small marina to arrange for sail repair. Except for a good bar, the marina lacked yachting amenities. A local upholsterer with dirty cloth and a heavy sewing machine, but no sail experience, did a fine job of repairing my staysail. I didn't realize, until years later, just what a fine job it was. I might have paid him more if I'd known it would save me in the North Pacific.

Columbus wrote that Jamaica was "the fairest island that eyes have beheld..." It is certainly the most beautiful Caribbean Island I saw, outdone only by the more spectacular of the South Sea Islands. High mountains rise steeply from the sea to seven thousand feet and are heavily forested with tropical trees. The island profile is sharp and varied.

Jamaica is an independent country populated largely by descendents of African slaves. They speak English and Creole. Port Antonio is small, crowded and, except for a day or two after the trash truck comes through, dirty. Prices for most things are surprisingly low, comparable to or less than U.S. prices. A small banana ship comes once a week to carry bananas and oranges to England. The primary export is sugar. The aficionados of spiced rum will want to stand, glass in hand, whenever Jamaica is mentioned. It is the long-time home and burial place of Captain Henry Morgan.

Jamaicans are not a happy people. The boat boys work for two dollars an hour and travel about the harbor on rafts made by tying 3-inch diameter bamboo logs together. One youngster, John, cleaned my topsides but banged his raft against my hull all the while.

Unemployment is high, and panhandling is endemic in Port Antonio. In daylight hours, men line the sidewalks and watch the cars and bicycles go by. School attendance to age seventeen appears high. Girls in blue and white uniforms and boys in khaki congregate in the ice cream parlors after school.

I had favorable winds sailing from Jamaica to Panama, but I relied on sextant navigation. The GPS, for all its great promise, would not operate after I left Port Antonio. I raised the mainland of Panama one afternoon some miles east and north of the canal entrance where the coast is high and rugged. As I headed on, keeping well off shore, I expected to fix position by the big light on Isla Grande, twenty-three miles from the canal. It should have been visible by dark. At 2130, I saw the line of ships ahead and realized the light was unlit. I hove-to for the night and went to bed.

Next morning, in the early half light, I was startled into frenzied activity. The huge and daunting point of Isla Grande was close enough that I saw breakers on the off-lying islets. I jumped on deck and yanked on the halyards to raise sail. A brisk reach in the northeast wind took me off this lee shore.

That afternoon I tied up at the Panama Canal Yacht Club in Colon. I embarked on hours of clearing papers with Customs, Immigration, cruising yacht control, and canal authorities. Panama is one of the worst ports for paperwork. I wished Faido were here to help.

Maggie and Jack Farrington flew in from Florida to act as crew for my canal passage. Jack ran into friends Joyce and Ken, staying on their yacht *Joya*. This vigorous young couple agreed to complete the set of required four line handlers. Yachts at that time transited the canal in convoy, rafted three abreast when in the locks. Transiting yachts are not a high priority, preference understandably given to commercial ships. We suffered one delay after another.

Finally, the day of transit arrived. The canal is fifty miles long through three main locks on each coast. Even though this was my third time through, I still marveled at the magnificence of this engineering feat. Construction was begun in 1879 by the French, who failed in the effort. Americans completed the job in 1913, on time and under budget, but at a cost of thousands of lives. Most died from malaria or yellow fever.

In the locks, *Idle Queen* was on the right flank of our three-boat raft. The pilot on the middle boat, who was in overall charge of the set, got taken with the euphony of the call, "Take up the slack, Jack!" and used it in the locks whenever the fancy hit. This amused everyone except Jack Farrington on IQ's starboard bow. Meanwhile, Maggie provided gourmet meals that proved embarrassing. The cheerful pilot on IQ bragged about them to the other pilots as we traveled on.

From the last lock, we motored to Balboa Yacht Club in Panama City. My crew dispersed. Ken and Joyce returned to their own boat while the Farringtons flew back to Florida. Before leaving, Jack introduced me to Captain Arthur Rowley (USN) and his wife Millie. Captain Rowley is the less formal, more intellectual-type naval officer. I thought him more like Admiral Nimitz, less like Admiral Halsey. Millie, Panamanian-born, is cheerful, buxom, and very proud of her husband's achievements. They chauffeured me about as I re-provisioned the boat, and entertained me as I awaited the return of my GPS, sent off to California for repair. I hoped the repaired GPS would mean the end to my taking sextant sights.

Millie introduced me to her relatives. She was born in the Canal Zone. "Not Panama," she said emphatically, "the Canal Zone." She knows the language, the people, and the routines. She spent several days chasing through the labyrinth of Panamanian bureaucracy to locate my returned GPS. The day after she successfully extracted it from Customs, I planned to leave.

That night, I splurged on dinner at the local YMCA. I found a pay phone afterward and called my four children and two siblings, and said my good-byes. I was nervous, but I felt my trip was finally getting back on course after the slow start and delays.

I was wrong.

I returned to Balboa Yacht Club about 2100. The yacht club mans a launch twenty-four hours a day to deliver or retrieve sailors anchored in the estuary. I was the only passenger when the launch motored off to the spot in the estuary where *Idle Queen* was tied to a mooring buoy. We arrived at the spot, but there was no *Idle Queen* and no mooring buoy. Puzzled, the launch operator and I stared at each other until realization hit. The mooring buoy had broken its chain and drifted away into the darkness, dragging *Idle Queen* behind.

I had lost my boat.

Chapter 4

A Stop in Galapagos

Life is either a daring adventure or nothing.
-Helen Keller

The launch operator hesitated, and then opened the throttle. We sped down channel and crisscrossed the area for about a mile. The night was moonless. The shore lights did not penetrate. Somewhere in this unsparing blackness, *Idle Queen* was hidden. We couldn't find her.

Depressed, I realized I was a sailor without a boat.

The launch operator headed back to the yacht club. Instead of dropping me off at the dock, he took me to *Hot Fudgie*, a boat owned by an American army officer. John was aboard and about to leave for his night shift. He listened attentively to my problem and immediately took command.

Calling army headquarters, he reported crisply, "I'll be indefinitely delayed."

By 2200 we were underway. While John maneuvered through the estuary, I stood on the bow and operated a powerful searchlight, turning it slowing from port to starboard and back, lighting up the sea. The minutes passed tensely and slowly. One hour passed, two hours passed. My eyes teared from the wind and the constant strain of peering into the darkness. After three hours, I was discouraged. I visualized *Idle Queen* hit by a ship and sunk in the dark channel. Or smashed on the rocky shores of an off-lying island.

"Let's give up!" I yelled from the bow. "When it's light, I'll see if Captain Rowley can send up a helicopter for a wider search."

"No, no," John countered. "I know we can find her."

We kept going, although I feared the search was futile. For another ten minutes I moved the searchlight back and forth with no expectation of success. But in one bright pass, *Idle Queen* stood out starkly. I froze, dumbstruck. Although hindered by the mooring buoy and its broken chain, she had drifted seven miles to sea.

John maneuvered *Hot Fudgie* to *Idle Queen's* side. I scrambled aboard. I was enormously grateful to John for having found her. I cut the mooring buoy loose—it was too heavy to lift into the boat—and got underway. I patted IQ and congratulated her for finding her way through a crowded moorage, across a busy shipping lane, and through the dozen or so anchored canal-bound ships, without touching a thing. I may leave the piloting to her.

I returned to the yacht club, filled my water tanks, and took off.

An El Nino year, with its lack of wind, is not the time to sail from Panama to Galapagos. During my crossing, the doldrums belt appeared to have expanded. At one point, I had no sailable wind for forty-four hours. After an interminable eighteen days and eighteen gallons of diesel, I covered the 850 rhumb-line miles to Santa Cruz Island, Galapagos, Ecuador.

As I arrived in Academy Bay, Sylvia and Mike on *Rite-Trak* put off in their dinghy to welcome me and help me get two anchors set in fifty feet of water. I met this young Australian couple in Green Cove Springs just before I left. Sylvia is the epitome of the fresh, outdoor and beautiful Australian woman. She is as much at home aboard ship as Mike, and he is a muscular ex-navy veteran. Mike told the story of being on a navy ship in the Tasman Sea on the west coast of New Zealand. The seas were so high and rough, they broke on deck and washed the lifeboats overboard. Australia paid a recovery fee to the New Zealanders who found the beached boats.

Visas are needed to stop in Galapagos, and visas are almost impossible to obtain. This can be overcome if a sailor has a problem and needs to stop. The thirty dollar per day harbor charge makes it easier for the port captain to see the need. I said my need was diesel fuel.

April is ordinarily in the hot, dry season in Galapagos. Of the five days I was there, it rained every afternoon, sometimes a steady downpour from noon until five. The rain inhibited my exploration afoot. The Galapagos support unusual fauna, including the giant tortoise. Charles Darwin's observations of these animals and birds during his visit in 1835 were significant in his theory of natural selection.

My greatest disappointment was my inability to visit Darwin Research Station. Employees were on strike and looked much too tough for me to nudge through the picket line. I saw not a single Galapagos tortoise. I photographed the marine iguanas, tame great blue herons, green lizards, and some of the landscape. In the harbor, the blue-footed and blue-faced boobies dominated the scenery. The almost tame Galapagos petrels flitted in and out among the anchored boats.

Puerto Ayora, with five thousand inhabitants, is larger than I expected. Souvenir shops, small restaurants, and mini-hotels are plentiful. The center of activity is on the north side of the bay. Many of the old houses on the opposite shore, including Gus Angermeyer's place on Angermeyer Point, look dilapidated and deserted. Gus was one of the early German settlers on these islands.

Standing in line one day at the post office, I had a brief conversation with a rotund Herr Gross who said he had lived in Galapagos for fifty-three years. I started to ask him about the scandalous affairs in *My Father's Island*, the book by Gus's daughter, Johanna Angermeyer.

"There's not a word of truth in it, just a pack of lies," he interrupted me. "I could tell you things that go on here that you wouldn't believe."

To my relief, he didn't.

On the next-to-last day of my approved stay in Galapagos, Montezuma's revenge caught up with me after a greasy lunch at the well-named Restaurante Pirata. The effects lasted several days. This prevented me from taking a guided tour to another island. On 29 April, I struggled to raise the two anchors and set off for Nuku Hiva. As I left the island behind, I felt mentally dissatisfied and physically, much worse.

Chapter 5

Island-Hopping across the Pacific

It is difficult to visualize the immense size of the Pacific Ocean from an armchair.
-Len Deighten, *Blood, Tears and Folly*

Bird life is scarce in this section of ocean east of Polynesia: an occasional shearwater and, when close to land, a few boobies. A sooty tern joined me to sit for almost twenty-four hours on deck. He was all black except for a white domino. One morning I found four eight-inch squids on deck. I don't know how they jetted there. Black ink stains remained for several days.

Squalls passed through at frequent intervals. Lowell North, the sailmaker, in a 50-plus footer, traveling a few days behind *Rite-Trak* and a few days ahead of IQ, was dismasted in a squall. Fortunately, he had enough fuel to motor to Hiva Oa.

I made the 3055 mile sail from Galapagos to Nuku Hiva, Marquesas Islands, in just twenty-nine days.

The Marquesas are high, steep-sided volcanic islands located in the South Pacific 900 miles northeast of Tahiti. The vegetation is lush, the climate delightfully mild. The islands were visited by a Spanish captain in 1595, but they are now owned by France as part of French Polynesia. The inhabitants are French and Marquesan-speaking Polynesians.

As I arrived in Taiohae Bay, Nuku Hiva, I looked around once again at the comforting hills and shoreline. The mountains are green and the frangipani and tiare are in bloom. Taiohae has expanded since Faido and I were here in 1980, but it's still small and a poor place to re-supply. The rains knocked out most of the vegetable crop.

In the 1970s, Frank and Rose Corser, former California schoolteachers, sailed *Corsair* to the Marquesas and stayed. They built a small inn comprised of a main building with dining room and five small cottages. The French authorities were not pleased with the enterprising couple. They obstructed them legally whenever possible. The Keikahanui Inn finally opened in 1980. Faido and I were there on opening night. The Corsers cleverly invited the French gendarme as their honored guest; they had no problem getting a permit.

I was excited to find the inn, with its panoramic view over the bay, still open. The chef creates amazing breadfruit dishes. In earlier days, lack of transportation hampered development, but now Nuku Hiva has an airport only a few miles and a boat ride away. After Frank Corser died in 1992, Air Tahiti took over the inn. Rose remained in the Marquesas.

The ocean swells roll around the headland of Taiohae harbor and discourage long layovers in Nuku Hiva. I stayed a week. In 1984 a tiki festival was held here and sample tikis were brought in from outlying areas as far away as Easter Island. The tikis are collected in a small waterside park. Intrigued by these carved images of gods and ancestors, I studied them curiously.

I spent one evening with John and Pat aboard their 65-foot steel schooner *Quest II* from California and discovered what cruising is like when surrounded with all the comforts of shoreside. This was a fortuitous meeting. In Tonga later, the crew rallied to my aid.

I left Nuku Hiva planning to revisit the atoll of Rangiroa in the Tuamotoes—Faido and I had been there—but it was growing dark as I approached this low island. I slid off and angled down into the channel between atolls Tikehau and Mataiva. In the middle of this blind passage, a vicious rain squall roared out of the dark. I lashed the tiller and reduced to the staysail alone. Under these conditions, the wind set my course. Driven away from Tikehau, I was much closer to Mataiva than I thought I should be according to the chart, although charts and GPS positions often don't agree. I strained my eyes looking for the white glow of breakers to leeward. I finally decided that I had squeezed past the atoll. I reflected that I might have been in trouble without the GPS. But without the GPS, I might have shown better seamanship and not gotten into such a tight position. I shook my head in disgust: I better shape-up before my next landfall.

Idle Queen and I careened on into Raiatea, still part of French Polynesia. As I anchored off its north coast and looked to the northwest, I realized why Bora Bora is universally considered the most beautiful island in the world. Although nineteen miles away, the aspect ratio is perfect. The two high cathedral spire peaks are set off by the lower level of the island which spreads out in each direction to just the right extent. On closer view, Bora Bora shows the deep green gashes in the mountainsides so characteristic of the volcanic islands of the Pacific. This feature is most easily viewed closer to home in the mountains of Hawaii.

Raiatea is neglected by the cruising fraternity in favor of the more famous Tahiti, but the anchorages are better here. The town of Uturoa has all the advantages of Papeete without the hustle and bustle. The French do a good job of keeping all their welfare islands neat and clean.

Most of the people in these Isles Sous Le Vent are Tahitian and speak Tahitian as well as French. They consider themselves more advanced than the Marquesans. I think they are more sophisticated. The Tahitian language has a word for "thank you" (*Maururu roa*), but the Marquesan does not. A Marquesan told me that in earlier days, and lingering still, anything that belonged to a Marquesan belonged equally to his neighbor; there was no need to thank anyone.

The marina lies near the town of Uturoa where boats can get water and fuel and, space available, tie up to the quay. When I arrived, I went to check in with the gendarme. He spoke no English and he could not understand my French. He gestured that I should come back when I was ready to check out. Several days later, ready to leave, I returned to the office. A different gendarme was present. Our conversation was painful. He had trouble with my desperate English, I with his baleful French. He glowered fiercely at me.

This was the gist of our conversation:

"You failed to check in!" he shouted. "That is a serious offense."

"I tried to check in," I kept repeating.

Stalemated, I left and got the harbormaster, a friend and a native whose name I Americanized to "Jim." Jim returned to the office to translate, or rather negotiate, for me. After a long discussion, it was determined that I must check out in Bora Bora.

Without thinking, I asked a brilliant question: "Is Bora Bora this island's headquarters then?"

With that, I was free to go. Later Jim explained, "The officials at the Los Angeles Airport gave the gendarme a hard time once, so he hates all Americans."

Heading for Samoa, I made a mistake in my choice of routes. Lying across the path are the Cook Islands, widely scattered in a north-south direction. The most accessible is Rarotonga in the south. Suvorov is in the north with Aitutaki in the middle. One of last summer's cyclones wiped out the small yacht moorings at Rarotonga. The pass through the reef at Aitutaki carries only five feet of water, and IQ needs all of five feet. I decided on Suvorov. This is the atoll where Tom Neale lived alone for sixteen years and welcomed passing yachts. The drawback is that the entrance pass must be dog-legged in through rough seas because of an unmarked shoal in the passage. On the day I reached Suvorov, the winter trades blew briskly, and a big sea broke over the reefs. The anchorage, partially visible behind the tree-capped hill, looked attractive, but I convinced myself that I needed a bow lookout to make it in. I passed up the visit, rounded the atoll to the north, and continued west. I settled for the easy entrance at Pago Pago in American Samoa.

The harbor at Pago Pago—for pronunciation purposes, put an "n" in front of all Samoan "g"s—is, for ships, the best natural harbor in the South Pacific. It is less delightful for yachts. The holding ground is poor, the bottom is cluttered, and moorings are in limited supply. Trash and oil from the purse seiners and long-liners often cover the bay. And, I discovered, poorly-secured oriental fishing boats are a hazard.

The wharf is stacked high and wide with containers, and large container ships come and go. The tuna fishermen are rafted deep at the main pier. Starkist has just broken ground for a new $10 million can plant, allowing Starkist to compete, at $3/hour wages, with the Bumble Bee operations in Thailand, paying fifty cents an hour wages. The Starkist and Van De Camp fish processing plants send out a continuous olfactory signal to advertise the general prosperity.

It was a welcome change to speak English instead of struggling with Spanish or French. Since I planned to stay at least a month for boat maintenance and to restock with familiar goods, I tied up to a big, sturdy ex-destroyer mooring. Don, a friendly middle-aged man on *Bag End*, whom Faido and I met in the California Delta in 1981, showed me about the town. Transportation is easy. The area swarms with little *aiga* (family-owned) buses which are cheap, profitable to their owners, and almost as convenient as taxis. They are brilliantly painted and striped, reminiscent of the Portuguese fishing fleet, and many are named. Don and I were driven around in one labeled "South of Pago Pago."

As I got in I asked the driver, "Is this named for the old movie?"

He nodded and grinned appreciatively.

The bus groaned in low gear on the road over the pass to the north side of Tutuila, the island on which Pago Pago is located. The island rises sharply from the sea with but few flat spots. Pretty little villages are strung along the crescent beach of Fagosa (Forbidden) Bay. The island is beautiful, the rocky headlands along the coast interspersed with palm tree-lined beaches. The reef is generally close inshore which leads to high surf along the coast. Off Fagaitua it was sad to see a yacht high on the reef, mast still standing. It had been there for several years. The captain mistook this bay for Pago Pago.

Samoans are friendly people. They are often overweight, but being big-framed, they carry weight well. They seem proud to be American nationals, ruled by a governor and legislature. The U.S. runs the postal service and programs such as Head Start. Many buses fly American flags. The people have some uncivilized habits: those sitting on aisle seats in the front of the bus get up and move to the rear when new riders come aboard. From the bus, I saw only one cemetery. Many people are buried in front yards with well-kept tombs.

Being unable to get charts to Apia harbor on Upolu Island of Western Samoa (a separate, independent country), I flew over to see the area that Robert Louis Stevenson loved so well. I picked the worst weather of my stay for the seventy-five mile sightseeing flight. The ride was bumpy in a De Havilland STOL Twin Otter (thirteen seconds from brakes to airborne). Once in Apia, I found my way up the hill to Vailima by luck. My taxi driver didn't know exactly where it was. Vailima, the old homestead of Tusitala (Teller of Tales), has fallen into disrepair. The government's restoration interferes with an appreciative view of the structure. I wanted to climb the mountain where "he lies where he longed to be," but I hadn't the time, and probably not the ability.

Interestingly, the popular beer here is Vailima, made in Western Samoa.

Upolu Island is much less mountainous than Tutuila Island, with a higher population and population density. Apia is a depressing town. Old, low, and dirty buildings are relieved only by the huge piles of green bananas in the market, and the smart and famous Aggie Grey Hotel. Aggie Grey started his establishment as a hamburger stand for American servicemen in World War II. Today the prices for food and drink are for a more selective clientele. I had one drink only.

Back in Pago Pago, rain and wind continued into the following day—forty knots according to the radio. That morning at 0725, Dave Berg of *Kismet*, in an outboard dinghy, pounded on my hull.

"Cut your lines and move!" he shouted.

A rafted pair of 200-foot long Oriental fishing boats had broken loose and, wind-driven, were bearing down on me at two to three knots. I barely got the engine started before the ships slammed into my twelve-foot diameter mooring buoy, spun it 360 degrees, and slid off to my left. I gunned the engine and maneuvered to the free side of the buoy. The ships went aground fifty yards away. Two tugs arrived an hour later to pull them back to their moorings. I was lucky. If the ships had hit me, the damage to IQ would have been extensive, if not fatal. It would have been the end of my voyage.

I thanked Dave for alerting me and showed my gratitude that night by buying Dave and his wife, Mary, a drink at the yacht club bar. They are a handsome well-traveled American couple in their forties. Mary, a brash brunette, was particularly fun to be around with her loud laugh and earthy sense of humor. She worked part time in one of the local bars, a job that soon caused a problem for the three of us.

When I went to the office to clear out of Samoa, I was told that I must first stop at the Customs dock for inspection. This was a new and strange procedure. Dave and Mary on *Kismet* also had to be inspected. The reason came out later: In her part time job as a cocktail waitress, Mary befriended a known drug dealer who could only be arrested if he tried to leave the country. The authorities were convinced that Mary would smuggle him out. Since Dave and Mary were my friends, I was also suspect. When Mary discovered the reason we were inspected, her outrage was heard all over Pago Pago. The story became a legend in that part of the Pacific.

After inspection, with no drug dealer found hidden in the engine room, I set off for Tonga. The 350 mile run from Pago Pago to Neiafu on the island of Vava'u, Kingdom of Tonga, should have been an easy, unexciting sail. Instead, after a brisk 144 miles the first day, miserable weather rolled in. The most intense lightning display of the voyage greeted me the second day out—not much wind but heavy rain and an evoking of welder's eyes. The next two days brought strong SSE winds, possibly thirty knots, which I bashed into on a southwest course under triple-reefed main. In the midst of this disturbance, three slide fasteners on the mainsail ripped loose, and I had to lower it for repairs.

Usually, I do only absolutely necessary maintenance when underway. A typical day starts after breakfast with an inspection of the ship. I look for chafe, loose wires or lines, anything sagging or rattling, blocks held only by safety wires, water in the bilge. On the Tonga trip I missed the fraying slide ties. Ordinarily an inspection doesn't take long. If no repairs are required, I settle down happily to cooking, eating, extensive reading, and an informal extension of the ship's formal log. At apparent noon I determine position—by sextant sights if the handheld GPS is not working—and calculate distances and course. I can't nap and gave up trying a long time ago. My day starts at sunrise and ends at sunset, at least in theory. A kitchen timer awakens me every hour throughout the night. I look for ships and check on course and weather. I try to avoid late-night adventures modifying sail spread by shortening down earlier, but I'm not always successful. If I've lost sleep because of weather, a short trip, such as Pago Pago to Neiafu, allows me to rest up in port. On a long passage, rest doesn't come easily.

I arrived rested in Neiafu. The widespread Kingdom of Tonga consists of many low islands and high volcanic islands. It is a constitutional monarchy dedicated to free enterprise. The people are Polynesian and speak English and Tongan.

After clearing in at the Customs dock, I slowly motored in a meandering path to find less than seventy feet of water in which to anchor. A sailor sitting in the cockpit on *Mary Stewart* directed me to an unused mooring. I tied up overnight, only to be kicked off by an irate boater the next morning. The sailor who offered the mooring was an aging British soldier who fought with General William Slim in Burma. After the war he taught history in Australia. Major James Wickenden was a stereotypical stiff upper lip ex-British officer. He had an erect, slim figure and a well-trimmed mustache. He could be called Major or James, but never Jimmy. He and I got along well despite his contrasting British formality. We explored much of Vava'u together.

A visit to the Vava'u section of Tonga is well worth the trip. The harbor is clear blue water, unsullied by commerce as is Pago Pago, and almost landlocked. The harbor entrance at Neiafu is deep enough for inter-island freighters. The islands are high enough to give good protection, over 600 feet on Vava'u, and are covered with tropical trees. In the Vava'u group of islands there are forty-two recommended anchorages. I visited only five of them.

Downtown Neiafu was a surprise. It is a wild west town: dusty streets, mostly dirt sidewalks, faded one-story buildings, population 5000. The people are friendly, even more so than the Samoans. Prices are surprisingly low. The one tourist hotel, Paradise Hotel, is a good-looking, well-kept, reasonably-priced tiered set of buildings overlooking the bay. I recommend it to nonsailors wanting to experience the South Seas on a budget. There's not a great deal to do here, but the scenery is beautiful, water is clear and clean, and the island clusters are typically South Seas. The fishing is said to be good. To me, hiking the hills, walking the reefs or exploring by taxi was more exciting. The area is popular with yachts; there are sixty in this harbor alone, many on moorings because of the deep water. These water-borne tourists crowd the several little cafes along the waterfront to eat, drink and chatter.

Many familiar boats were here: *Le Galion, Quest II, Bag End, Kismet.* I had met these sailors before. I found it easier than expected to forge friendships. I'm shy. In the past I relied on Faido to make social contacts. Faido was a gregarious woman. In Virginia in the 1950s, she hosted a radio show. In the 1960s she was the women's page editor of a daily newspaper. Faido loved meeting people and learning their history. I was amazed whenever an hour passed in a new port, and she had not asked a sailor over for Happy Hour or dinner. Now I discovered that sailors traveling alone, or with only a spouse for company, are eager to meet others when ashore.

I became friendly with David Smith on *Le Galion.* David has a round, Charlie-Brown face with a blond swatch dipping over his wide forehead. Although not well versed in sailing, he was taking care of his father's boat while his father was in the U.S. on business. David acted as my water taxi operator and social secretary. Trying to be helpful, he once cautioned me: "It's hard these days to get a girl in bed on the first date."

I met two couples who became long-term friends and who would be met again and again in my travels. Bob and Rose Selfridge on *Fair Rose* were retired Americans. Bob was a tall, broad, bald man, quiet and competent. He towered over the diminutive Rose who, despite a perilous background, possessed a soft voice, a sweet smile, and twinkling dark eyes below short black hair. As a young Jew in Belgium, Rose just managed to stay out of the clutches of the Nazis. At the end of the war she emigrated to the United States and found work. Bob was her supervisor.

"You shouldn't date a subordinate," I told Bob.

"It was Rose's idea."

The second couple were young newlyweds, Kris and John Fulton on *Mew.* Kris came up only to John's chin and wore her brown hair like a cap covering her ears. John's receding brown hair was offset by his beard. They met in Alaska where Kris was a pharmacist and John, a U.S. Coast Guard officer. Kris owned a sailboat. After they married, they decided to sail around the world before starting a family. A social couple, they often hosted dinner for a cabin full of sailors. After dinner they entertained us with music, Kris on the violin and John on the concertina.

Kris and John were snorkeling off one of Tonga's colorful reefs when I was introduced to them by another young couple. Larry and Sheri are professional yacht deliverers, boat carpenters, and expert sailors who are widely known among the visiting yachties. Sheri is a petite dynamo, Larry an atavism to square rigger days. Their yacht, *Queequeg*, is a beautiful 61-year-old, 35-foot ketch.

Larry and Sheri took David Smith and me on a day sail to the better snorkeling spots. The coral gardens of Ava Island have the most spectacular shapes and colors in coral that I have seen anywhere. The ubiquitous parrot fishes and the yellow-black banded variety ("Manihi" in Tongan), along with strange looking gar fishes, weave in and out along the reef front. Swallow's Cave is a high vaulted hole in a cliff invaded by sea water. Local literature calls it a miniature version of the Blue Grotto. The sea snakes I saw had black and white bands and yellow snouts.

I accompanied Larry when he experimented erecting a mast and sail on a dinghy. We took it out in calm seas to see how it would perform. It was a warm day, and I leaned back on my elbows and started to whistle.

"Don't do that!" Larry snapped. "Don't you know it will bring on a gale?"

He and Sheri are both superstitious, a trait I discovered among several sailors. Rose Selfridge does not set sail on Friday. I suggested she write her insurance company, explain that she never leaves port on Fridays, and ask for a lower rate. I myself have admonished revelers not to click glasses after a toast.

"A sailor will die at sea," I say, quoting what someone once told me.

King Tuofu IV and his queen spent several days in Neiafu and opened the Agricultural Fair on a day following a night of heavy rain. David Smith and I sloshed through the fairgrounds, a huge mud puddle dotted with soggy islets. Many people struggled to set up the exhibits and were rewarded with a series of long speeches by government officials. The king said only a few words, but the queen handed out an extensive series of awards. The king is a huge man, over six feet tall and three hundred pounds. He could be recognized even without the large wraparound sunglasses.

The Tongans have stolen a march on the rest of the world: they consider themselves to be west of the dateline, even though they are really east of it. Their motto is: "Where Time Begins." The inscription on one of their coins reads "Planned Families—Food for All." Large families are usual. One young woman, selling papayas from a canoe, told me proudly that she was one of thirteen children and that she, in her mid-twenties, already had five. The people are highly religious. They are strict churchgoers and do no work on Sundays. The Mormons have poured a lot of concrete on this island.

The most impressive funeral march I ever saw, outside of New Orleans, was one which ended at a little church on the hill directly above my anchorage. I heard a bass drum, perhaps a quarter mile away, before the procession hove into sight. Behind the mourners came a huge bass drum hauled on a cart. Every two seconds the drum boomed across the harbor and the marchers took a step. I still recall the gripping solemnity of that booming drum.

On 17 September I motored up to the concrete fuel wharf in Neiafu to fill a water tank. With no one there to take a line, I leaped ashore. I landed heavily, and painfully, on my right heel. Dr. Alfredo Carafa, the young doctor from his Italian Clinic, came to the boat and bandaged the sprained ankle. He told me to stay off it for three weeks. This delayed my planned return to the States.

Two Tongan dock workers helped me get IQ to a close-in mooring. The next day Alfredo and his Tongan wife, Vika, came aboard and brought me lunch and crutches. A boat-call by a doctor in Tonga costs 15 Pa'anga ($12), including bandages and a dose of Voltaren. Who needs medical insurance?

Over the next week Larry and Sheri shopped and took care of my mail. In the evening they came aboard with a bottle of rum. Rum cost a dollar per liter. After Larry and Sheri left to deliver *Le Galion* to Fiji, John and Pat on *Quest II*, first met in Nuku Hiva, often brought me meals. And such meals! Roast lamb and breadfruit fritters, among the specialties of the ship.

Quest II inadvertently provided me entertainment. One of the ship's guests was a young female doctor. One evening she went ashore with a friend. Returning quite late, they stood on the shore and hollered at *Quest II*, trying to rouse someone to pick them up in a dinghy. Desperate, the young doctor stripped off her clothes and swam out to the boat. Fortunately, a bright moon illuminated the way. I sat in IQ's cockpit, my foot propped up, and watched as she swam close by *Idle Queen*'s stern. I almost called out to suggest she climb aboard and take my dinghy.

Other sailors stopped by to keep me company. Naturally, the conversation turned to sailing. I told them how I bought *Idle Queen*'s fiberglass hull, rigged her, and designed and finished the interior. I told them how, on our maiden voyage, Faido and I sailed her to the South Seas. Needing little encouragement, I related *Idle Queen*'s construction and that first voyage.

Chapter 6

I Build a Boat

The sea finds out everything you did wrong.
-Francis Stokes

Three years after my retirement, Faido and I knew we needed a heavier boat for serious ocean sailing. We sold our original *Idle Queen* to a couple who planned to cruise Chesapeake Bay.

We weren't sure what kind of boat we wanted or where we would find it. Our criterion was simple: a boat we liked, that was adequate for our purpose, and that we could afford. We bought a camper and started the search. We traveled from coast to coast, visited boatyard after boatyard, and talked with sailors. Nothing sufficed until we visited the Dreadnought boatworks in Carpenteria, California. Here unfinished Dreadnought 32 fiberglass hulls were built and sold. The hull lines are the same as the Tahiti ketch, a proven design for ocean sailing. I was excited at the prospect of taking a hull, installing the interior, and rigging it myself. Faido was less enthusiastic; she doubted my ability. We talked to owners who had done what I planned. Jean and Dolly Gendreau of Palo Alto gave us an exuberant report, verging on the excitement of a used car dealer's pitch. Faido was convinced. We ordered a hull.

We parked the camper in the driveway of my mother's house in Cupertino, California, and used this as our base. My mother Floss was then 92 and welcomed our company.

While I awaited delivery, estimated to be one year away, I designed the interior based on drawings of the hull. I studied Richard Skene's classic, *Elements of Yacht Design,* which gave such vital information as how wide a settee should be and how high off the floor, how heavy the mast and riggings, etc.

Faido wanted a large dinette on which to set a typewriter and spread papers. An indifferent cook, she did not need a big galley. We both wanted lots of bookcases and storage bins. In place of the usual ladder into the cabin, on which one tiptoes down, I designed a platform companionway of solid steps that Faido appreciated.

I slowly acquired the tools needed for the project. Any money left over from the weekly household expenses went into a tool fund. One week I bought a vice, a level, and a plane. Another week I added a saw or a power drill.

For necessity and practice, I built a workbench and a wooden dinghy. I disguised the mistakes on the latter by covering it with fiberglass. If an item called for three layers of fiberglass, I used four or five to make up for my lack of artistry. I built the bowsprit and boomkin. From a ten-foot piece of Sitka spruce, I fashioned a boat hook. Meanwhile, Faido signed up with a temp agency and spent her days as an office worker.

As the date for the hull delivery approached, I searched for a suitable place to work on it. I found a house in the neighborhood with an empty backyard. To my surprise, the homeowners, the David Lloyd Georges (no relation to the more famous one), agreed to let me use it. I paid them thirty dollars a month for the privilege. The yard was two blocks from Floss's house.

In January 1977, after several delays, the hull arrived. It came with a Sabb engine, a deck, and a yawning interior.

Now my work really began. Six days a week, as soon as it was light enough to see the sidewalk, I walked to my boatyard. At lunch I walked home to eat, then worked until time for cocktails and dinner. Sunday was my day off.

My work uniform was holey, cut-off shorts, a torn and stained shirt, and a greasy cap. I dragged my tools and supplies behind me in a red wagon. Some neighbors thought I was a bum on my way to the local dump; one offered me a used bedspread.

Work was slow but steady. Through weekly reports, I can still view the transformation. Writing weekly is a habit begun in college when my parents insisted I send them a postcard a week. Now my correspondents include my children and my two siblings. These letters form a diary of my progress.

13 February 1977: The third water tank is in the boat, and the fourth is ready to go in. We've just made the horrible discovery that we have greater storage capacity for water than for liquor. We may convert one thirty-five gallon tank to whiskey, so we can have running bourbon at the kitchen sink.

27 February 1977: I installed a muffler for the engine exhaust (even through the exhaust line itself is not in), secured the joists for the main cabin sole, weather-stripped the fore cabin and lazarette

hatches, and cut out bulkheads for the fore cabin and chain locker. We found some Plexiglas for windows.

13 March 1977: During the week we made our first holes in the boat hull below the water line, one to provide an outlet for sink, wash basin, and cockpit drains, the second to install the transducer for the depth sounder. Some may think that adding a depth sounder is premature, but Faido is always concerned about my getting in over my head.

10 April 1977: The first two boat windows have now been installed. Six more have been manufactured and remain to be put in. These homemade port lights, like no others you've seen, lend personality to the boat. At least, that's what we call it.

17 April 1977: The windows are finally installed in the boat, all eight of them. This gives us light with which to work below deck, at the same time eliminating one of our alibis for poor workmanship.

24 April 1977: This was delivery week on boat items. We received tank doors from England, engine controls from Norway, and the rudder from Carpenteria. Jean and Dolly Gendreau helped me mount the 200-pound rudder. The samson posts and bowsprit are also on (for temporary fitting), so we look much like a boat right now.

In June 1977 I summarized the progress:

The first six months of boat building are now behind us. Changes in the boat are significant and obvious, but the launching ceremony still looks to be a long beat to windward. The forward exterior of the boat, with bowsprit and samson posts, is set to take the standing rigging. The aft end, with boomkin to take the backstay, is in initial stages of construction. The remainder of the exterior—mast, lifelines, winches, running rigging, sails, etc.—is well in the future. Below deck, the fresh water system is ninety-five percent complete; the diesel fuel tanks are in. The engine water and exhaust systems are connected up, and the fuel supply system is not far behind. As far as accommodations are concerned, only the double bed in the forward cabin is complete. The dinette, settee, galley, bathroom, cabinets, electrical system, permanent flooring, interior decorating, etc., are but floating visions.

17 July 1977: We mocked up the companionway ladder into the depths of the boat this week. The entrance is really a series of platforms at different levels. The Admiral gave her grudging OK to the setup; she really had in mind an elevator or, as a distant second choice, an escalator.

24 July 1977: Having secured the dinette sole to the hull, I have once again turned my attention to the hatches. The stainless steel runners for the sliding hatch are in place, and I'm struggling to commingle properly the runners and fiberglass hatch cover by means of precisely put-together wood strips. We just hope it all floats.

7 August 1977: The sliding companionway hatch is finally installed. I didn't want it to slide too easily, since an easily-sliding hatch can be a guillotine at sea, so, of course, I made it too tight. I hope to condition it over the course of time, although it may do the job on me first. After I get a hasp affixed, we'll be able to lock the boat, and I can leave my power tools aboard. When I stop hauling tools back and forth in my little red wagon, much amusement will disappear from the lives of the small neighborhood children.

A month later I hit a stumbling block. A discrepancy in two drawings left me unsure of dimensions and location of the boomkin. I called the naval architect, W. I. B. Crealock, who designed the Dreadnought's cutter rigging and sail plan. He lived in Carlsbad, California. I explained the problem and asked how much the clarification information would cost. Crealock assured me there would be no charge if new drawings weren't required. (They weren't.) He asked me to call back that evening, as he was on his way out to an important appointment. When I called that evening, I learned that Crealock was still out on his important appointment: he had not yet returned from sailing.

When we spoke, Crealock couldn't reconcile the drawings, either. Over the phone, he gave me dimensions of the boomkin and the new sail plan. *Idle Queen* is a unique Dreadnought, different on the outside as well as the inside.

9 October 1977: Half the necessary walls are in place around the bathroom. Faido is not happy with the size of the bathroom, saying this will not be her favorite room on the boat. But then, I ask myself, why should she want it her favorite room?

23 October 1977: I installed a diesel fuel transfer pump, completing the fuel system on the boat. Advances were made in kitchen cabinetry, and in bathroom bulkhead installations. I'm waiting for rain to soak some wooden rubrails, so I can bend them in place.

In January 1978 I had been at it for a year. I sent out a status report:

Exterior: all work below deck level is done except for painting the bottom, the boot topping, and the rubrails. The boat could be put in the water on short notice. The biggest item remaining outside is to erect mast and standing rigging. The smaller necessities include bow and stern pulpits along with the life lines and running rigging. We are some time away from being able to sail.

Interior: All the major items below deck are roughed into place. The engine is ready to run. The toilet and stove are ready to go. A relatively small amount of work remains to hooking up the fresh water supply system, the waste drain system, plus wash basin. If the boat were put in the water, we could move aboard and camp out.

The electrical system, interior and exterior, remains untouched, but we have a layout in mind. Thousands of cabinets, shelves, lockers, bookcases, etc., remain to be designed, made and installed. The final, and perhaps the major, job is the decorative finishing of the interior, including insulation. We haven't decided how to do this yet.

12 February 1978: The boat has a rough–finished dinette. (I guess you know the operable word there.) The varnished mahogany table looks incongruous mid the acres of unfinished fir plywood and rough fiberglass.

26 March 1978: I dedicated recent work to the interior of the boat: the pantry bins and hanging locker are roughed in and the forecabin dresser and head cabinets are well advanced. I'm also continuing to experiment with putty mixes to provide a coating for the rough bulkheads prior to painting.

18 June 1978: We have on order both the standing rigging and the working sails. These are the last of the big ticket items (about $2400 total). We are starting the documentation process. The authorities advise us to save paperwork by calling Norfolk, Va., our home port. This doesn't have the glamorous ring of a San Francisco, but we'll accept the advice anyway. Last week we touched up paint and varnish, and washed and waxed the hull. It does seem tragically ironic to have to perform annual maintenance on an unfinished hull.

2 July 1978: The caprails (which go on top of the bulwarks) are fitted and trimmed, ready to be fastened and painted. I started on the caprails last January, which goes to show that in the boat building business, no matter how long you wait, the nasty jobs just don't disappear. The staysail boom pedestal finally arrived. The boat was measured for documentation purposes (11 tons net), and the papers forwarded to Norfolk.

Mid-July marked a year and a half of boat building. Although a lot remained to be done, I could see the end:

We have had the boat for eighteen months. Below decks we still lack many cabinets and fixtures, insulation, a heater, handholds, much interior trim, and prettying up. The lighting system is almost untouched, and we are mostly without cushions and upholstery. Nevertheless, we could now move aboard and live in reasonable comfort, considering how tough we are. On the exterior, we lack lifelines and handrails in addition to the rigging. The spars are ready to go, but the wire and wire terminals have not arrived. The rope and blocks for running rigging haven't been ordered.

24 September 1978: Our Hong Kong sails have arrived, and they look excellent. These represent our last big-ticket item. We have $29,000 invested in the boat with about $1500 more to go. The name *IDLE QUEEN,* NORFOLK, VA painted on the stern, gives the boat a personality of its own. The documentation is complete.

A month later, *Idle Queen* was seaworthy enough to be moved into water and far enough along for us to live aboard. We located a temporary slip at Redwood City Yacht Club and paid Ivan, a professional boat mover, fifty dollars an hour to transport her there. Launch Day was 21 October 1978.

That morning, Faido and I arose at 0600, too excited to sleep longer. I dressed, ate breakfast, and hurried off to the boat. Dolly and Jean Gendreau, my sister Florence Mary and her family, Floss and Faido joined me about 0800. Several neighbors, including Tim, a mechanic, arrived to watch the proceedings. The homeowners, who had seen the boat hull transformed into the *Idle Queen,* brought out chairs for the dozen spectators.

Ivan pulled up an hour later. He backed his large red-and-white truck into the backyard, hopped out, and surveyed the boat.

"We have a problem," he announced.

The problem was that his truck bed was two feet higher than the bottom of the boat. *Idle Queen* had to be jacked up two feet so the truck could get under her. Ivan got out jacks, and a half dozen of us unloaded wooden planks from his truck. Ivan jacked up the bow a few inches, and we shoved the planks underneath the keel and along the sides inside the cradle to keep the boat upright. After the bow of the 19,000 pound boat was up a few inches, Ivan went to the stern. He jacked on one side while Tim the mechanic jacked in unison on the other. Armed with sledgehammers and pieces of wood, we stood ready to help, pounding in the planks of wood, as needed, to stabilize the boat.

At one point, Ivan exclaimed loudly, "I hope the boat doesn't tip over."

As a precaution, Ivan sent Jean Gendreau and me to the lumber yard for ten-foot planks to use as props. Finally, at noon, the truck bed could slide under the keel. Ivan expertly tied the boat to the truck and drove off.

I wanted to spend the night on *Idle Queen* at the Redwood City Marina, but Faido wouldn't hear of it. Leftover construction scraps lay in the companionway and across the unmade bed. They blocked access to the galley and the head. Cupboards overflowed with tools and parts. Reluctantly, I agreed to return to Floss's house until we cleaned up the boat.

Soon after we moved aboard, we motored *Idle Queen* a mile down Redwood Creek and back to test her diesel engine. This trial went without incident. Dolly and Jean Gendreau joined us on our first shakedown sail, otherwise known as a Chinese fire drill. It turned out that some outhauls and downhauls were too short, and some downhauls too long. We unraveled things eventually, and the boat did well in the light prevailing airs.

In early December, we sailed up the San Juaquin River to Stockton where a permanent slip was available. Faido again signed up for temp jobs. I continued to work on *Idle Queen*. I installed storage bins and bookshelves and finished the interior. Faido sewed curtains, cushions and sail covers when she wasn't working.

Nine laborious months later, in September 1979, I wrote the family: "We now consider that construction of *Idle Queen* is complete. A long list of projects remains, but this will always be the case. We have carried out the precepts of that ancient South African dictum, enunciated by sailor John Guzzwell, to the effect that a man should plant a tree, raise a son (women libbers: modify as required), and build a boat. Furthermore, we have even received compliments on our trees."

Having been on land for most of the previous two years, I was anxious to return to the sea.

Chapter 7

Idle Queen's Maiden Voyage, Part 1: The Untested

*Twenty years from now you will be more disappointed by the things
that you didn't do than by the ones you did do.
So throw off the bowlines. Sail away from the safe harbor.
Catch the trade winds in your sails. Explore. Dream. Discover.*
-Mark Twain

I needed a break. I suggested to Faido that we take a shakedown cruise, a year's circuit of the Pacific. We could sail to Mexico, across the Pacific to Tahiti and Hawaii, to Alaska, and back to San Francisco. Besides really testing the boat, we would discover what further equipment we needed and what modifications in interior design we wanted. Faido made a list of supplies and we started stocking the boat for a September leaving.

The night before their departure, the Stockton sailing community gathered in Idle Queen's *cabin for a farewell party. They toasted Dad for creating* Idle Queen, *and they toasted his dream of crossing an ocean in her.*

One sailor said, "Knowing you, Harry, has been the most rewarding experience of my life."

That evening, Dad called Floss to say good-bye. "We'll be back in a year," he promised. "Don't worry about us."

The next morning, 15 September 1979, they set off.

They started the trip cautiously. They sailed to the California Delta and spent several days in The Meadows, author Erle Stanley Gardner's favorite Delta spot. Here Mom read a cruising book: "What a time they had," she wrote the family. "Miserable. The hatches leaked, the portholes leaked, the rudder came off. None of that will happen to us. We have such a well-built boat."

Leaving the Golden Gate Bridge behind, they ran into near-gale conditions. Mom described the experience:

About 4:00 A.M. the first night, we had the main and staysail up, running before the wind. In a sudden wind shift, the main screamed across in a jibe, and tore through the end of the track. The stopper on the traveler splashed overboard. I yelled for Harry who came bouncing up from the cabin in his stocking feet. He refused to put on his shoes or his safety line, as he hurriedly leaned over the water and tried to pull the main in. He couldn't; the wind was too strong and the topping lift was wound around the rigging. He cut the topping lift, and the boom plunged into the water. We struggled and struggled to recover the boom and the main. Finally, we started the engine and headed the boat into the wind and were able to get the heavy boom into a slot in the boom gallows. Meanwhile, the boom gallows was damaged, as the boom slammed back and forth. I am leaving out some of the nightmare, but when we finished, it was light.

The next day we tried to raise sail, but we were unable to lift the boom without the topping lift. We sailed that day under genny alone. That night the wind came up, and we were under bare pole. The wind whined continually. The seas towered behind us, as tall as a two-story building. *Idle Queen* strove ahead, her pointed end dividing the seas neatly. On we tore through the moonlight. Looking aft, the scene looked like every snapshot of a storm at sea. I felt as if I were rounding treacherous Cape Horn. Whenever I awoke after my fifty-seven minutes of deep sleep, I hoped the wind had abated, but it still moaned and screamed in the rigging. In the morning, the wind and waves were down, and up went the genny. By noon we saw the Cape Martin light. No, not Cape Martin, but Piedros Blancos twenty-five miles farther on. We really screamed along under bare pole. We went into the hairy entrance of Morro Bay at six o'clock.

Harry thinks it great that the grandchildren's sixty-year-old grandma is fighting a gale off the California coast. Actually, I am only fifty-nine. And the gale wasn't frightening since *Idle Queen* is such a heavy safe boat, and I had the radio to listen to.

Sometimes, I wish the man I married had a passion for growing hollyhocks.

At Morro Bay they made necessary repairs. The topping lift, a traveler stop and most of the boom holders on the gallows had been damaged. It was less than a month since they started.

Weather continued to be a factor as they proceeded down the coast. Days later, they left Cojo Bay headed for the Channel Islands near Santa Barbara. Mom reported:

The wind and sea swells were right in our face, and we sailed in light winds. During the first hour, we averaged only two knots. The next hour, we were still thirty miles away from the Channel Islands because we had been swept north. By one o'clock Harry announced we couldn't possibly make the anchorage. Why didn't we jog on through the night and see where we were in the morning? I rebelled and insisted we go back to Cojo Bay. We were both tired from the tiring day and night before, and I was tired from being at the helm all day while Harry put genny up, genny down, main up, etc., trying to get more speed out of the boat. He was dreadfully cross with me, since he doesn't approve of going back, but I pulled my admiral rank and we returned, getting back to our original spot in two hours, so little progress had we made. He had been too tired to agree to start the engine.

I have full confidence in my boat. I think our only danger comes from Harry getting so tired that he doesn't make wise decisions. He doesn't realize that he isn't thinking straight. Back at Cojo, with a fishing boat for company, we ate dinner, and Harry was asleep by seven.

The next day, again in light winds, we made it to Santa Cruz Island. The day after, the lighter winds flared into a gale. *Idle Queen* raced along, heeled to the extent that water rushed in through the scuppers. Harry reefed the main, then took it down, as the wind continued. Under just staysail, *Idle Queen* bowled along. At one point a U. S. Coast Guard helicopter approached. A coastguardsman braced himself in the open doorway, staring down at us, until Harry waved that we were all right.

When the wind abated and I went below, I was shocked. The cabin floor was a foot deep with papers, pans, apples and oranges. I forgot to pack away and tie down loose objects. Even the large radio and TV, tied down on the table, were upended by the virulent weather.

When they reached Avalon, where Dad's family often vacationed, Mom was enchanted:

It was like being on the stage of a huge amphitheater. On the shore was a sandy beach with a road beyond, not for cars, but for bikers and walkers. Above this main thoroughfare, four streets rose steeply into the hills. On the cliffs, the houses perched close together and peered down on us, a beautiful sight at night with their shining lights. We ate lunch, went ashore and walked the road. We looked in the beautiful quality shops, read the menus of the fine restaurants, and strolled to the point and the famous casino. This impressive round building is a movie theatre now, but in the twenties and thirties, Glen Gray and his Casaloma Orchestra played here and broadcast across the country.

The next morning, we walked up a road that led back into the hills. After three blocks, we left the houses behind and were in country covered with palms, cactus, and flowering shrubs. We passed a golf course and tennis courts. As we climbed, the canyon walls closed in on us. At the top of the canyon was a botanical garden, and against the canyon wall was a huge memorial to William Wrigley, who used his chewing gum money to buy Catalina Island. His wife, interested in botany, was responsible for this garden which preserved trees and flowers endemic to the Channel Islands.

From Avalon Mom and Dad sailed overnight to San Diego, the last American port before Mexico. During the day they restocked the boat. In the evenings they pored over the Seven Seas Cruising Association's bulletins. Written by sailors whose main residence is their boat, the bulletins list the latest information on harbors: how to clear into them, who to see, where to get mail, etc. The information, Mom wrote, "makes where you are going so vivid. You know just where to anchor, where the Port Capitan is, and in the Marquesas, you have your mail sent to Maurice's store!"

As they sailed south from San Diego, Mom kept the family apprised of their progress:

When we left San Diego, we started the definitive test. We would sail more than seven hundred miles down the Baja Peninsula without stopping. If we couldn't manage that, we'd never be able to cross an ocean.

That night the wind died briefly, then came in strongly from the north. For the next twenty-four hours, we tore along, being slewed every few seconds by every wave that came by: thrown to the left as the force of the water caught the stern, tossed to the right as the wave passed under us, then over to the left again. Pause. Next wave: left, right, left.

Cooking the evening meal was impossible; likewise, serving any meal. One night I planned chicken á la king on rice. I made the rice and put the pan on the counter where it slammed against the bulkhead, spewing rice everywhere. I heated up a can of stew in a pan for Harry. He ate, and in the same pan, I heated up the chicken for me. The next evening, I opened a can of corned beef hash, broke eggs on top, and we took turns eating out of the frying pan. At night, we just flopped down on the cabin sole. I didn't even take off my shoes; too much effort to brace myself to put them back on.

Sunday morning the wind lost its grip, and we stopped being tossed about. The waves calmed down, too, and I was able to clean the kitchen. Every pan I owned had been used twice; food was stuck everywhere. I felt great after everything was washed and put away. When I finished, the wind began to blow again. We put up the genny and sailed along. We had gone 200 miles in forty-eight hours which was good; 560 to go.

That night was calm, but Harry thought we should keep a watch. How hard it was to sleep just an hour and then be awakened. That was the hardest part of the trip, especially hard in the 2:00 to 5:00 A.M. period. Hated to hear that voice calling me out of a deep sleep.

One night I was on watch about 2:00 A.M., listening to the radio. I heard of a terrific storm that came down from the northwest and hit San Francisco with eighty knot winds. It was 100 miles south of San Francisco at Monterey. I told Harry when he came on watch. He thought we were sitting ducks, and we should turn on the engine and get the boat as far south as we could. We motored south until the wind came up enough to hoist the genny. We also headed back to the Mexican coast where the winds were supposed to be lighter.

Monday morning there was another lull in the wind. I cleaned up the cabin and shook the rugs. I also washed my face for the first time since leaving San Diego. Our position was confirmed as we approached the coast and saw land: the high mountain on Cedros Island. It was Christmas Eve.

I loved Christmas Eve. The San Diego radio station played Christmas music all night. Never had the mystery of the Incarnation seemed more vivid, as I guided my boat along under the stars. I'll never forget that night.

When Harry came on watch at 6:00 A.M., the sky lightened and was covered with clouds, an ominous sign that the storm was on its way. To the east, close to the horizon, was still an open spot through which the sun's first rays made the bowl of clouds above us glow in pinky rose.

"Look in back of you," Harry suddenly said in awe.

Christmas 1979. God had given us His Christmas present early. Rising out of the ocean to the east and stretching high above us and then arching back into the sea in the west was a perfect rainbow. Never had I seen a rainbow in which you could really distinguish the bands of color, and while these blended at the edges, the colors were gorgeous: the top of red, then orange, yellow, then green, blue and violet. They lasted a long time.

The wind and waves surged, not so violently as on Saturday, but exhausting nevertheless. On watch, my hand gripped the tiller and tugged it back on course after the waves slewed it off. My left hand and arm had to hang on to the stanchion to keep from being thrown out of my seat. One hour was about all one could take, and I felt I was developing the most tremendous biceps. Down below was positively dangerous. If I didn't have a good grip on something, I would be slammed across the cabin. While taking off a jacket, I got caught and thrown into the stove. There was no thought of opening Christmas presents.

The night was worse. We left as much sail up as long as possible, willing to put up with discomfort to get farther away from the storm which was hitting Los Angeles and due the next noon at San Diego. During the night came the time to reef the main, and reef again a few hours later. We haven't done enough reefing to know how to do it easily, and things went wrong. Gear broke. Knots got jammed. It was one hour of sleep to two hours of struggle, holding on with one hand, pulling the tiller back with the other. I was exhausted.

"What we have to do," Harry said, "is just concentrate on keeping the boat going, eating and sleeping. Everything else has to go."

I was never scared. *Idle Queen* wallowed on, taking the waves and heeling without a struggle. If we were caught in a gale, I'd just as soon shut up the boat, go below, and let her handle the storm. She is a wonderful boat.

The next day the sky began to clear. We tore south for Cabo San Lucas, 280 miles away. By afternoon, the clouds dissipated, the wind dropped, and the waves calmed. We had a good night. The self-steering finally took over, so we let it do so while we made quick watch changes, one going down and taking outside gear and shoes off while the other put jacket and shoes on. The wind held steady, and we made good mileage. But by supper, the wind came up again, this time from head on. We were so near Cabo San Lucas that we didn't want to alter course to accommodate ease of motion. We were laid over with each slam of the waves. I tired quickly; my upper arms and shoulders ached. This was my sixtieth birthday and perhaps our last night at sea for a while. How heavenly to be able to get my raunchy clothes off and to sleep without having to be awakened through the night! Land people just don't appreciate their blessings.

Our last day. Dried food adorns the galley. Damp clothes are tossed under the table. Only the settee where we sleep is clear. We have one piece of bread left. Oranges are long gone, but the apples are holding out. I am able to nap during the day, but Harry isn't and so can't catch up on his sleep, and he is worn out. It shows in his face and temper.

Toward dusk Cabo Falso, the lowest point of Baja California, was in sight. We had to round the point which had a light. We were too far off shore to make a quick rounding, and the tidal current must have been pouring out of the Sea of Cortez, for it took us hours to get around. Thank God for the almost full moon. It was 2:00 A.M. when we gingerly felt our way into this mile-long indentation in the coast, located another boat at anchor, and put ours down nearby. While Harry did things with lines, I cleared off the bed, piled high with everything that needed to be gotten out of the way or that had fallen on the floor during the last—just found a hat Harry thought he had lost in San Diego!—nine days. We had hot chocolate and crackers and then, for the first time since leaving San Diego, got out of our clothes and into nightclothes. Maybe tonight I'll take a bath! And sailing is supposed to be romantic.

We slept until almost nine and then went out to look around. The long beach is almost empty, and behind it rise stark, barren, rocky hills. Lots of boats are anchored here, since everyone stops at Cabo San Lucas either going north, south or up the Sea of Cortez. It is a beautiful day, and to recount the tale of our stormy trip, I have to refer to my diary. Already the memories of the weariness and pounding are fading.

Cabo San Lucas is just one paved street, badly pockmarked with potholes and sand. There are no curbs or sidewalks. The small houses are separated from the streets by a cement wall, and lots of little shops dot the roads, for Cabo has lots of tourists. Visitors with campers can park along the beach for $1.50 a night. Lots of open-air restaurants cater to them. The town has small grocery stores, a bakery, a couple of hardware stores, and two beautiful hotels. In the harbor are boats seen in San Francisco, Morro Bay and San Diego.

We stayed in Cabo a week, visiting friends we made, getting advice, trading books, and eating out in the village. I could have spent the winter, and some boats do. But we had a schedule to meet, so after a week of socializing, we left for Isla Isabella where the Mexicans have fish camps.

At dusk, we became apprehensive when a powerboat came up behind us. Harry got out our handheld VHF. Soon a cheerful male voice called the "sailboat off my starboard bow." He and a friend were on their way to Isla Isabella. Since so many people were afraid of pirates, he liked to introduce himself. He and Harry talked for quite a while and agreed to get together at Isabella. The powerboat skipper signed off by saying he would monitor Channel 68 all night in case we had any trouble.

In Isabella, we anchored next to our new friends. I invited them over for Happy Hour. They arrived bearing a huge dish of shrimp that fisherman gave them, cocktail sauce, and a pitcher of ice cubes. After we stuffed ourselves on shrimp cocktail, I fixed dinner, and we continued to talk. That evening was one of the most enjoyable of the year.

As they traveled down the Mexican coast, Mom and Dad's reports were sometimes markedly different. About San Blas, for example, Dad wrote:

The dry rugged mountains of Baja have given way to lush palm greenery and jungle around San Blas and south from there, but still mountainous. Ensenada Matenchen, as lovely a tropical bay as you will find anywhere, is dominated by 7550 foot high Cerro San Juan. San Blas itself is an intriguing 200-year-old town. Junipero Serra's mission trek started from here. San Blas was once the center of government for western Mexico, the principal port in early days for imports from the orient, and claims to be the mother of all Pacific ports. Of course, we negotiated the tricky, new, unmarked channel over the bar and up to town, because Longfellow's last poem was *The Bells of San Blas*. The bells are still there in the crumbling old church.

Mom's description: Spanish ruins, an old church with bells, narrow, dusty cobblestone streets, little shops. A town square by the church with fountain and statue. Groups of Mexicans talking together and Spanish music emanating from the shops. It looked like a set for an opera. I fully expected Carmen to come bursting out from the cigar factory and start the Habanera.

As they wended their way down the coast, Mom continued her reports:

We anchored in bays beside thatch-roofed villages. Local fishermen often stopped by to give or sell us a fish, and we invited them aboard to talk. Another delight was the teenagers who swam out to the boat to practice their English as we, dictionary in hand, improved our Spanish. They were marvelous young people, and the future of Mexico seemed bright. There were visits from boating friends we met in Cabo who were also traveling south. We were having such a heavenly time, and we had an astonishing realization: we weren't spending much money! With few marinas in Mexico, we anchored out. We ate the canned goods we brought, with an occasional inexpensive meal or snack ashore. To help the local economy, I bought crafts, and I gave generously at local church services. Sometimes we met friends who had engine breakdowns and repairs of several hundred dollars, but since we seldom used our Sabb diesel, that didn't happen to us. Harry's pension and Social Security checks were piling up in the bank.

When they reached Manzanillo, Mexico, friends flew down from Houston for a week. They toured in a whirlwind of activity. With the friends' rented car, Mom and Dad provisioned the boat for the journey's next leg. After their friends left, Mom and Dad needed only 140 gallons of water and fifty gallons of diesel. But nowhere near the harbor could they find either. Mom used her social skills to solve the problem:

For diesel, there's a gas station about two miles away, and we could lug the diesel up the hill and down, several times if we had to. Someone suggested that perhaps at the *palapa*—a thatch-covered beach food stand—we could buy water. If the *palapa* would let us fill our jugs, we had the capacity for seven gallons at a time, which would mean rowing to the boat, emptying the jugs, and rowing back to shore twenty times, but it had to be done.

On the return trip from Manzanillo by bus Friday, we decided to have a beer at the *palapa* and befriend the young manager. Unfortunately, he wouldn't sell us water.

Next door to the *palapa* stood a beautiful three-story home, a big front porch on each story. As we walked past, two American couples greeted us warmly. Since we were the only boat in the cove, they enjoyed our comings and goings and acted as if they knew us, perhaps from hearing our voices across the water.

Inspired, I stopped and called to them, asking if they had an outside spigot and would sell us water. No, they replied, they wouldn't sell us any, but we could take all we wanted. Moreover, Mr. Stein thought that if we backed our boat close to shore, between his hose and ours, we could fill our tanks easily. Which we did. Both couples enjoyed helping us, and it was a relief to have full water tanks again.

That left us with only the diesel problem. We took the bus to Manzanillo again. The long distance phone was in a small restaurant. While I waited for the operator to reach my daughter, Faith, I joined a Canadian couple at a table—Harry had gone to the post office—and we got chatting. They were so nice, staying in a trailer park. Sometimes I embarrass myself with my deviousness, but I made a long story out of getting water, and added that all we had to do was lug the diesel. *Oh, couldn't we help? Please, let us help.* They had an empty five-gallon jug. So we spent the day with them, visited the farmer's market, took them to the hotel for lunch, got the diesel, visited their trailer park, they came to the boat...

With the boat fully provisioned, Mom and Dad were ready to conquer the Pacific Ocean.

Chapter 8

Idle Queen's Maiden Voyage, Part 2:
The Stress and the Triumph

To the question, "When were your spirits at the lowest ebb?"
the obvious answer seemed to be, "When the gin gave out."
-Sir Francis Chichester

Sailing across the Pacific should feel like a romantic vacation, an all-inclusive cruise of sea and sun. In reality, close-quarter living for weeks on end tested Mom and Dad's good humor. Mom lamented:

Our thirty-six year marriage was rapidly unwinding. I found the constant motion aggravating. In my usual way, I made out a list of the chores to be accomplished: dishes, kitchen cleaned, table in order. Completing the whole list takes forty-five minutes, but having to hold on with one hand, sometimes two, made it endless. Nothing would stay put. One day I handed Harry's breakfast out to him in the cockpit, and then put mine down. My plate went sliding, but the corned beef hash and egg slid faster and landed in the dirt. Another day, Harry put my breakfast plate down on the cockpit floor. I carefully backed down and put my bare dirty foot into my French toast and syrup.

One morning I stood in the galley and just screamed! This is the first time I've done that, and probably the last, but I was so frustrated at being thrown around and slammed this way and that.

Our main problem was lack of sleep. Our night started at 7:00 P.M. when I went to bed for two hours. That was early, and I slept only one hour. From nine to eleven I sat in the cockpit listening to the radio while Harry was below, and so on during the night for two-hour periods. With sail changes and delays of getting out of bed and dressed, it would be nine in the morning before we each got— supposedly—six hours of sleep. For the first few days, we thought, "How great, we can get along on six hours of sleep." Actually, it was nearer to five. I didn't realize how tired I was until something went wrong, and I lashed out at Harry. When he asked me something like, "Why don't you throw out the egg shells?" it didn't come out pleasantly. It came out, "You dumb ox, why in hell don't you throw out the damn egg shells?" He didn't say that, but it sounded as if he had, so I flared up. After a few days of that, Harry decreed we each would take a morning and an afternoon nap.

Our routine settled down, and we vowed to be polite and loving to each other no matter how tired and irritable we felt. Harry finished his sleep about nine. While I got breakfast, he worked up the sun sights he took earlier. After breakfast, I did a few housekeeping chores—dishes and laundry—and went to bed to sleep as long as I wished, usually until noon. After lunch, Harry went to bed for a couple of hours, and I took books to the cockpit and settled under the awning. When Harry woke up, we had a nice chat and an early dinner. We watched the sun set and the stars come out. I went to bed about seven.

Weather occasionally disrupted their routine:

At seven degrees north of the equator, we saw the doldrums stretching across our path with dark clouds. At six we headed under them. Harry was at the helm about eight when a squall line approached. We got the mainsail down prudently, leaving up just the jib and staysail. Then wham! We were hit by sixty knot blasts, and *Idle Queen's* starboard rail went under, flooding the cockpit. Blinding lightning exploded around us. It was all I could do to hang on to the boom crutch stanchion and stay in the boat. Harry, almost vertically above me, grimly held on to his stanchion with one hand, as he steered with the other, pulling on the tiller with all his might to keep us from capsizing. An hour and a half passed before the wind let up. We took the staysail down, and the boat coped with the wind. In the lightning flashes, we looked like every movie of a hurricane—seas pounded by rain so just peaks, like cake icing, stood up, the waves torn off horizontally.

With the staysail finally secured, we rode out the other squall lines, and about 4:00 A.M. it cleared for a while. The next day at eleven, another squall line hit us with sixty knot winds. Over we went again, and this time it was more traumatic as we knew what to expect. That night was worse, because the wind and storms raged unrelentingly. The third day saw constant rain. For the next five days we encountered squall lines.

The trades petered out as we neared Hiva Oa, French Polynesia. Our Wednesday arrival stretched to Thursday and then Friday noon, and we motored the last ten hours. Ten boats were here, six from Cabo San Lucas. Two men in dinghies rowed out to meet us and offer advice on anchoring.

With anchors down we had a quick supper and, tired, went to bed. But we accomplished a milestone: we crossed an ocean! The 2840 mile passage took thirty-five days.

The next morning, a Saturday, we cleared in with the French gendarme. We asked about changing money, but the banks were closed. I longed for fresh fruit and vegetables. The gendarme pulled a wad of five thousand franc notes from his pocket and insisted that we could pay him back when the banks opened. Later, we realized he gave strangers $130 for groceries.

After resting a few days, we sailed the ninety miles to Nuku Hiva and picked up mail at Maurice's store, just as the South Seas Cruising Bulletins advised.

There are about ten islands in the Marquesan group with two official French check-in points. On Hiva Oa it is about a mile to town from the small cove where the boats anchor. We never walked far. Passing cars always stopped and offered us rides.

Harry learned not to give money for favors. We were out in the dinghy one day when we passed a Marquesan boat full of fish. "Would you like to sell one?" Harry asked the young men. He figured they could use the cash for gasoline.

The men looked at each other for a moment. "No," one said.

We asked our friend Philippe, a French school teacher, why they wouldn't sell us a fish.

"They would never do that," Philippe explained. "They were probably planning a family party. If they had more fish than they needed for themselves, they would have given you one. But never would they have taken your money."

As our shakedown cruise continued, we regretted more and more the deadlines we set. In Nuku Hiva, fresh fruits and vegetables come from a Japanese farm four miles back in the mountains. One day a charming young man gave us a ride back from town. As we were let out at the boat harbor, the Marquesan youth remarked, "I'll be glad to drive you to the Japanese farm tomorrow."

My thoughts raced. If he did that, then we could invite his family to go sailing, and then they might invite us to their farm to watch the copra being harvested. Wouldn't that be marvelous? Then I remembered: we were leaving the next day for the Tuamotoes.

Dad described this passage:

From the Marquesas, we sailed to Papeete, Tahiti. The direct route is blocked by the Tuamotoes, also known as "The Dangerous Archipelago." These coral atolls rise only a few feet above the sea. We planned to stop at one of them if we could. Chances began to look poor when we ran into a late-season frontal system two days out of Nuku Hiva. We had headwinds, rain and heavy overcast for five days. At one point, we sailed two days with only one sun sight, and tacked away from Ahe and Manihi to avoid coming on them in the dark of the moon. The next day the sun was out, and in late afternoon the palms of Rangiroa rose out of the sea. We found Tiputa Pass and anchored in a delightful traditional South Sea island lagoon. Clear water, white sand and tall coconut palms made it one of our most rewarding stops.

Tahiti was a highlight for Mom:

The main street of Papeete runs along the waterfront. On the sidewalk passes all Papeete. Such handsome men, such beautiful women. It's a regular fashion parade since no two dresses are alike. There are many dress good stores here, and the women make their own beautiful clothes, usually a form of the *pareu*. No shoulders, but the material is held up over the bosom by a drawstring and then billows out. It is so hot here, the women don't wear bras, just panties under the billowing material, a flower behind their ears.

Neither Harry nor I felt tip-top in Papeete, maybe because of the heat in the cabin, perhaps because of the dark-looking water from Nuku Hiva. I didn't entertain, which is such a great way to get a place's history. We went to one party on an adjoining boat, and we took a bus trip around the island. We went on almost daily shopping trips in our eight days. The officials were charming, and the ladies I bought shell jewelry from, very loving. I bought a few things and was given a present of something else!

We had a pleasant sail eleven miles across open water to Moorea, Tahiti's sister island. Tahiti is mountainous, but Moorea's mountains resemble cathedral spires and are spectacular. By mid-afternoon we found the pass we wanted through the reefs, and anchored near three other sailboats. A young couple from the next boat rowed over as I finished my swim. I invited them aboard, but they were going snorkeling and would join us later. As we finished dinner in the cockpit, Christie and Doug arrived. Christie brought me a beautiful shell.

Doug is an oceanographer; Christie has a master's degree from Stanford in water pollution control. They decided to leave their state jobs, take the money in their retirement funds, and spend three years on Doug's sailboat going around the world before settling down and starting a family. One of the pluses of our lifestyle is that young people are happy to spend time with us. They must assume, since we live as we do, that although our bodies are old, our spirits are young. Which, of course, they are! We just loved Doug and Christie, and we chatted on long after dark. Christie was out of reading material and was reduced to reading the encyclopedia they had on board. I sent her off with several books I had read.

The next morning, as we sailed off, Doug blew his conch shell. This is the third time we've been tooted off on a long journey. This must be a sailor's tradition.

It was a cloudy, rainy day, and windless. For three days we sat on a glassy sea with Tahiti, Moorea, and Tetiaroa in sight. Tetiaroa is Marlon Brando's South Pacific pad. We were becalmed so long, I thought Marlon would motor out and insist we come in and wait for wind.

Sunday the wind came up, and our trip really began. The first two weeks we were hard on the wind, but the wind was not particularly strong, and I didn't mind. We sailed through numerous squalls, but on this passage we were not so gung-ho to make time as we had been on earlier ones.

Getting from Tahiti to Hawaii is not as easy as it looks. The current pushed us west fourteen to twenty miles a day. The northeast trades on the other side of the equator set us still farther west. On the advice of more experienced sailors, we tried to get as much easting as we could while we were in the South Pacific's southeast trades. This meant being hard on the wind for the first ten days or so, hoping to get as far east as 143°. As one sailor remarked, "Which would you rather do—be hard on the wind for ten days, or for a whole month?"

The doldrums were good to us; lots of squalls without much wind in them. The last night featured ominous dark clouds, and lots of putting up and taking down of the main as we passed under the black bridges overhead. In the morning, the wind came in strongly from the northeast, and we eased sheets and laid a course for Hilo.

For the next two weeks we rocked back and forth. I hated the twenty knot winds with their accompanying steep seas. I swore and got thrown about and finally gave up doing much boat keeping. Occasionally the wind eased and the seas went down and acted like a lady, but the trip was the most unpleasant we had.

On the San Diego to Cabo and Manzanillo to Marquesas runs we did lots of sail changing at night. If the wind lightened, Harry went out on the bowsprit and worked from the heaving platform in the dark taking down the jib and attaching the genny, a job of at least an hour, especially since at night we were both conscientious about wearing the harnesses which attached us to a lifeline.

If the wind increased, the genny would come down and the jib would go up. Up to three reefs might be taken in the main, another long job. This time we took it easier, and probably more sensibly. At dusk the genny came off and the jib went up or, if it was too windy, we left it off. The main was reefed once or twice, and we jogged on easily until dawn. We still called the other on deck if a squall line appeared, and played it safe by fastening the main boom into the boom crutch. Our days soon settled down into our passage routine.

Our most firmly fixed time was 6:00 P.M., after supper. Harry went to bed on the settee mattress on the cabin sole. I sat in the cockpit and enjoyed the sunset. My portable radio, after getting doused with sea water, no longer worked. No music or news from America, no discussions from Papua, New Guinea, which used to entertain me. I worked on my novel mentally or, if the sky was a bowl of stars with no squalls, I dozed for short periods. At eight, the dinger went off, and I woke Harry and we changed shifts. With less sail handling, the shift changes went smoother. Harry's last shift was from five to seven A.M., when he usually took a morning sun sight. He worked up the sight while I got breakfast and we listened to the weather on the cabin radio.

Hawaii broadcasts the time ticks, and at forty-eight after the hour, it gives the gales and storms in the western Pacific; at forty-nine after the hour, it does the eastern Pacific; and at fifty after the hour, tropical southern Pacific south to 25°. Almost always it was the same: *There are no warnings in the tropical Pacific. Repeat: There are no warnings in the tropical Pacific.* I found this very comforting.

After I did the minimum of boat keeping, Harry went back to bed until noon to supplement his six hours of interrupted sleep. I took my Bible and related books to the cockpit for a serene morning of study while the sheet-to-tiller rig continued to steer *Idle Queen* on its course with no fuss or complaint. When Harry awoke, he got the noon sun sight which he worked up while we ate lunch. It was fun to find out how far we had gone and how much farther to the equator and then Hawaii.

After lunch, I went to bed to sleep as long as I wanted. I woke up slowly, with no one standing over me waiting to get in bed as soon as I arose. As I got supper, Harry drank his cocktail. Until he ran out of liquor. What a calamity!

On our final day in Papeete, we bought last-minute groceries, including a bottle of gin. Everything was hastily shoved out of sight. When Harry finished his current gin bottle, he couldn't find the new one.

"My mind is shot, just shot," he complained.

"You couldn't find anything when you were thirty," I reminded him.

We searched the boat, but didn't find it. I remembered that when the Gendreaus gave me a stuffed mouse, they inserted a pint of brandy to give me further comfort. I retrieved the pint of brandy. Mixed with pineapple Tang, Harry made it last a week. Then he reluctantly started on the bottle of fine wine he had given me.

One day I had the main rug up, as I cleaned the boat. "I'm sure it isn't there," Harry said, "but check those little bins, will you?"

I lifted a narrow cover and there, grinning up at me like a baby lying on its back, was the bottle of gin. By careful rationing, Harry made it last to Hawaii.

On Saturday, 24 May, we were coming up to Hilo too far to the east. For the first time since Moorea, we jibed the boat, following Harry's calculations. Our landfalls weren't very exciting; we both had such confidence in Harry's sight-taking ability that we were always sure of where we were. This confidence was reinforced when we were puzzling over the entrance to Rangiroa in the Tuamotoes. Was that division in the coconut palms the pass, or just a low spot in the reef? Harry took a sun sight and announced that we were opposite the pass. We turned and, sure enough, it was the pass.

Now Harry guided us toward the lighthouse on the point, and after midnight we picked up the light which is visible for nineteen miles. Shortly after dawn I closed the coast and jibed to westward. A small power boat with two men aboard rushed toward us. I was apprehensive about how much we would enjoy Hawaii. Many magazine articles said the Islanders were very unfriendly; they didn't really want mainlanders coming over in their sailboats. The powerboat slowed beside us.

"Where did you come from?" asked the Hawaiian.

"Tahiti," Harry replied.

"You're the first people we've talked to in a month," I added.

"Welcome to Hawaii!" they called, as they sped off.

We reached Radio Bay, a protected corner of the Hilo Harbor. Two men helped us tie up. Since Monday was the Memorial Day holiday, and Sunday the office was closed, we would have to pay twenty-five dollars to get cleared in from a foreign port, or else stay on the boat until Tuesday. We opted to stay aboard, of course, although I did long for some groceries.

"Where did you come from?" asked a man who helped us dock.

We told him and asked where he was from.

"I live here," he said.

Later Ross returned with his beautiful Hawaiian wife. "Can we get you anything from a store?" he asked.

I asked for a loaf of bread, a dozen eggs, and something sweet. We were starved for sweets. They brought us a chocolate cake with whipped cream frosting. We ate the whole thing right then.

My sister, Faith, and her husband flew over to vacation with Mom and Dad who gladly scratched Alaska off their itinerary. The day after their guests flew home, Mom and Dad started their forty-two day sail back to San Francisco. Dad wrote:

The trip home was mostly a slow dull grind. IQ's bottom was so foul, it took a gale of wind to move us at more than four knots. The North Pacific High, which we would ordinarily go north around to get fair winds for the trip, was sitting so far north (as high as 44°N) that we deemed this route infeasible. As a result, we had the wind dead ahead of us for ninety percent of the way. At least we know for sure we can go to windward over long distances. The main enlivening on the trip came when we caught a forty-seven inch mahi-mahi.

We sailed under the Golden Gate Bridge in the early morning of 15 September 1980. We had been gone a full year to the day. After a few hours sleep, I went ashore in early morning to call Floss and tell her we were back.

"Were you worried?" I asked.

"No. You said you'd be home September 15. I was sitting here by the phone waiting for your call."

Mom summed up their successful maiden voyage:

The only breakdown in our gear was a staysail block which Harry easily replaced. The engine started when we needed it. The mast stayed up.

Our guest book contained the names and addresses of wonderful people. Our photograph albums would refresh our memories of unbelievably beautiful scenes. We returned to Stockton with renewed enthusiasm and a list of seventy-two modifications and items for the boat.

Harry redesigned my galley so cups and pans wouldn't flip over. He didn't like the way the boat trimmed with a big water tank in the bow and moved it. We needed more bookshelves. We hadn't planned on a dodger but now felt it essential. We no longer wanted a steering vane. We did want a knotmeter. We had a better feel for the food and clothes to take on our next trip. Most gratifying of all, we were sure we could afford a cruising life, and oh, it was such fun!

How could we live any other way?

Chapter 9

No Going Back

He travels fastest who travels alone.
-Anonymous

The three weeks of boat rest slowly passed. As I recovered, I formulated a new plan. Other sailors shared their plans to continue on to New Zealand. The prevailing currents favored sailing in that direction. I decided to do the same.

Larry and Sheri returned from Fiji with my mail. Assuming I would visit Fiji, friends and family had written me there. I told Sheri I'd like to visit Fiji. Concerned about my health, Sheri offered to sail there with me. After some thought, I turned her down for two reasons: the cyclone season was rapidly approaching, and I didn't want to sail with another person. The demands of sailing solo appealed to me. It tested me physically and mentally, and what better way to stay active and alert? Although I was seventy-six, I felt fit enough in both respects to rise to the challenge. I wanted to complete this voyage on my own.

My first challenge was the weather. There is much concern, even trepidation, about weather in the yacht fleet headed south in November. Andy and Sandy on *Jakaranda* are professional sailmakers. They pointed out periodically on the morning VHF radio net that it was best to get sails in top condition, fully repaired, before leaving Tonga. It was likely, they said, that at least one gale would be encountered before covering the 1300 miles to New Zealand. I hired them to tighten the leach on my Yankee jib.

"A Chinese sail," Andy noted.

"Yes, I buy cheap sails, so they blow out before the rigging goes."

"Ah, a much neglected principle," Andy said, tongue-in-cheek.

I was charged only ten dollars for the repair, and knew I was given a discount. You can't pick up a needle and thread for only ten dollars.

The local weather turned fine on 3 November, and I set out to ease my way southwest through the maze of chart vigias—reefs, rocks, shoals, "discolored water," "volcanic activity," "obstruction reported"—that officially and unofficially splatter the area about Tonga and south to Minerva Reef. *The Magellan GPS had better keep working*, I thought, as I passed through this area. It did.

Along my route one of the sight oddities is the view of Fao and Tofua islands. These two, juxtaposed in the sea, look like educational blocks in a toy store. Fao is 3000 feet high and a smooth cone; Tofua is 1500 feet high and pancake-flat.

As I passed Minerva Reef, the mild southeaster that had been blowing backed into the northeast. Amazingly enough, this fair wind blew from NE or ENE—generally at a friendly velocity, sometimes blustery, wet and overly muscular—all the way to New Zealand. Twelve days out of Neiafu, I covered the 1300 miles and anchored one late afternoon in the Hatea River just downstream from Whangarei. My trip into Neiafu had been unexpectedly rough, the trip out unexpectedly mild. No doubt this supports Emerson's Law of Compensation.

Hurricane seasons have a useful purpose for the circumnavigating small boat sailor. They force him to make detours, to get out of the comfortable trade wind anchorages and into more rugged territory. I picked a spot well south in which to spend the 1992-'93 southern summer. Where does one find a spot that is all-weather, nothing bigger than ripples on the harbor water; has secure tie-ups and a good dinghy dock; is within four blocks of the town center of 40,000 people and within two blocks of a large supermarket; has haul-out facilities within a half mile of town with skilled, cheap labor; and, is in a subtropical climate with pleasant hilly and wooded environs? I found it in Whangarei on New Zealand's North Island.

While I checked in, I rafted to a Danish boat. I had to cross this other boat, stepping down several feet from the dock to its deck, to get to *Idle Queen*. Once I stepped on the lifeline instead of a stanchion. No damage was done, but the boat's captain erupted from the cockpit in a rage. The word "apoplexy" flashed through my mind. He shouted at me in English and Danish. The English was repeatable, but I doubt the Danish was. The captain's wife stood behind him, open-mouthed, and slowly shook her head. I was too shocked to offer an apology, and slunk across the deck to IQ. Soon afterward, the boat was put in the hands of a broker and the couple flew back to Denmark.

The marina was a magnet for sailors traveling across the South Pacific. Among them were Mary and Dave Berg on *Kismet*, Kris and John Fulton on *Mew*, and Canadian Dave, a commercial fisherman with his teenage son, Michael, on *Blue Serenity*. Other sailors represented South Africa, Germany, Japan, and Italy. Politicians wouldn't believe the camaraderie of international sailors when they get together in a foreign port.

On Thanksgiving Day, Kris and John entertained ten of us aboard *Mew* for a traditional turkey dinner. I met Jean Giquel (*Judikael*), a tough, outspoken, ex-Parisian gendarme. At age 59, Jean was the oldest singlehander in the group until my arrival. Jean's wife, Collette, refused to sail. Even when she visited Jean in ports around the world, Collette stayed in a hotel rather than on the boat.

Jean was socially expansive. He cooked gourmet meals for ten in a cabin even smaller than *Mew*'s. At one of Jean's dinners, a New Zealander named Bertil awakened everyone with the statement that it was a New Zealander who made the atom bomb possible. After ruminating, I remembered that Ernest Rutherford, who worked in England, was a New Zealander. Rutherford won the Nobel Prize for Chemistry in 1908.

At another dinner I met "Massa" Masato, a Japanese sailor who was circumnavigating the world in a 21' sailboat. His wife accompanied him until she ran out of birth control pills on the seventy-four day sail from Japan to Hawaii. The resulting pregnancy forced her to return home. Masato, his wife, and their baby were Jean's guests. The party included another Japanese sailor, two Frenchmen, and me. The conversation was in English, even though only one of us is at ease in the language. We stayed away from politics and international trade, concentrating on the virtues of wine (Neufchateau du Pape) and beer. We agreed that the best New Zealand beer is Speights, a rich dark brew from Dunedin.

Although Jean loved to cook, he hated washing up. One night I watched as he dunked the dirty dishes in a pan of clear cold water and sploshed them around. After drying them, he stacked them back on the shelf, ready for the next dinner.

I held my dinner parties at restaurants. After one of those dinners, Jean, Dave (*Blue Serenity*) and I wandered the back streets of Whangarei where we came upon a massage parlor. Jean and Dave went upstairs to price the operation. I lingered in the street below. Shortly they returned.

"Sixty-five dollars!" growled Jean. "I hate professional women."

Despite our language difficulties, and probably because we were the oldest, Jean and I spent a lot of time together. One day Jean told me about the can of powdered milk he bought. The can wasn't his regular brand, but he knew it was milk because a baby was pictured on the label. He added a spoonful to his coffee, took a mouthful, and almost threw up. He showed me the can; it contained detergent for washing diapers.

I told about my excursion to the post office. I asked the clerk how long it took mail to reach the United States.

"You mean a liter?" the clerk asked.

For a moment I wondered if I looked like a wino. Then the translation dawned: "Yes," I answered, "a *letter.*"

Besides sailing friends, I was fortunate to have relatives in New Zealand. My brother John's wife, Catherine, a native of England, has a brother and two sisters living in the Auckland area.

"You'll enjoy Patricia and Anne," Catherine said.

Patricia married a tea taster out of Hong Kong, and the family lived there until her husband's untimely death. Anne, a former nurse, was divorced. She and her ex-husband's second wife, a Chinese lady, became best friends and talked often.

"But," Catherine warned, "be careful of Tony."

True to Catherine's word, I enjoyed Patricia and Anne and their offspring. Perversely, Tony and I took to each other immediately. Under a shock of white hair beamed a cherubic face. In his seventies, Tony was a divorced, retired school teacher. A typical New Zealander, he shunned shoes. When we entered a bar, Tony had me walk directly in front of him so no one would notice.

On Boxing Day I took the bus to Auckland for a family picnic. The three-hour bus ride from Whangarei passed through rolling hills, along the coast, and over a small mountain range. This area of North Island is forest and pastureland with grazing cattle and sheep. Everything was green, including the giant ferns.

I was impressed with Auckland. The downtown area contains an eye-catching mixture of modern skyscrapers and well-maintained buildings that may be a century old. The area across and around the city is dotted with long-extinct volcanoes that offer a myriad of viewpoints to look over the spacious harbor and surrounding islands in the gulf.

In Auckland, Patricia found an engineer for a project I long had in mind. I gave him IQ's rudder and boomkin measurements so he could create a rudder-trim-tab and steering vane for me. This would provide a better, easier to adjust, system for the boat to steer herself.

I'm getting too old for this sheet-to-tiller steering and its need for attention.

At Anne's place, thirty people gathered for swimming and tennis. That day I lay in the sun and thought how much I preferred this to past Christmases where I had to wear ear muffs and mittens. The next day Tony drove me around to show off the beauty of the pohutukawa tree. These large trees bloom around Christmas and are known as the "Christmas trees" of New Zealand. With their brilliant red blossoms, they add a festive splash of color to the otherwise green landscape.

Tony expressed an interest in sailing, so I invited him to join me on a fifty-mile cruise to Great Barrier Island. We anchored that first night near the mouth of the Hatea River. Next morning Tony, who acted as deckhand, strained to haul up the anchor. I went to the bow to add a hand.

"You're half my size and older," Tony wheezed in protest, as sweat wreathed his round face. But he accepted my help.

We ran into strong southeast headwinds as we sailed toward Great Barrier Island. We would not make land before nightfall. Tony wasn't too disappointed when we turned back. He said later, he left the contents of his stomach in the heaving seas, and nearly his upper dentures. That night brought a thirty knot southeaster and heavy rain punctuated by thunder and lightning. The radio reported that four men were rescued from a capsized catamaran off North Cape. Tony and I were glad to be tied to a dock.

Tony's girlfriend, Billie, is a petite, dark-haired librarian slightly younger than he. Over several days, they drove me on a tour of North Island. The Northland countryside is green, the hills wooded and indented by deep inlets and quiet rivers. About halfway between Whangarei and Paikia is the Glow Worms Cavern. This limestone cave is a hundred yards long and encloses a small stream. Limestone deposits on the walls and ceilings give off a greenish-yellow light. Our tour guide was a young Maori girl who took pride in recounting stories of her ancestors as she showed us around.

We stopped at Kerikeri and at Paikia on the Bay of Islands and looked at the treaty house at Waitangi. The British signed a treaty with the Maoris in 1840. The Maori and English language versions of the treaty do not agree, exacerbating difficulty between the races.

On Saturday evening, we missed by one minute the last ferry of the day in the wilds on the north side of Hokianga Inlet. We sat with the car lights on in front of the ferry slip, as we pondered the hundred mile detour we faced. As we watched, the ferry made a U-turn and returned. I was amazed. This is the only time that I've seen a ferry come back for a late fare.

We had dinner and drinks and stayed that night at the ancient, two-story wooden Masonic Hotel in Rawene. Rawene bills itself as the "place where sun rises and sets." Later we spent hours in Waipona Forest looking at the ancient and famous kauri trees which go back to the early days of the island. These slow-growing giants, as big but not as tall as the redwoods, are no longer allowed to be cut. New Zealanders look up in awe at kauri trees the same way that Americans stare in awe at the redwoods.

On the way back to the boat, Tony stopped to give me a treat. The famous kiwi, national bird of New Zealand, is difficult to see in the wild. They are nocturnal. At an aviary that specialized in kiwis, we watched behind a glass screen in a dark room as a group of these small, chicken-like birds, pounded on the dirt for food. I was excited to add the bird to my life list.

Back in Whangarei, I had *Idle Queen* hauled out at Austral Marine for maintenance work. The Canadian boat, *Blue Serenity*, was hauled out as well. When *Blue Serenity* went back in the water, the effervescent Dave got aboard, gunned the engine, turned to wave to the crowd on the wharf, and smashed head-on into a piling.

A few days before Christmas, Austral Marine hosted a big December barbecue for employees and customers. I went along with Jean Giquel, Kris and John, and Mary and Dave. The late afternoon affair took place on a flat area of green overlooking the river. Six fifteen-kilogram, eight-month-old lambs were roasted over mechanically turned spits. The meat was surprisingly tender. This kiwi specialty was my first such barbecue; I could become addicted. Faido would have enjoyed it.

At Austral Marine, I met Paul and Elizabeth Farge, a prominent political couple. I spent Christmas with them. Paul is a Frenchman who sailed to New Zealand in 1954, stayed and married. He remains French. He wears a beret in the picture of local heroes displayed on the town billboard. As a professional photographer, Paul knew and photographed many of the great early singlehanders: Tambs, Gau, Allcard, Moitessier, and many more. He added my picture to his set.

Paul also photographed and had an extensive collection of nudes. I got hold of one—the photograph, not the nude—and had Elizabeth sign it: "To Jack, in remembrance of old times, with much love,

Elizabeth." I sent it to Jack Farrington in Florida. Maggie Farrington noted that the photograph was mailed from New Zealand, where I just happened to be. Jack kept it anyway.

After Christmas I explored New Zealand's South Island on my own. I flew to Christchurch and took a bus around the area. I marveled at the variations in the island. The northern, southern, and eastern coastal plains are used for farming. Cattle, deer, and sheep graze across the green land. The interior hill country is arid, almost desert, and supports only merino (wool) sheep grazing. Along the west coast lie the Southern Alps. Their snow-covered peaks with glaciers and deep fjords run into the Tasman Sea. Mt. Cook, at 3763 meters and with ice far down its steep sides, looks like a Himalayan peak.

I took the cruise boat down Milford Sound. The Tasman Sea was uncharacteristically quiet. Mist surrounding the waterfall-streaked tops of the peaks rising sheer out of the fjord gave a romantic cast to the scene.

On my last day in this area, I visited Invercargill, the world's most southern city except for Punta Arenas, which is slightly smaller. Invercargill is 2600 nautical miles from the South Pole. I was sorry to leave this part of the country, for the views were spectacular.

Back in Whangarei, brash Mary of *Kismet* discovered that 17 February was my birthday. She organized a surprise party at Austral Marine. Sailors from ten boats and the dozen or so workers at Austral Marine crowded into the meeting room. I was deeply touched. *This may be my lucky year*, I thought, *with two sevens in my birthday.*

About this time Jean Giquel sailed off for Australia. As May approached, I was also anxious to be away, but I still awaited my new self-steering gear from Auckland. It had been promised in early March, then mid-March and finally the end of March. I couldn't be launched from the yard at Austral Marine until the rudder trim tab was received, installed, and painted. If I missed high tide on 8 April, the next possible date to be launched into this shallow river would be either two weeks or possibly four weeks later. To my relief, on 5 April, the steering apparatus arrived. Peter from Austral Marine installed the unit in time for a 0700 launching on 8 April.

The other navigational device I needed was a GPS. The Magellan had again been sent off for repairs. Because New Zealand does not charge import duties on a GPS, I ordered a U.S.-made Trimble as a backup. I also ordered a new solar panel from Australia. When installed, it would give me about sixty watts of power, enough to keep the navigation lights aglow.

While I waited for these deliveries, *Mew*, *Kismet* (who was participating in the race to Japan), *Blue Serenity*, indeed most of the boats whose sailors I palled around with, sailed off. Most, like me, were headed to Australia. I hoped to meet them somewhere along the way. Months earlier we had spread out charts and discussed which route to take and where to stay.

Those who enjoy the quiet, relaxed life find it hard to leave New Zealand. It's especially hard for the small boat sailor who must leave as winter approaches. Cold fronts sweep off the Tasman Sea with distressing speed and frequency. Weather maps, covering twenty degrees of latitude, can show three cold fronts moving simultaneously across the islands. I got lucky. I waited out a twenty to thirty knot northwester for two days and caught a one-day lull. I cleared from Whangarei on 6 May, and rode off on a thirty knot southeaster which pushed me along for two days toward Australia.

The sea area north of New Zealand and south of 30° S is an aviary. With Peter Harrison's *Seabirds* in hand, I spent hours struggling to identify the many species. I was most excited by views of the red-tailed Tropic bird, and that most graceful and beautiful of flyers, the wedge-tailed shearwater.

Three days after passing just north of Norfolk Island, I ran into a broad, deep cold front. The steady northwester headwind blew up to perhaps thirty to thirty-five knots, but the front was peppered with squalls of much higher velocity. I hove-to under triple-reefed main with the tiller tied down. The boat rode comfortably. Late one night, I awakened to a sharp rattling noise. I stepped into shoes and climbed into the cockpit where the sound was even louder. Leaning over the fantail, I saw that a stainless weld on the new steering apparatus had broken. The control rod dangled over the water, shaking and rattling with the surge of the waves. Leaning over still farther, I grabbed the rod before it was lost to the sea. The self-steering apparatus was now useless.

The next morning I was in for a greater shock. My tiller had been showing signs of delamination over the past year. I had made patchy re-gluings as well as I could. That morning I watched as bits of laminate broke off. I was dismayed at the extensive delamination. Then I heard loud cracks and started. The tiller was breaking apart. In the middle of the South Pacific Ocean, I was on a boat I might be unable to steer.

Chapter 10

Cruising Down Under

Land was created to provide a place for boats to visit.
-Brooks Atkinson

I flew below and riffled through my supplies. Rushing back to the cockpit, I hastily wrapped the tiller tightly over its entire length with small diameter rope. Next I lashed on a six-foot piece of 2x4. I stood back and surveyed my work. The tiller looked like a broken arm with an unsightly cast. I treated it gingerly thereafter, uncomfortable with my doctoring. Two weeks later, cast intact, I reached Australia.

Cape York is the northeast corner of Mainland Australia. Alan Lucas writes in his *Cruising Guide to the Coral Coast*: "Cape York provides tolerable anchorage and intense gratification that the top of Australia has been rounded." He could have written "intense gratification and intense relief."

The coast of Queensland stretches for 1100 miles from Brisbane north to Cape York, most of it tucked in behind the Great Barrier Reef. It should be a delightful winter cruising area—protected waters, tropical climate, steady trade winds. Instead, it was a wonderful feeling to have it behind me, something I have not said about any other cruising area. The channels inside the Reef are deep and well marked at strategic points, but they are lined and dotted with submerged reefs and low islets. Currents are strong. The anchorages are often more than a daylight sail apart for slower boats. They are often desperately uncomfortable with a punishing southeasterly swell warping around the headlands.

Traveling inside the Great Barrier Reef, I had to anchor every night. I started out early every day, while it was still dark, hoping to reach an anchorage while it was still light. With the uncomfortable anchorages and the early-morning starts, I slept little.

A gusty southeaster was blowing at the time of my arrival in Gladstone in Queensland. The watchful, empathetic, local liveaboards in the marina lined the wharf to help me into a slip. The town itself, separated from the marina by a small river, seemed less friendly, a hilly, dull, overgrown hamlet. A broken lift bridge made access to the town a long bus ride.

The metal and woodworking shops on the marina grounds gave me prompt attention at a price I could afford. They welded and strengthened my steering vane gear and made a new laminated teak tiller. Meanwhile, Fred and Roma, a couple sailing north from Brisbane on the 51-foot catamaran, *Roam Free,* entertained me with home cooking and provided tips for sailing up the coast.

Of the four Queensland towns I visited on my way north, Bowen was the most interesting. It serves the surrounding farming area and might have been lifted from the center of Nebraska. Bowen was laid out to be the capital of Queensland, but the politicians were not as adept as the planners, and the capital went elsewhere. The streets are as wide throughout as the Avendida da Liberdade in Lisbon.

The town was friendly. At the local supermarket, employees insisted on driving sailors and their groceries back to the yacht basin. The yacht club was crowded on Friday nights. I enjoyed a buffet dinner of range-fed local beef prepared, surprisingly, by a French chef.

When I asked how he happened to find himself in Bowen, he said, "*cherchez la femme.*" The Australian lady smiled brightly at me.

North of Bowen I sailed in behind low, windy Cape Bowling Green and found that neither of my depth sounders worked. A depth sounder is invaluable when coming into strange and poorly charted anchorages. I scrambled through lockers and seized my lead line. By dropping it repeatedly to check the depth, I crept into shoaling water. I spent the next day taking the motor out of one depth sounder and installing it in the other. In Townsville I installed a new digital depth sounder, far superior to the earlier dial read-out types.

Townsville is a city of 100,000 people, touristy and expensive, with a large modern marina and a seaside park. The park sports the huge Moreton Bay fig trees with a multitude of widespread roots dropping to the ground from the lower limbs. A tasteful low-key monument commemorates the Battle of the Coral Sea, fought off Townsville in 1942. Chiseled in the red marble is a map and the story of how the American-Australian forces, in spite of heavy losses, stopped the southward advance of the Japanese.

The Queensland coast is not a scenic area. The hills are low and drab with few palm trees in this part of the tropics. Beyond Cooktown the face of the cliffs show occasional splotches of brilliant white silica to enliven the view. Certainly the loveliest part of the coast is just north of Townsville: Hichinbrook Island. A navigable passage leads between island and mainland and provides a switch to calm and secure anchorages, surrounded by sharply jutting peaks densely wooded with rain forest. I luxuriated for two days in Gayundah Creek with egrets, herons and boobies the only neighbors. I looked for but saw none of the notorious saltwater crocodiles. I did not go swimming.

The town of Cairns—"Pronounced just like a can of beans," Sylvia of *Rite-Trak* had told me—has a distinctive look from the sea. The white buildings, including a number of tourist high-rises, lie along the face of the crescent waterfront, well indented from the surrounding area and horseshoed in by a range of low green hills. Sylvia and Mike live here. We had kept in touch and when I arrived, I called them. Mike was working, but Sylvia hurried down to the marina with her beautiful welcoming smile. We went out to dinner and caught up on our news.

The couple sold *Rite-Trak*, built a house, and returned to the world of paying jobs. Mike skippers either one of two Ocean Spirit's large (85 and 100 feet) sailing catamarans, taking tourists out to view the reefs. He took me along as a guest one day. It was educational to watch him muscle the big vessel into a narrow protected spot in the reef where the passengers could go ashore on a sand spit. I opted for a glass-bottomed launch ride, but was disappointed in the coral gardens. They lacked the color and variety of coral structures around Tonga. I will look for Sylvia and Mike to go circumnavigating again when they recognize once more how dull shore life can be.

A day sail north of Cairns, I maneuvered into a quiet harbor to set anchor. Few boats were there, but I recognized one. I anchored beside it and yelled.

Jean Giquel poked his head out of *Judikael*'s companionway, and rushed on deck. Raising both arms, he shouted, *"Fantastique!"*

I was surprised and pleased to see him. He left Whangarei well before me, and planned to sail directly to Cairns. In IQ's cabin, over a bottle of Australian red, Jean told his story. Forty miles south of Cape York he had in sight a "fire," the light on Cairncrosse Island. He had not allowed for leeway and had not checked his GPS. That night, he ran *Judikael* up on a reef. Jean abandoned ship. His life raft wouldn't hold air, so he and his puppy took off in the dinghy. A passing cargo vessel picked them up and took them to Cairns. There Jean learned that *Judikael* had washed over the reef and onto the mainland beach. A motorized barge recovered the boat, and in Cairns the minor structural damage was repaired. Jean was undaunted. Early the next morning I went on deck to wave him off.

The scenery may not be exciting along the Queensland coast, but the historical spots definitely are. Off Cooktown lies Endeavour Reef where Cook, with strangely poor judgment, ran his vessel aground at night. If the struggle to free the ship had been unsuccessful, Australia might be French-speaking today.

Farther north, off Cape Grenville, I passed within a few hundred meters of Sunday Island, a green-treed, reddish lump in the sea with a pretty little white sand beach on the leeside. Here Bligh, during his small boat voyage after being kicked off the *Bounty*, almost had a second mutiny on his hands. With no hostile natives on this island, his group landed for a period of rest. Bligh was challenged for leadership, but the challenger backed down when the swords were drawn.

Gove Harbor lies across the Gulf of Carpentaria from Cape York. This comfortable harbor is well protected. The company town of Nhulunbuy, manicured and neat, is not far from the harbor. The area is populated by those connected with the bauxite mining and alumina extraction by Nabalco, a $350 million investment. The operation is in the middle of an Aborigine reserve. The Aborigines drifting about the town seem the most unfortunate of the world's indigenous peoples, far worse off than the Maoris or the American Indians. They seem unable to adapt themselves to modern society. In the Aborigine craft shop, I purchased six small items. The clerk tried twice to add them up, then turned the job over to the white store advisor.

At the yacht club bar, I was adopted by a young Aussie couple, Dani and Bob. They showed me around the area by car and helped out with all my little supply and fix-it problems. A day later, Kris and John dropped *Mew's* anchor near me, and all five of us celebrated. It was impossible to match the Aussie capacity for beer drinking.

Dani and Bob, along with a pair of their friends, Audrey and Graham, took us three Americans for an all-day picnic in the outback near Cape Arnhem. We swam in the Arafura Sea. After the swim, Bob pointed out that he was the last in the water.

"Women and children first," he said. "It's always wise to let them check out the croc situation."

The vicious saltwater crocodiles are abundant in this area. Someone always keeps a sharp lookout for moving logs in the water. The next day Audrey and Graham took us to the Aborigine village of Yirrkala, but the Elders only let us visit the craft shop.

In Australia, a boat must sail the same day it is given outbound clearance. It is the only country I know where a vessel is not given at least a twenty-four hour grace period. The regulation was troublesome for me at Gove. The wind tends to lull during the night, then comes up strongly by midmorning. On 4 August, my clearance papers were not ready until 1000. The crowded anchorage was a mass of small whitecaps. Kris and John came aboard and helped control *Idle Queen* while the chain and anchor were raised. Otherwise, I might have blown into another boat before getting underway.

Other regulations reveal the Australian government's unfriendly attitude toward foreign yachts. The quarantine inspection on entering Australia cost me US $90, even though all my stores had been purchased in New Zealand where quarantine regulations are just as strict. New Zealand does not charge for inspection. In New Zealand, a sales tax refund (around twenty percent in both countries) is granted at time of purchase for things installed in an outbound foreign yacht. In Australia, the refund is often not available. When it is available, it must be applied for by mail and sent only to an address outside Australia. Not all Banana Republics grow bananas.

The first two days out of Gove brought brisk winds. Much to my surprise, a little black cormorant, perhaps blown off one of the neighboring islands, landed on the boat that first afternoon. He disappeared during a rough night. Several days later, a beautiful adult crested tern joined the crew. He was a fine specimen with a shaggy crest and an oversized greenish-yellow bill. Occasionally he would fly off for an hour, then return. I could tell from the state of my deck that he was feeding well, and I welcomed the day he moved from the bridge deck to the side deck. He did not leave.

As the days passed, he grew weak although he didn't appear sick. At times, I imagined he welcomed my help when I lifted him under the lifelines and over the bulwarks when he obviously wanted to be airborne. Occasionally, I bounced him up and down on my palm to encourage him to fly. One morning I found him lying dead on the deck. I knelt and slipped him overboard. As the day wore on, I found that I missed his company.

The 2400 mile passage to Cocos (Keeling) Islands was marked only by several days of heavy winds in the usually calm Timor Sea and by several days of light wind in the usually boisterous Indian Ocean. Cocos (Keeling) is a dreamer's dream atoll: palm trees waving in the breeze, clean white sand beaches, a lagoon with the myriad shades of blues and greens reminiscent of the Bahamas, a quiet yacht anchorage off uninhabited Direction Island. As I dropped anchor, I raised a mental toast to those early singlehanders, Joshua Slocum and Harry Pidgeon, who found their way into this same cove years earlier when distance sailing was so much more difficult. When I arrived, seven yachts, including *Mew*, who had passed me on the way, were in the anchorage.

For a week, I swam, ate, and watched the wildlife. The lagoon sports a variety of fish, including the odd hump-backed Napoleon fish, but no sharks. Kris, John and I spent hours sawing—by means of a saw blade on a long pole—green coconuts out of the shorter palms. John is addicted to coconut milk. We visited the two inhabited islands on government launches. Aside from the occasional call to prayers and the head coverings on the women, the Muslim community of Malays on Home Island seemed no different from island communities I'm familiar with.

Australian officials on Cocos (Keeling) had not been properly indoctrinated. They thought part of their mission was to help, rather than hinder, the yachties. Brian Shields, the marine officer on Home Island, could be relied on to locate almost anything a cruiser needed. He and his chic Indonesian wife, Herni, often joined in the barbecues on Direction Island beach. Once they supplied the fish. Kris and John provided the music for an ad hoc dance after one barbecue. The music was far better than the dancing, as sailors stumbled about the deep sand, drinks in hand.

The Indian Ocean remained unusually placid for my passage from Cocos (Keeling) to Mauritius. I had two days of flat calm in an area and season where the average is one day of calm in a hundred. The wind vane self-steering gear, made in Auckland, proved a disappointment; it was not nearly powerful enough to handle IQ's large rudder. I reinstalled the old sheet-to-tiller system. I kept the Auckland steering vane on duty to hold course during sail changes.

Mauritius is a volcanic island, thirty-eight miles long and almost as wide, lying in the Indian Ocean approximately a thousand miles east of Africa. It was discovered by Portuguese explorers, settled by the Dutch, and ruled subsequently by the French and then the English. Ninety percent of the people are trilingual: Creole, French, and English. It is a struggling independent country, and the third worst overpopulated in the world. There is no longer room for the dodos.

Port Louis is a crowded, undistinguished, waterfront town. Unemployment is not as bad as expected because of the sugar cane and textile industries. Everyone wears designer clothes; they are made here. I bought Saint Laurent shorts for US $7.95 each. Prices are as low as anywhere I've been.

The yacht anchorage is at Grand Baie, twelve miles north of Port Louis in a more pastoral setting. Royal Palms line the street leading from the harbor to the capitol. The dozen boats anchored here represented the U.S., Canada, France, Norway, New Zealand, Switzerland, Holland and Great Britain. During my stay, the Francophonies congregated for their periodic conference to promote French language and culture. French President François Mitterand addressed the group. During his visit, the area swarmed with police and coast guard crews. We had to move our boats out of gunshot range. I found French officialdom disgustingly provincial.

Kris and John befriended a pair of Mauritian men, Anwar and Hashad, who were so delighted to meet foreign yachties that they took us for a tour of the island in their own car and refused our offer to buy the petrol. The interior of Mauritius is covered with small trees and sugar cane. Some impressive deep gorges cut through the low mountains. The densely populated areas remind me of Mexico. The botanical gardens at Pamplemousse and the bird park at Casella would give credit to a much wealthier nation. In the bird park the rare Mauritian pink pigeon is neighbor to the American wood duck.

A Mauritian of Indian descent told us a joke: An American, an Indian and a Mauritian were sitting in the cockpit of a boat. The American took out a handful of dollar bills and threw them into the water.

"Why did you do that?"

"Oh, in America we have lots of dollar bills."

The Indian took out two handfuls of *roti* (bread) and threw them into the water.

"Why did you do that?"

"In India we have lots of *roti*, more than we need."

The Mauritian picked up the Indian and threw him into the water.

Ile de la Reunion is but 135 sailing miles from Mauritius, but what a contrast. Reunion is owned by the French who pour money by the shipload into the place: four-lane divided highways; ultramodern, upholstered-seat buses; and chic ladies on the streets of Saint-Denis as fashionably dressed as those in Paris. The population is half that of

Mauritius although the island is slightly larger. Cost of living is higher even though there is little industry and much unemployment.

Kris, John and I traveled by bus from our base at Port des Galets to the mountain cirque village of Cilaos over a world-class spectacular mountain road which is built out from the cliff wall in spots. At one white-knuckle hairpin turn, the bus had to back and fill to get around. The views were awe-inspiring.

A few days later, I sailed away from Kris and John headed for South Africa. Known for bad weather, this passage is considered the roughest of a normal east-to-west circumnavigation. Eight days out of Port des Galets and ready to corner the south end of Madagascar, 135 miles to the northwest, the wind began to rise. This is a particularly bad place to be during a gale. The seabed shelf, extending south from the island, creates turbulent conditions. By nightfall I ran in an easterly gale with a reefed staysail and the tiller tied off. I prepared the boat. I closed the hatches, plugged the ventilators, and put in the washboards fronting the hatch. The barometer dropped 11 mb.

During the night, the boat began to pound. I stirred, but I was too lethargic to get up. At 0200, a loud crash abruptly awakened me. Books flew over my head. Crockery fell in the galley. The cabin tilted. I had waited too long.

Idle Queen had been knocked down.

Chapter 11

The Wild Coast

Cruising teaches a man to rely on his own judgment and skill.
-Eric C. Hiscock, *Cruising Under Sail*

Idle Queen quickly righted herself, but for a moment I was too scared to move. Crockery and glass from the galley littered the cabin. Sea water poured in around joints in the washboards and soaked the cabin sole before running off into the bilge. A heavy book just missed my head. I waited until my heart slowed, then rolled out of the bunk. I stepped into my shoes, unmindful that shards of glass might be embedded there. Thoughts rushed through my mind. If the rigging, the outboard rudder, or the tiller were damaged, this was a desolate place to seek help.

I slid back the hatch and climbed onto the deck over the washboards. In the tumult of breaking seas, the waves glowed faintly in the darkness. I peered around. The dodger and weather cloths around the cockpit were gone, but no critical items had been swept overboard. I lurched to the fantail. The tiller and rudder were intact. I crawled forward over the wet deck. The rigging looked stable. I clawed down the staysail. Under bare mast, the boat rode surprisingly well. I felt elated, as I crawled back below, closed the hatch, and started the clean up. Dawn broke as I finished.

The sharp depression moved on rapidly and left a windless but turbulent sea. A second gale blew in several days later, but I rode this one out in comfort; the Indian Ocean had gotten my attention.

With a sense of pride, I finally sailed into Richards Bay, South Africa. The gales had delayed me. Kris and John on *Mew*, Jean Giquel on *Judikael*, and Roger Fawer on *Balbu* were already docked. Each harbor becomes a reunion, as sailors discover, with relief, that friends have made it into another port. *Idle Queen* is so slow a boat that I am surprised, even knowing other boats' routes, that they are still in harbor when I arrive. We did not travel together. The ocean is too wide and unpredictable for that.

Roger in *Balbu* experienced the same gale I had. We had been about seventy miles apart. Roger logged the wind at fifty to sixty knots. His boat suffered no damage, but he said, "Next morning, my jaws were sore from having gritted my teeth all night."

A Swiss engineer, Roger built his forty-foot yacht. He's a big man with a heavy black beard, and looks like a reincarnation of the pirate Blackbeard. Unlike Blackbeard, who inspired fear, Roger is solicitous. He looked at my obstreperous steering set up.

"The designer didn't know what he was doing," he said. "I'll fix it for you."

Roger had a machine shop on board *Balbu*. After a day of cutting and welding, he presented me with a new and efficient (as it turned out) self-steering apparatus. The charge was one bottle of wine. Another cruising handyman, Andy on *Nina*, made me a new canvas dodger and installed a replacement solar panel. Andy is typical of sailors who pay their way along the ocean routes by doing odd jobs on yachts. He had never made a dodger, but this didn't prevent him from turning out a professional job. These two men alone made my stay in Richards Bay logistically memorable.

Shortly after I arrived, the group of yachties decided to celebrate Thanksgiving together. We pitched in for a large turkey, but none of the boats had an oven big enough to handle the bird. It was sent out to the yacht club chef for roasting. The turkey came back just in time for dinner, but was too undercooked to be safely eaten. Each woman took a chunk of the turkey and hurried off to roast a portion in her own oven. Apparently, large turkeys do not get roasted whole in Richards Bay.

The small town center is four kilometers from the waterfront, and the taxi cartel charges R30 (about $10) per trip. Robert Duvivier, a local printer, delights in letting his wife, Doris, tend the business while he stops almost every morning at the yacht club to drive sailors to town. Robbie would arrive, a big smile affixed between his graying hair and his bright shirt, honk and escort us into the car. Robbie was born on Mauritius of French lineage. He enjoyed exercising his rusty French with Roger, Jean, and later, Jean's visiting wife, Colette.

Robbie, Doris, and their pre-teen daughter, Jeannine, took a small group of us to the Hluhluwe (put an "s" in front of the "h"s for pronunciation) Game Park. Along the route, the distinctive round Zulu huts are scattered across the hillsides, sometimes picturesque, sometimes squalid. In the park, I was thrilled to be close to wild animals in their own habitat. The buffaloes, giraffes, nyalas, impalas, wildebeests, elephants, warthogs, baboons, and zebras kept a conservative distance. Robbie became nervous when a white rhino poked an inquisitive snout within four feet of the car. We stayed well clear of the crocodiles when we stopped, ignored regulations, and stretched our legs outside the car.

The Duviviers entertained a group of us in their home on several evenings. We met and talked with local people, mulling over politics and the future of South Africa. This was in late fall 1993. The elections which would bring Nelson Mandela and the ANC to power were not scheduled until spring 1994. In Zululand the mood among white people was generally pessimistic and resigned. Most of the whites carried handguns in their cars. We met two families, and crossed paths with others later, who planned to flee the country on boats.

The Burgers were among the South African families I met. Kuss, a trim, muscular man who had won many karate competitions, ran a karate school with his blonde wife Ida. They had two teenagers. The family was sailing to Florida and I recommended the Green Cove Springs Marina as an inexpensive place to dock their boat, *Scot Free*. They followed my advice.

Dave Savides, editor of the *Zululand Observer*, interviewed me and put a short article and my picture in the paper. He thought I was too old for this type of venture and wondered whether I was brave or just stupid. I think he had his own idea.

On the same page was an article about a man who was motorboating around the world. Ahead of his time, this man used vegetable oil as fuel. I heard nothing more about him, but much about vegetable diesel fuel.

In the Zululand Yacht Club, I met Gary and Bill on *Amadon Light* out of Los Angeles. The men made their money in real estate and decided to sail the world. They collected friends along the way. Gary, quiet and intellectual, often lectured on marine communication to ad hoc groups via the ham radio. Bill, the outgoing ambassador of the pair, arranged their elegant dinner parties. On *Amadon Light*, wine was served in crystal goblets, a marked contrast to the normal dinners served on boats.

The most astounding and unexpected meeting in the course of meandering around the world came in Richards Bay. One afternoon as I stood on the knoll above the wharf where IQ lay, an unmistakable big red sloop flying the German flag came into view around the end of the pier.

"*Freydis!*" I exclaimed.

At the same time, Heide and Erich Wilts spotted *Idle Queen*.

"Ahoy, *Idle Queen*!" Erich called. He saw me running down the hill, waving, and yelled, "Harry, may we raft to you?"

Faido and I had met the couple in 1982 at the Panama Canal.

"How do we arrange to get through the canal?" they'd asked.

"Come over for Happy Hour," Faido countered.

"What's Happy Hour?"

We shared many Happy Hours together. As we caught up on our news, Heide and Erich were saddened to learn of Faido's death.

The Wilts were preparing for a ten-week cruise to Australia, touching at islands off the Antarctic continent on the way. Over several dinners we discussed these plans. The Wilts have received many awards and honors for Heide's books and Erich's photography. They have sailed around Cape Horn eight times, and now lead charters to Antarctica. You can read Heide's many adventurous sailing books, but only if you read German.

Pleasant as Richards Bay is—in memory it remains one of my favorite stops—these social days at the Zululand Yacht Club represented the last gathering of many friends with whom I traveled across the Pacific and Indian Oceans. Jean and Colette I was to see in Durban, but the rest went on ahead. Many who went to sea to get away from it all were on the way back home. Those who set out eagerly to see new places viewed the remainder of their voyage with less enthusiasm.

The prospect of leaving generated unease, as we gathered around the boats with weather faxes. We studied the weather reports, discussed the outlook, took our chances and left. The run south from Richards Bay to the Cape is along what is known as the Wild Coast, named for the unpredictability of its often severe weather.

"I would rather go around Cape Horn," Erich Wilts said, "than sail the southeast coast of Africa."

Kris and John Fulton on *Mew* left one afternoon for the ninety-mile jump to Durban. A good weather report was well confirmed. At two the next morning, concerned friends helped them back into a berth at the Small Boat Harbor, as a southwest gale drove them to shelter.

I picked good weather to leave for Durban, so good that I had to motor all the way.

Durban is a mixed city architecturally. Well-kept, old historic buildings are nestled in among thirty-two-story skyscrapers. Stores have not moved to the suburbs, an advantage to having a population that has not yet discovered the necessity of an automobile. The Point Yacht Club in Durban is as pleasant a place to wait out weather as a sailor is likely to find—hospitable, inexpensive (for foreign yachts) with a well-chefed dining room and bar overlooking the harbor. I celebrated Christmas here with Jean and Colette, who flew in from France. The dress was formal, no shorts allowed in the dining room.

During the run south from Richards Bay to Durban, IQ's engine throttle control began to stick. In Durban I hired a man named Aubrey to repair it, and we became friends. Aubrey told me that he and two of his brothers had been declared "black" by the government. The three remaining brothers had been classified "white." Although Aubrey could easily have been considered white, his closest friend, George, had distinct negroid features. We three had dinner on their boat, since I couldn't meet with them in a public place.

Aubrey's girlfriend, Esme, was strictly white Afrikaner. She didn't know that Aubrey was classified as "black." I sat with Aubrey and Esme at dinner one night, saddened to think of the outcome of this relationship if Aubrey's background became public.

After the start of the new year, the faster boats went on ahead. Or was it the boats with livelier, more vigorous crews? I hung around with another singlehander, Kevin Foley, on *Connemara*. I first met Kevin in Neiafu, Tonga, but had not seen him since. He is an ex-Green Beret from San Francisco, tall and dark-haired, with a mustache. We once walked into a Customs office and the young female clerk's eyes bulged.

"Oh, Magnum P.I.!" she cried.

Kevin looks like Tom Selleck.

In Tonga, Kevin had been with a statuesque blonde, a physical therapist on her way to Australia for some special course in her field. I thought their future prospects seemed dim: her heart was with her parents in St. Louis while Kevin can't live far from the sea. I was not surprised to find him alone in South Africa. I didn't ask about the blonde.

At some time, I had to head south from Durban. In sailing the southeast coast of Africa, there are three related problems to be faced: the unpredictability of the weather, the effect on sea conditions of southwest gales blowing against the strongly south-setting Agulhas current, and the shortage of harbors. Weather forecasts are for twelve hours only, insufficient to cover the 255 mile run from Durban along a bare coast to East London. It is not unusual for the weather to shift from a northeast gale to a southwest gale in but a few hours. A southwest gale, blowing against the four to five knots of Agulhas current, can produce steep waves twenty meters in height. These have broken and sunk large ships.

Chris Bonnet of the Ocean Sailing School in Durban gives free lectures on tactics to use. He points out that a careful analysis of barometric pressure trends can indicate when a sufficiently lengthy weather window is opening for a yacht to make a safe passage. He says, in brief, "Leave Durban at the tail end of a southwesterly blow, but only after the barometer has risen to 1020 millibars."

I disregarded this advice the first time I left Durban and was lucky not to suffer for it. After a spell of bad weather, the barometer started rising. The local weather bureau predicted forty-eight hours of favorable conditions, enough to get to East London. A call to the East London weather bureau confirmed the analysis. *Connemara*, *Scot Free*, and *Idle Queen* prepared to leave. I was away first, shortly after noon. The barometer read only 1011mb. At 1600, I made a scheduled radio contact with *Connemara*. I was about eight miles down the coast.

"Get back here," Kevin Foley said. "They've changed the forecast. A southwest blow is due to arrive by sunset."

I returned in time. That night I listened to the southwester rattle the rigging, happy to be back in port.

Kevin and I found agreement on the weather patterns, and we traveled the route to Cape Town at the same time. The northeast gale, that was predicted to blow us along before we reached East London, failed to come up to full force. The weather around Cape Agulhas was pleasantly breezy. The Cape of Good Hope held one last thirty-five knot gale in store, and this from astern and out of the Agulhas current. As we finally rounded the continent, I sat in the cockpit and admired *Connemara*'s lines. I called Kevin on the radio.

"Looking good, Kevin," I said.

"Thanks. The boat doesn't look bad either."

The three places we visited along the route from Durban were quite similar in most respects. East London, Port Elizabeth, and Mossel Bay all have limited and generally poor facilities for visiting yachts. But the yacht clubs continue to demonstrate the South African dedication to hospitality for the visiting cruiser.

East London, situated on a hill high over the sea, is an undistinguished town: a little industry, a little business, a little residential. Below the town on the Buffalo River is a new waterfront development replacing the old dilapidated waterfront. This practice is occurring in many cities around the world. A plaque on the boardwalk notes that here in 1938 was landed the first coelacanth, the fish thought extinct for seventy million years.

Port Elizabeth, in the English-settled part of South Africa, is a substantial city with a varied downtown district and some true English pubs. The city is not named for a queen, but for the wife of Sir Rufane Donkin, the town's founder. The statue in the town center is of Victoria, not Elizabeth. The Campanile looks to be a duplicate of that in Berkeley, California (and perhaps a duplicate of the original), except that it is constructed of red brick. David Davies, commodore of the Algoa Bay Yacht Club, drove me around the town and countryside. Many of the 1820s-vintage houses are in fine restored condition. The Zwartkopf Yacht Club, a few miles out of town, proudly displays a Red Ensign that a member filched from Robert Scott's visiting ship.

One night Kevin and I splurged on a fancy dinner at the Sir Rufane Donkin restaurant. On the way up the hill we passed a young black man going down.

"Where are you from?" he asked.

"We're Americans," Kevin called back.

"You are my Jesus!" the black man shouted.

David Davies says, "Of course, white South Africans are friendly to visitors. They have a guilty conscience."

Mossel Bay is a hillside Afrikaner town of neat houses, clean sea water, and rough moorings. The harbor surge is incessant. For its size, Mossel Bay has perhaps the best museum I have seen. It features a massive, sixty-foot long replica of the caravel that Bartolomeu Diaz sailed into Mossel Bay in 1488, his first stop after discovering the route around the bottom of Africa.

Not far northwest from the bottom of the continent is the entrance to Hout Bay, where the cliffs rise sharply and majestically. The prevailing southeast wind drops down the precipices, picks up velocity, and churns the bay into a blanket of white caps even inside the harbor jetties. For this reason it is best to arrive and get well secured early in the morning. When I arrived late in the day, a half-dozen local yachtsmen, plus Kevin, helped warp me into a slip. Hout Bay Yacht Club embraces foreigners with the type of welcome we have come to expect. But for the first time, the tie-up charges were more than minimal.

Cape Town is north of Hout Bay, forty-five minutes by bus along a strikingly scenic coast, reminiscent of stretches of California Route 1 north of Morro Bay. The rugged range of low peaks along this coast is dominated by the massive bulk of Table Mountain. Cape Town is a much livelier town than Durban, and a good choice for South Africa's Olympic bid.

Kevin and I took a bus tour of the area's wine country, sampling the wares of the region, as we proceeded east from Cape Town. The countryside is a series of green valleys and low mountains, neat and prosperous looking except for the shanty towns. Bantu shanties line the main highway for miles outside the city and give a depressing view of South Africa's future. The government supplies water, builds latrines, and lays concrete pads on which the natives build scrap wood and iron shacks. Where the Bantus scrounge the raw materials and how they manage to survive are questions to which I found no answers.

The university town of Stellenbosch, in the wine country, showcases early Dutch architecture. The style is plain, brightly white and unexciting. The area is in the heart of Afrikaner culture. We stopped briefly to sample a remarkable South African version of sherry in the wine town, Paarl, where the first dictionary of the Afrikaner language was compiled.

We also saw the final prison—with tennis courts and swimming pool—from which Nelson Mandela was released.

Back in Hout Bay I prepared to leave South Africa. Kevin planned to follow my route, and I expected to see him along the way. The eighth of February was a rare day of light wind sweeping Hout Bay. I cleared for St. Helena, a British crown colony, 1200 miles west of Africa. The island, because of its remoteness, was Napoleon's final forced exile. Before the opening of the Suez Canal, St. Helena was a stopping point for ships bound around the south of Africa.

I made a mess of anchoring there. The waterfront at Jamestown provides the only suitable landing spot on this thirty-mile diameter, steep-sided island. While exercising the engine 540 miles east of the island, I discovered diesel fuel spurting from a hole in a chafed-through spot in the fuel line. When I bought the engine seventeen years ago, I purchased a spare fuel line. I was upset when it didn't fit. As I result, I sailed into Jamestown.

The Jamestown anchorage is an open roadstead, rolly and twenty meters deep. I reached a suitable spot, dropped sails, and went forward to lower the anchor. At that moment, a williwaw from Jamestown Valley caught the boat and threw it across another anchor line. I was able to avoid the other boat, but the anchor lines were miserably entwined. I couldn't free my anchor chain; I needed a diver. Helmut, of the South African boat *Lazy L*, had scuba gear and volunteered. Authorities on St. Helena, because of the valuable ancient artifacts on the bottom of the harbor, demand that all divers get a permit and pay for an official dive observer. Helmut decided to avoid this hassle by free diving, that is, diving without scuba gear. I worried that he was down sixty feet for an interminable time, but he cleared my anchor. His reward was a bottle of wine. I shared it with Helmut and Trisch at dinner on their boat. The couple was headed for Brazil and I never saw them again.

St. Helena looks dark and barren from the sea. Bare cliffs rise precipitously on all sides. The high interior of the island catches rainfall, and all is green and enticing there. The landing at Jamestown is guarded by castle walls, moats, and heavy smooth-bore cannon. This seems unnecessary since it is such a hazardous undertaking to get ashore. Skilled launch operators deliver passengers with perfect timing to the stone steps in the sea wall against which the surge rolls unceasingly. There is no breakwater in the harbor.

Connemara sailed in a few days later, and Kevin helped me solve a financial problem. I arrived with only a few South African rand in my pocket, expecting to get local currency through my Visa card. To my surprise, the only bank on St. Helena could not handle Visa cards. They suggested I have my bank wire money to the London representative of the St. Helena bank. This would take two weeks, by which time I would be gone. I relayed all this to Kevin. Unperturbed, Kevin walked into the bank as if he were Magnum, P.I., and talked the banker into accepting a personal check on a San Francisco bank. We celebrated his ingenuity at the local bar. On his money.

St. Helenans are derived from a mixture of British, Asian, and African forbears. Britain puts nine million pounds per year into the island, and the 7000-plus people are not inclined to exert themselves. The flax industry died in 1966, but the raw material still grows with gusto over the island. A meticulously maintained 1929 Chevy bus took us on a tour. The roads are more vertical than horizontal, and bicycles are not allowed for fear of brake failure. We visited Napoleon's home, Longwood House, which is kept in display condition by the French government. The rooms are many but small and filled with memorabilia. Did Napoleon play backgammon? There is also a large snooker table. The St. Helena tomb of Napoleon, now empty, his remains in Paris, is in a quiet glade. It is surrounded by massive Norfolk Island pines that may have been there in Napoleon's day.

Jacob's Ladder is Jamestown's most famous attraction. It consists of 699 almost vertical stairs up the hillside and provides a challenge for local athletes. Kevin ran all the way up in what must have been record time. I took a bus to the top. From the top, one has an all-inclusive view of Jamestown's castle, St. James church, the public gardens, and all the rest of the little town's attractions. Kevin ran all the way down the stairs. I clung to the iron rail every step of the way.

Kevin left the island before me and, regrettably, our paths did not cross again.

Eight days out of St. Helena I sighted Ascension Island off the port bow. I wanted to look at this tracking station outpost. During World War II, Air Force planes refueled here on their way to North Africa. The island has a more varied profile than St. Helena and wears its cloud cap perched at a more fashionable height. The masked boobies and the island specialty, the Ascension frigatebirds, came out to greet me. The small settlement at Georgetown, low down on the flats, looked dreary compared to Jamestown. No yachts and only a few fishing boats were moored in the open roadstead. I sailed on.

A few days out of Ascension a black noddy spent the night dozing on the boom gallows, occasionally flapping a wing to counter the scend of the sea. The next night there were three of them aboard. Having in mind my meager clean-up crew, I thought of shooing them off. Then I remembered the experience of the fellow with the albatross and decided not to. Over the course of the next week, I had noddy friends aboard every night.

I planned to stop at Fernando de Noronha. The island has an outstanding point of recognition: a high, lopsided peak that looks like a huge green broken thumb giving the high sign. There were no yachts in the anchorage and the landing looked rough. I was thoroughly jaded at this point and sailed past without stopping. I jibed the boat and headed north for the equator, as a wet sloppy convergence zone descended on me. The doldrums presented no problem, and I made good progress northwest. I looked forward to my arrival on the island of St. Lucia. This would mark the formal end of my circumnavigation of the world for I stopped at the island on my return from Portugal in

1991. On 9 April, I happily calculated that I was but a thousand miles from this goal.

The next morning my euphoric feelings evaporated. My right arm went numb.

Chapter 12

Medical Emergency

The journey not the arrival matters.
-T. S. Eliot

I had just taken *Idle Queen* off the self-steering mechanism. I settled onto the cockpit bench and adjusted the sails. When I grasped the tiller, a warm tingling sensation spread up my right arm, from fingertips to shoulder. Within seconds my arm was numb. My hand fell off the tiller. I stared at it for a moment, then shifted seats and grasped the tiller with my left hand. I propped my right arm on my lap and pushed down my panicked thoughts. I reminded myself that I had, on several occasions, experienced similar brief episodes. I waited for the numbness to pass.

It didn't.

I tested my speech by reciting aloud Henley's first stanza of *Invictus*: "Out of the night that covers me, Black as the pit from pole to pole…"

My speech was not slurred, but my right arm remained useless.

I sailed on.

A half hour later a blur appeared on the horizon. I watched until I recognized the lines of a freighter. I hurried below to the radio and hailed them: "Calling the west bound ship, this is sailing vessel *Idle Queen* two miles abeam of you to starboard."

The freighter was identified as the *Arcona* out of Cyprus. I requested the captain. After we introduced ourselves, I asked Captain Herman Willen if he would call my oldest son, Harry Third, collect and relay my symptoms and my position.

After assuring me that he would, Captain Willen tried to persuade me to come aboard and see the ship's doctor. To do so, I would have to abandon *Idle Queen*. I would have to open her seacocks and flood her with water so that she would sink. Left afloat she would be a shipping hazard. I had had *Idle Queen* for twenty years. Between sinking my boat and suffering a stroke, I preferred the stroke.

Captain Willen acquiesced. I watched until the freighter disappeared from sight. Half an hour later Captain Willen radioed that he had reached my son.

I sailed on.

Unbeknownst to me, Captain Willen's phone call set up a flurry of activity. Harry Third alerted the rest of my family. My sister, Florence Mary, is a nurse. She concurred that my symptom sounded like a stroke. The family agreed that I needed help.

My daughter Faith contacted the U.S. Coast Guard with my last known latitude and longitude, my medical problem, and a passionate plea that a rescue plane be dispatched immediately. It wasn't, of course. Finding a drifting 32-foot sailboat in the Atlantic Ocean, allegedly skippered by a septuagenarian sailing solo around the world, was not a task to be considered lightly.

In Florida, Jack Farrington called, not the Coast Guard, but entertainment mogul Ted Turner. Jack had worked for a company that had been bought out by Turner's. Turner, Jack knew, was a sailor. He was also wealthy enough to launch his own rescue for, say, the exclusive rights for my story.

On day two, Faith phoned the Coast Guard again. And again on day three. In Florida, Jack Farrington also called the Coast Guard. For some reason, Ted Turner was not taking Jack's calls. Worn down by Faith and Jack's persistence, and convinced that I might indeed need help, the Coast Guard authorized a search plane from St. Lucia.

The morning after my contact with the *Arcona*, my arm, inexplicably, was back to normal. No stroke after all. I was relieved. I wanted to let my children know, but no other ship appeared to relay a message.

A few days later, I spotted a U. S. Coast Guard plane flying high overhead, headed toward South Africa. I wondered why. Near dusk, I saw the lights of a ship and I turned on the radio to advise it of my presence. I overheard an official voice, a coast guardsman, say: "…he's a seventy-eight-year-old man traveling alone…"

I broke into the conversation. "Are you looking for me?" I asked.

I was embarrassed at the fuss and worry I had caused. After locating me, the Coast Guard informed my children that I had been found, but not how that had been achieved. My daughter, Florence, imagined that the discovery went something like this:

Coast Guard: Captain Heckel, I presume? We've found you!

Capt.: I didn't know I was lost.
CG: You're seventy-five miles from St. Lucia.
Capt.: That's what my sextant told me at noon today.
CG: Maybe we should get one of those. We missed you the first pass over.
Capt.: Well, it's a big ocean, and I should know. I've sailed it from one end to the other.
CG: How's the arm?
Capt.: I can still hoist a Manhattan.
CG: Good, we'll have a few waiting for you in St. Lucia.
Capt.: Well, as long as you're buying, my ETA is 1400 tomorrow.
CG: You probably don't drink before five, but in the Coast Guard we have a saying: "It's 1700 somewhere in the world!"

The Coast Guard plane monitored my arrival into Rodney Bay, St. Lucia. I arrived on 20 April 1994. I was seventy-eight years old. I had completed a solo circumnavigation of the world.

Two of my children, Harry Third and Faith, and friends Jack and Maggie Farrington flew in to help celebrate. The Burgers—Kuss, Ida, Henk and Elbe—from South Africa were also in port and joined the party. Word of my accomplishment spread through the yachting community. Sailors from surrounding docks came by to shake my hand or called out congratulations. The celebration and camaraderie lasted for several days.

When my guests flew back to the States, I went with them to see a doctor. The diagnosis was displacement of vertebrae in my neck, which pressed on nerves and caused my occasional numbness. I attributed this to my repeated jerking on the halyards due to corroded sheaves in the masthead. To prevent a recurrence, the doctor suggested that I change my lifestyle. Not go sailing? I merely grinned.

"Well," the doctor said, "if you insist on sailing, at least modify your methods."

That seemed reasonable. Later I installed halyard winches to raise the sails. For now I flew back to St. Lucia and sailed *Idle Queen*, uneventfully, home. I arrived 11 June 1994. The Farringtons greeted me with champagne.

Lee Werth, the philosophy professor at Cleveland State University whom I met in Bermuda on my shakedown cruise across the Atlantic, occasionally sends me appropriate little quotations. When I was just starting to singlehand in 1990, he quoted Melville (*Redburn*):

"Though his craft was none of the largest, it was subject to him; and though his crew might only consist of himself; yet if he governed it well, he achieved a triumph which the moralists of all ages have set above the victories of Alexander."

Later, when I considered pushing on around the world, he cited Chekhov (*Gooseberries*):

"It is not six feet of earth, not a country estate that a man needs, but the whole globe, the whole of nature, room to display his qualities and the individual characteristics of his soul."

As I considered my next cruise, noting that I am getting along in years, will Lee, I wondered, bring up Joyce (*The Dead*)?

"Better pass boldly into that otherworld in the full glory of some passion than fade and wither dismally with age."

VOYAGE II

1995 - 2005

Chapter 13

I Set Out Again

I travel for travel's sake. The great affair is to move.
-Robert Lewis Stevenson

I was tired when I completed my circumnavigation, so bone-achingly tired that I intended to give up long-range sailing. I left the boat and took Amtrak around the country, visiting my children and my siblings, Florence Mary and John, on the west coast.

I spent Christmas in Florida with Maggie and Jack Farrington. For my Christmas present, Jack sought to include me in the *Guinness Book of World Records*. He sent the group documentation to prove that I was the oldest man to sail solo around the world. *Guinness* replied that it "is no longer interested in assembling statistics on elderly round-the-world sailors." According to Jack, they didn't want to encourage "this kind of behavior." Apparently, it was too dangerous.

As the months passed, I recovered from the strains of the voyage. I found myself longing to go to sea again. I had seen much of the world, but I had left much unseen. I wanted to visit the countries of the Mediterranean and the Far East. *Did I have the stamina to circumnavigate again?* I asked myself. Long days at sea would test my endurance, but I reminded myself that I could rest up in port. Sailing solo had become an obsession. At my age, now seventy-nine, the challenge of a second circumnavigation was invigorating. It gave purpose to my life. I decided to accept the challenge.

On 13 June 1995, I motored away from Green Cove Springs Marina. This time I planned a west-to-east circumnavigation. I headed across the Atlantic. I arrived in Bermuda well after the start of the summer hurricane season. When I left the island, tropical storm Chantelle was forming in the area. Apprehensively, I followed the storm's progress. Initial projections had it headed well west of my position, so I continued heading directly north to 39-40° before turning east. As the days passed, each succeeding weather projection had the storm bending to the northeast and then east-northeast. I feared that Chantelle and I could be on a collision course. Over the afternoon and night of 19-20 July, I spent a sleepless twelve hours driving into a thirty knot southeaster under triple-reefed main and staysail. My concern was that I not be driven farther north into the path of the storm. Sometime after midnight, Chantelle reached its point of closest approach, and then retreated. The wind lost its intensity. I slacked sheets and eased off to the east-northeast. I went below and stripped off wet weather gear. I added a dry layer of clothing, mixed myself a nightcap, and relaxed.

The next morning, I slept later than usual. As I dawdled in the cabin over coffee, I chanced to look aft through the open hatch into a misty rain. I was startled to see a stopped ship lying athwart my stern a half mile away. I switched on the radio and called.

A grumpy voice replied, "I have been calling you for half an hour. Do you need any help?"

I had not yet raised enough sail to get the boat underway. I assured him I was fine, thanked him for asking, and took charge of the boat.

When I reached the Azores, I passed up the island of Faial—I had been there on my first Atlantic sail—for a stop at the smaller island of Corvo, southeast of Faial. Corvo is a truncated mountain rock with only a handful of inhabitants. This remote island supports a large colony of shearwaters. I motored among them, as I anchored close in. I caught up on my sleep before I sailed the short hop to the island of San Miguel.

San Miguel is now my favorite island in the Azores group. It is called *Ilha Verde*, even though all the Azorean islands are green. A large flotilla of boats docked off Ponta Delgada, the island's main city. Ponta Delgada is bigger, busier and more modern than Horta on Faial. The high-rise hotel and the expansion of the shopping district along the waterfront are slowly obliterating the unmistakably Portuguese look of the town from the sea. Much of the *duende* is gone. The sidewalks are still laid with the black-and-white patterned *lajes*. The ancient statue of Cabral still stands in the town square.

Unlike quiet Corvo, the tourists flock to San Miguel. The big draw is hot springs. I took the bus out to see them. They are notably less spectacular than those in Yellowstone Park. The volcanic countryside is set off by clusters of wild hortensias with their tall spiky clusters of golden flowerets.

A twenty foot tall statue, Lutice, faces the Atlantic on the east side. I took a bus up to visit her. I walked along the statue base and admired the view over the Atlantic from the spit on which she stands.

She is a magnificent landmark. When I sailed away two days later, I could see Lutice in my sights for most of the day. She inspired me:

The yachtsmen sail to San Miguel, away across the pond
They rest while summer days grow short, then linger on and on.
I sailed myself to San Miguel, you know I have to sail.
I found the reason yachtsmen pause along this ocean trail.
It is Lutice with shining smile, her office fronts the sea
With eyes alight and hair aflame, she makes us feel her glee.
I almost tarried here as well, I knew I could not stay,
Just once I saw Lutice glum: 'twas the day I sailed away.

Late one night, I awakened to the strange sound of a geyser. I stumbled on deck to find the source. Staring aft, I was shocked to see the pouf of mist rising above a massive body. He was twenty feet behind me. I was uneasy; whales can easily crush and sink boats. I stood in the cockpit for almost half an hour hoping he would get bored and submerge for good. But he kept bobbing up, the same distance back. He seemed content to follow in my wake. *Did I look like a mama whale?* I concluded that he was no threat but remained as my rearguard. I went back to bed. The next morning he was still with me. Sometime during the afternoon he disappeared. I sat in the cockpit and stared about for a quarter hour without spotting him. I was disappointed; I missed this fellow traveler.

Otherwise, wildlife away from the islands was sparse: a few dolphins, one turtle (I almost ran over him as he looked up in wonderment), one squid on deck, a few Wilson's storm petrels, many Manx shearwaters. Wildlife was a welcome diversion since otherwise I endured a boring passage. From San Miguel to Lagos, Portugal, I was beset by head winds or no wind at all. As was Browning, I was happy when "Nobly, nobly Cape St. Vincent to the northwest died away."

I had visited Lagos with Faido ten years earlier on our European tour. On a hot dusty day, we were stuck in a traffic jam trying to find our way out of an unpleasant maze of streets. This time I found Lagos intriguing with its narrow winding hillside byways, many not permitted to cars. Unfortunately, the tourists have also discovered Lagos. The marina is just over a year old and is thoroughly modern.

Mainland Portugal is noticeably less conservative than the Azorean islands. Widows (until they remarry) dress all in black, including the headscarf, but more so in the islands; their granddaughters go topless on the beaches, more so on the mainland. Change is coming to Portugal.

When I think of tiring passages, I think of the one from Lagos to Gibraltar. I knew it would take forty-eight hours, but I planned to sleep at night. The fishing boats were so numerous, that I couldn't afford to sleep. They pressed around me like partiers in Times Square on New Year's Eve. I slipped and slid my way amongst them, like a reveler avoiding pickpockets. I stayed alert and ever watchful.

When I docked at Shepherd's Marina in Gibraltar, I was too tired to cook breakfast. I walked the half mile into town to a restaurant. At the restaurant, I realized I had forgotten to bring a credit card. I turned around and walked back to the boat, got the card, and plodded off to find a bank to get cash. The breakfast may have been worth the trouble, but I can't remember.

One morning I took a cable car to the top of the Rock. On a clear day, you can see across the straits to Morocco. This was a clear day. Monkeys cavorted around the peak and among the tourists, and their antics amused me. After an hour or so, refreshed and entertained, I took the cable car down. I returned to the marina and motored off to find my winter quarters in Spain.

Chapter 14

Wintering in Spain

A journey is best measured in friends, rather than miles.
-Tim Cahill

Estepona, Spain, is twenty-five miles northeast of Gibraltar. It is more Spanish than English in its aspect, a rare quality on this touristy coast. Blocks of hotels do not mar the landscape as they do in Malaga and other coastal towns invaded by British tourists. I spent hours sitting on a bench under the orange trees in the central plaza, beer in hand, people-watching. A library opened onto the plaza. Sometimes I amused myself by scanning through its outstanding array of reference books.

The marina uses Mediterranean-style moorings. The skipper docks his boat by backing into a slip while simultaneously tying the bow to a mooring buoy and stern to the dock. For the solo sailor, it seems a system invented by Satan with an attitude. Luckily, willing hands helped.

Among marina neighbors were three convivial couples who became close friends. Two were Scandinavians: the Swedes, Per and Mona, on *Windfall*, and Norwegians Elisabeth and Martin on *Navsika*. Mona and Elisabeth were slim, attractive blondes. The men were sturdy, sea-going types. Per had a white beard and was a retired submarine captain. He told gripping air and naval stories. Martin, distinguished by a gray mustache, was once a union negotiator. He had an uncompromising firmness concealed under a warm personality. Both couples were retired and experienced travelers.

The third couple, Larry and Jay, were novice British sailors on *Inner Vision*. Jay was a breath-taking, graceful blonde. Larry was stereotypically short, dark and handsome. Unmarried and in their early fifties, the couple met through a personal ad. They bought *Inner Vision* to learn to sail so they could travel. The experienced man they expected to sail with them backed out at the last minute. Larry and Jay set out on their forty-foot sailboat anyway and made it to Spain.

One late afternoon as I sat below decks enjoying a cup of coffee, I heard a shout from the dock. I went on deck.

"*Idle Queen, fantastique!*" Jean Giquel cried. He rushed up onto my stern plank and assaulted me on both cheeks. "How can the ocean be so big and the world so small?" he cried

We had not seen each other since Christmas dinner at the Point Yacht Club in Durban. We celebrated our reunion over the course of two days. One early morning, I helped Jean with lines, as he sailed off once more, headed for India. I wondered if I'd run into him again somewhere down the sea lanes.

After Jean's departure, I readied the boat for company. Son Carl and his wife, Dixie, arrived to explore the area. Our first sightseeing trip was a sail to Gibraltar. When Carl took the helm, I recalled how the family learned to sail. Our first boats had been old wooden fishing boats, 39- and 40-footers to accommodate the family. After a decade of power boating, I decided to switch to sailboats. I knew by then that I wanted to travel after I retired, and by boat. Wind being cheaper than diesel, a sailboat would be the economical way to go. Before we got our first sailboat, we learned to sail. The dining room table was our classroom.

During dinner we did more than eat. We took turns reading aloud a poem a night. Once we read a play, each of us taking parts. In the early '60s, we read how-to-sail books aloud. After dinner we practiced tying bowlines and clove hitches on the dining room chairs. Then we adjourned to the living room, formed two facing lines, and tossed a medicine ball back and forth to strengthen our arms for quick sail changes. Dixie, no doubt, was happy to miss all that activity; Dixie learned to sail on the boat.

Although we sailed to Gibraltar on a nearly windless day, the trip was exciting. Halfway there, we heard the boom of heavy weapon gunfire. Beyond us, the sea erupted. We looked seaward and saw a target float being towed behind a naval vessel. Even in the light winds, our sails were up and made us more visible. The shore battery paused and allowed us to pass before they resumed firing.

When we reached Queensway Quay Marina in Gibraltar, we encountered what was said to be the worst southwester in two-and-a-half years, steady wind at fifty knots, gusts to sixty. The weather was so violent that the cable car up the Rock was not running. Carl and Dixie missed seeing the view and the Gibraltar monkeys. We ventured out to tour the town, letting the wind blow us along.

Gibraltar is a British colony, recognizable by the red post boxes and the bobbies. Marks & Spencer, a British department store, is here.

At the governor's residence is the traditional British changing of the guard. Trafalgar Cemetery contains the graves of British sailors killed in the Battle of Trafalgar in 1805. As we walked the cemetery paths, I thought of my mother, Floss, who liked to read the headstones in the family cemeteries on Virginia plantations. In Trafalgar Cemetery, I read the headstones of these fallen sailors.

After sailing back to Estepona, we traveled by car to see Ronda, Seville, and Doñana National Park. Ronda is divided into two towns by the gorge of the Rio Guadalquivir. The gorge is deep and the view spectacular, particularly the sight of houses clinging to the cliffs. The town is known for its closely-packed whitewashed houses, the Pueblos Blancos. Ronda had grown considerably in the tourism market since Faido and I visited in the mid-1980s. Cars are not allowed in the immense shopping area. We parked underground. The Plaza de Toros, Spain's oldest bullring, was closed for the season. When Faido and I were here in 1985, we put on a mock bullfight. I played a matador and held out a cape as Faido charged me with a closed umbrella. This historic event is preserved in a family album.

The draw for me in Seville is that this is a river port town; Columbus docked here after returning from America. The twelve-sided Torre de Oro, its gold covering long since stolen, overlooks the river. It is a maritime museum, filled with drawings of the Seville port. We were disappointed that the Alcazar, a fourteenth century palace and the oldest royal residence in Europe, was closed this day. Faido and I toured it on our European trip. Carl and Dixie missed seeing the replica of the *Santa Maria* inside.

Cathedral de Seville is the largest cathedral in Europe. The huge quantity of gold decorating the interior was stolen from the Incas. Columbus' tomb is here, mounted on four statues, although his body is buried in the Dominican Republic. Carl and Dixie studied the cathedral's main focus, the altarpiece with its carvings of a thousand Biblical figures. Near the cathedral is the Giralda Tower, built in the twelfth century and Seville's most recognizable monument. Carl and Dixie walked the thirty-five ramps to the top while I sat and read in the nearby plaza.

The Santa Cruz section is a quiet residential area. From its narrow streets can be seen orange trees, gardens, and patios overflowing with flowers. We walked through this area and enjoyed the smells and the sights on an afternoon of bright sunshine.

Doñana National Park is one of Europe's most important wetlands; six million birds spend part of the year here. In the spring, flamingos and storks arrive, many to nest. We were sorry it was too early in the year to see them. Carl and Dixie bought a Spanish bird guide at the visitor center and went to work identifying what they saw. A dozen of us, mostly Spanish tourists, took the four-hour tour of the area in a 4-wheel-drive Land Rover. The tour guide's commentary was in Spanish. Luckily, the scenery needed no interpretation. The park is a mixture of beach, river, marshlands, and a forest with lollypop-shaped pines. We expected help to identify birds, but the guide was more interested in other wildlife. We slowed for deer and wild boar and came unexpectedly upon one boar eating a deer he had just killed. Carl and Dixie were able to identify twenty-three new birds, surely a record for a half day in this area.

After returning to Estepona, my guests bade good-bye to my sailor friends. They left with an old Spanish saying: *Salut, armor, dinero y tiempo para gostarlos* meaning: "Health, love, money, and time to enjoy them."

With their departure, I went back to maintenance work on the boat. At 1030, ready for a break, I went to the marina restaurant for coffee. Martin always joined me. Three or four other sailors gravitated to our table. This was the start of the coffee klatch, a congenial get-together that I held in ports around the world. While we drank coffee, we discussed various topics, usually world events. Perhaps because of my age, I led the discussions. I listened to the British Broadcasting Corporation on the radio for news and points of interest.

One of the outsiders who frequently joined us was a fiftyish American graduate of Wharton School of Business. After owning a restaurant in France, he retired to Estepona to smoke pot. He had written twelve novels, none of which had been published. He asked me to read one and offer criticism. I couldn't get past the first chapter.

My other established break occurred on Wednesdays. Every Wednesday, the sailors met at 2000 to socialize at Club Nautico. To my relief, English was the common language. At one of these fun affairs, an Italian pantomimed his reception by strutting officials in Albania. At another, someone observed that if you call for the stewardess in Spanish (*azafata*), make sure you are on a Spanish-speaking airline.

Bad weather hampered my boat maintenance in the wettest December seen here in a decade. The reservoirs overflowed, the sea became murky with silt, and people died in floods as several frontal systems swept through. Because it was too wet to work, I sat and read. I finished Patrick O'Brian's seventeen-volume masterpiece of life in Nelson's navy, and read two books by George Stewart, *California Trail* and *Explorations of W.H. Ashley and Jedediah Smith*. One of the Brits insisted that I read *Slow Boats to China* by Gavin Young. Not a sailing book, it provides a hitchhiker's view of commercial shipping in some of the backwaters of the world. Given the current state of affairs, Gavin Young's trip would be far too dangerous an undertaking today.

Twice I ventured out for cultural pursuits. Jay knew a flamenco dance teacher and arranged a successful evening of flamenco for about thirty-five yachties. An Italian sailor and his German girlfriend struggled to cruise and stay solvent. It was difficult, because Ulrica is a stage set designer and Antonio, a classical musician and conductor. Neither occupation blossoms well in a marina. One Thursday Antonio gave a Bach concert and lecture—free, donations accepted—at Club Nautico. It was an educational evening for me; I learned how a fugue is put together.

I turned eighty in February 1996. Mona and Per had flown back to Sweden to visit, and I was surprised when they returned earlier than expected. Their reason soon became clear: they organized a surprise birthday luncheon at El Cazador with Elisabeth and Martin and Larry and Jay. Afterward, Mona and Per invited us back to *Windfall* where we had coffee, Swedish cakes, and cognac. That evening we walked to the town center to see the Estepona carnival. At midnight we stopped in at Club Nautico for a final nightcap. The rest of the yachties were waiting to wish me happy birthday and buy me a drink. As Swedish Mona said, it was "a whole day." I was touched by all the attention.

After a memorable winter, my birthday signaled the advent of spring. The change of season meant a change of venue. It was time to explore the islands in the Mediterranean.

Chapter 15

Sailing the Mediterranean

The grand object of traveling is to see the shores of the Mediterranean.
-Samuel Johnson

In April, I roused myself and sailed into new territory, Aguadulce, 130 miles east of Estepona. Larry and Jay followed in my wake and imitated my moves. Since the experienced sailor had abandoned them, they asked if they could travel with, and learn from, me. I enjoyed their company, and the feeling I got pretending to be an expert sailor.

The trip was typically warm-weather Mediterranean sailing: one day of good sailing, one day of poor sailing, and two nights of flat calm. The coast was uninspiring with barren rocky crags, more arid than around Estepona. More exciting was the sight of the early morning sunrays scintillating on the snowy peaks of the Sierra. An early riser, I sipped coffee as I enjoyed the view.

After we docked in Aguadulce, I flew home to Virginia for my annual medical check-up. On my return trip, I was in Malaga, Spain, at midnight outside a bus station that closed at 0100. The bus to Aguadulce stops outside at 0300. I decided to lug my fifty-seven kilos of luggage to an all-night restaurant reputed to be nearby. Along the way in the dark street, I stopped a young fellow to confirm that I was on the right route. The "young fellow" turned out to be a young female. She suggested that I solve my problems by spending the night with her, but I wended my way onward.

After returning to *Idle Queen*, I sailed the 382 miles from Aguadulce to Port Mahon on the Spanish island of Minorca. *Inner Vision*, *Navsika* and *Windfall* had gone on before. I was frustrated by unremitting headwinds, and almost driven back by a 35 knot northwester. I fought my way into the long narrow channel, squeezed in by the island's low hills, which led to the town's moorings. I docked and was reunited with my friends.

Port Mahon is the second largest natural harbor in the world after Pearl Harbor. This port was headquarters for the British Med fleet during the Napoleonic wars, and the American navy was present from

1822 to 1847. Nelson supposedly entertained Lady Hamilton here. The town today is nothing special; it is no longer militarily strategic.

The 190-mile trip from Port Mahon to Alghero on the northwest coast of Sardinia involved considerable motoring in light to no wind. As expected, the other three boats reached Alghero before *Idle Queen*. As I motored in, I spied *Navsika* and headed for dock space nearby. I threw a line to Martin on the wharf. He pulled it in only to discover that I had not secured my end to the boat.

"Harry, we might be able to find a course in elementary boat handling here in Alghero," Martin said, his mustache twitching.

Alghero, founded by the Dorias from Genoa in the tenth century, could be the setting for a mystery novel with its narrow winding streets. The Old Town and its multi-storied stone houses reminded me of the Alfama district in Lisbon. Alghero was one of the most satisfying and piquant spots I visited.

One night we sailors celebrated Jay's birthday at Ristaurante La Singular. The group consisted of French, Norwegian, and British couples, plus one old American. The *maitre d'hotel* arranged the group dinner. The French couple, Eliza and Guy, who speak Italian, guided us along the way. The restaurant staff knew no English and could not take plastic money. They see few tourists. It is already clear that Italian cuisine is far superior to that in Spain.

Our flotilla sailed from Alghero around the top of Sardinia to the little town of Stintino. Stintino, once a fishing village, has reinvented itself as a tourist town. I would have preferred the fishing village. Our sight-seeing tour continued by bus across the flat coastal plain to the busy, dirty, refinery town of Porto Torres. In this cattle country, I enjoyed the pastoral view of rolled-up hay bales.

Bonifacio Strait, which separates Sardinia and Corsica, has a reputation for bad weather. For several days we anchored at Capo Testa awaiting good conditions. We finally sailed off, only to be blasted by a forty-knot westerly on our way to Porto Vecchio on the southeast coast of Corsica. The final stretch of this run leads up a long narrow valley and directly into winds that funnel down between the hills. Per and Mona had little trouble with their large engine. *Inner Vision* passed *Idle Queen*. I struggled with my small engine and motored in two hours later. Mona was pacing the dock when I arrived, worried that I might not make it.

Like Sardinia, Corsica has more inclines than flats. We traveled in Per's rented car south from Porto Vecchio to Bonifacio, northwest to

Sartene, and back east across the island to Porto Vecchio. The harbor town of Bonifacio sits in a spectacularly beautiful setting on the side of a deep slice in the mountains. The sea, intruding into the cut, makes the harbor. Villages across the green backbone of Corsica are distinctive with their red tile roofs over low stone houses, all dominated by the lowering presence of the gray stone church spires.

We were lucky on our passage from Porto Vecchio to Fiumicino, the port closest to Rome. We missed by one day a southwesterly gale that would have put us on a lee shore with an impossible harbor entrance. As it was, *Navsika* and *Windfall* arrived before *Inner Vision* and IQ.

Rome is vastly different from any city I have ever seen. The area is peppered with amazingly crafted and ancient stone and marble monuments, buildings, statues and relics. They would be fenced off and heavily guarded elsewhere. Here they are casually patted or ignored by passersby. We gawked at the Colosseum (How did they get those huge granite blocks cut and fitted?), craned our necks in the Sistine Chapel (I have not learned to appreciate this type art), and scratched our heads among the ruins of the Roman Forum. We watched Jay cool her feet in *Trevi* (Three Coins) Fountain, cooled ourselves in the depths of the Catacombs, admired St. Peter's (smaller than St. Paul's, a fraction of the size of Seville Cathedral, but better kept than either), saw where Horatius kept the bridge "in the brave days of old," visited the Pantheon, saw Villa Borghese, and a hundred other sights.

"There is beauty everywhere I turn," Jay said, her blonde hair swinging.

"I have always dreamed of visiting Rome," Larry said. "I'm overwhelmed by the power of its antiquities."

From Rome, our fleet day-hopped south down the coast of Italy. I was surprised at how long the coast is. The many harbors along the way are crowded and expensive. San Felice Circeo, the legendary home of Circe, is where Odysseus lingered for a year. The magic has gone, and one day was enough for us. A few miles farther along lies Gaeta on an outstanding promontory with an impregnable-looking fortress perched high on the cliffs. John Cabot was supposedly born here. An American warship is on permanent station in the harbor. Ischia, just off the Bay of Naples, is a beautiful island. In the town of Casamicciola, an Italian pointed out the white house halfway up the mountain where Henrik Ibsen wrote *Peer Gynt*.

Naples is reputedly a trashy, crime-ridden city. We passed it up in favor of the faded beauty of Amalfi. En route, we sailed close by the romantic but expensive Isle of Capri with Vesuvius dominating the skyline to the east. After our boats were moored in the breakwatered harbor of the sleepy old town of Agropolis, we backtracked by train to visit the ruins of Pompeii. The remarkable job of excavating a well-preserved city of 20,000 showed just how people lived in 79 A.D. The columns are standing upright, walls and some roofs are intact, and even pictures painted on the walls are still colorful and legible. The pictures demonstrate that Pompeiians were a lascivious people which, of course, do not distinguish them from today's society.

Reluctantly, we hopped on the train for the one-hour trip back to the boats. This was the last night we would all travel together. We shared a farewell dinner at a restaurant just off the marina. The next day, *Idle Queen* and *Inner Vision* continued down Italy's coast. *Windfall* and *Navsika* sailed ahead to other ports.

The most picturesque town along the southwest coast of mainland Italy is Cetraro. Perched high on a hill, it overlooks the sea and the small, almost deserted, fishing port. The bus ride up the mountain is a horn-blowing, brake-slamming adventure. We hove-to off Stromboli the next night. This island-volcano, which usually produces fireworks, only smoked weakly. We continued on through the Strait of Messina and tried to tie up in Sicily. We found no facilities and settled instead for the dirty mainland town of Reggio Calabria. This gloomy town with its paper-strewn streets is rumored to be a breeding ground for the Mafia. Scilla and Charybdis gave us no problems in the Strait, and we saw not even a Fata Morgana.

We traveled northeast along the foot of Italy to the heel at Sta. Maria di Leuca, supposedly the poorest part of Italy. I think the people are more slovenly than poor. Dust and papers float through the streets, garbage piles up, downtown residences advertise the dreariness of flaking paint. In contrast, the countryside is mountainous and eye-appealing right down to the sea. Old castles dominate the landscape. The hills are only slightly greener than those of southern California.

A heavy thunderstorm descended on *Inner Vision* and *Idle Queen* as we lay at anchor in the harbor. Ensconced in IQ's cabin, I heard a loud sizzle and a deafening thundering boom. I poked my head out from the companionway and looked around.

"We've been hit by lightning!" Jay yelled. Their boat was dark.

I struggled into wet weather gear and hurried over. All the electronics, lights, most of the wiring, and alternator were destroyed in that sudden burst of energy. Jay and Larry were lucky to be uninjured. Larry was able to start the engine, and we decided that repairs could be better made in the Greek island town of Corfu. We sailed there the next morning. Larry and Jay were told that repairs would take several weeks. To take advantage of the lull, I ordered a sail and a solar panel from the U.S.

Corfu is a touristy, very British town, on a high green island. Although I enjoyed the modern part of town, despite the hordes of tourists who cluttered the shopping districts, I was most interested in exploring the ancient sections. Priests strolled through the streets in their full black robes, long gray beards and round brimless black hats. The older monuments and fortresses are Venetian in character. Venice ruled the area for 400 years starting in the fourteenth century. This is a good place in which to get used to the Greek alphabet and pick up a few words of the language, for the locals are always helpful. Greek food is more varied and beguiling than that of either Italy or Spain. (My earlier report on great food in Italy should have been limited to Sardinia.) I attended an evening of Greek dancing put on by a local group; the Rockettes it was not, but excellent for its style.

Greek officialdom is not as laid back as that of Spain or Italy, but there are some strange compensations. Italian Customs wanted $500 (30% import duty plus 20% Value Added Tax) to allow me to import a U.S.-made sail. Greek Customs didn't even raise a question when the sail was delivered. I bought four liters of engine oil in Corfu for $13; in Italy the same item was $37. I am a convert to setting monetary exchange rates on a commodity index.

The Greek outlook is backward in many ways. Wendy and Chris Weigman, an American couple on *Spirit Of Delft*, arrived several days after I had. Wendy did the clearing in.

"Who is the captain?" the official asked her.

"I am, Wendy Weigman," said Wendy.

"No," the official said, and repeated the question.

Wendy insisted that she was the captain.

"Poof," said the official, and wrote down "Chris Weigman."

Chris and Wendy were an atypical cruising couple. They bought a stripped-out 60-foot aluminum racing hull in Holland and converted it to a comfortable live-aboard boat. Chris has remarkable mechanical skills formed during his years as an airplane mechanic. I think the couple would rather work on, than sail, a yacht.

After my shipment arrived, I installed the two solar panels and sailed off while *Inner Vision* was still being repaired. I planned to meet visiting friends in Athens in early October. It was hard to leave Larry and Jay, the beer and *souvlaki* lunches in Corfu, and even the picturesque town, but I finally had to.

My first stop was the little island of Paxos, lying just south of Corfu. It has an almost land-locked anchorage but no flat land that I could find on two bus trips from one end to the other. The steep slopes are covered with stone-walled terraces supporting 160-year-old olive trees. There is neither bank nor post office. In the village of Lakka, I learned to enjoy Greek coffee while I watched the old men spend afternoons and evenings playing backgammon in the coffeehouse. The house provided boards for the eight or ten tables scattered around the bare room. If a woman stepped inside, she would not be Greek.

Greek coffee must analyze about 45% coffee, 45% sugar, 10% water. It is always served with a full tumbler of water—for good reason. Actually the coffee is tasty, but the Greek retsina wine is another matter. I couldn't swallow it.

At Lakka, Jay and Larry caught up with me. We sailed together to the mainland at Prevesa. Here I left them once again; they wanted to go in one direction and I in another. They were now confident sailors. I proceeded south through the Ionian islands and east into the Gulf of Corinth. South of Levkas Island is possibly the best cruising area in Greece. Part of the Ionian here is almost an inland sea, surrounded tightly by a multitude of high islands. I wanted to stop at Ithaca, but the anchorages around Ulysses's island are poor, and the weather continued to be never satisfied with itself.

The entrance into the port of Mesolongion, off the Gulf of Corinth, looked unapproachable, so I passed up the place where Byron died of a fever in 1824 while fighting for Greek independence. As I prepared to dock in Patras, Chris Weigman hailed me and asked me to berth near them. I rounded up and headed in, moving too fast and at a bad angle.

"Reverse, Harry!" Chris yelled. "Reverse!"

Over *Idle Queen's* engine, I couldn't hear him. Nor did I notice that my bowsprit was aimed at an expensive Super Maramu. Chris jumped on board the other boat just as my bowsprit threatened to wipe the

GPS antennae off its rail. He quickly lifted my bowsprit and stopped my forward progress. Chris is 6'2" and about 220 pounds.

"Is everything all right, Chris?" I called.

All was well. Chris stepped aboard *Idle Queen* and his foot promptly went through the wood at the bowsprit platform. Our laughter relieved the tension caused by my poor docking.

The Weigmans and I left Patras together and sailed into the Gulf of Corinth on our way to the beautiful island of Trizonia. In one place, the Gulf narrows to its smallest point, and a sandbar sticks far out from the south side. This caused the Weigmans more frightful moments. They told me later that they could see the sandbar, and I was headed right toward it. They called me on the VHF, which I had off. They shouted and whistled, but I didn't hear them. As they prepared ropes to pull me off, I became aware of a calming change in the water. I looked about and spotted the reason. I threw the tiller sharply over and paralleled the sandbar toward deep water. Afterward, I admitted to the Weigmans that my eyesight was not as sharp as it used to be. Sometimes good friends can substitute for good eyesight, even at sea.

I was running behind in my scheduled meeting in Corinth with my friends, Lyn and Juan Morales of California. They were touring Europe on land, and we agreed to meet on a certain date. I was stuck on Trizonia Island for three days due to wind and rain. I set off once, only to be driven back to its secure little harbor, a comfortable enough place except for uncertain phone links. I couldn't phone Harry Third in Virginia to relay a message in case the Moraleses called. As I waited for the weather to break, I wondered if I would make it to Corinth before Lyn and Juan had to travel on. And when I finally arrived, where would I possibly find them?

Chapter 16

Turkish Delight

History is about people, and there is nothing more fascinating to people than other people living in a different time, in different circumstances.
-Stephen E. Ambrose, *To America*

I finally sailed from Trizonia Island across to Corinth and into the marina at the west end of the Corinth Canal. After I docked, I pondered where I could find one visiting couple in a sizable Greek city. But first things first: I went to the post office to pick up my general delivery mail and write postcards. I stood at a counter and scribbled away.

Behind me, someone said loudly in English, "Hello!"

I turned, and there were Lyn and Juan! We shook hands, hugged, and laughed. What were the chances that we would find each other in a post office?

Over several days we reminisced of our sails together through Central America, as we toured Ancient Corinth and Athens. Ancient Corinth, on the plain above modern Corinth, flourished in the seventh century BC and was destroyed by the Romans in 146 BC. The people of the time built columns and carved statues which survive to this day, many in a well-preserved state. I was mesmerized.

After Rome, Athens was a disappointment. A city of three million, Athens could be almost any overgrown village anywhere. Only the Acropolis in its magnificent location on a high hill overlooking the whole of Athens, stands out as a remarkable feature. The Parthenon's tall, massive, marble columns are perhaps more striking than any single site in Rome.

After Lyn and Juan left Corinth, I became acquainted with Tommy Fortas, a Greek-derived henchman of the Chicago Daleys, returned to his ancestral home.

Tommy said, "The old Greeks in the out villages do not like Americans. They are Communists and will never change."

I found the Greeks not unfriendly, but not as friendly as I found the Turks.

I sailed to Turkey without ever being out of sight of land. The arid rocks that are the Greek islands lie like huge pebbles scattered in the Aegean Sea. They are sparsely covered with low bushes and sometimes a little grass, but are rarely wooded. The stark-white houses of the *choras* scatter up the hillsides and cluster around the peaks. I felt welcome in the tight little harbors in Egina, Serifos, Amorgos, and Rhodes, among others. I was blown out of Amorgos by a summer's rare thirty-knot norther and broke a staysail halyard block in the process. The Colossus is gone from Rhodes, but ancient forts and citadels make this island a worthwhile visit.

I entered Turkey at the port of Fethiye and browsed for a couple days through this old town. On the street I stopped a man only slightly younger than I to ask directions to the "posta."

"Aleman?" he asked.

I shook my head and said, "American."

"Bush-Clinton?"

I smiled and nodded.

"Saddam?"

I passed a finger across my throat. He laughed, threw an arm over my shoulder, and led me to the post office.

I discovered in small heavily Islamic towns, such as Fethiye, one has to be watchful walking the streets during Ramadan. The Moslems, prohibited from swallowing during daylight hours, spit their saliva onto the sidewalk.

After I left Fethiye, *Inner Vision* sailed in. Here, I learned, Jay and Larry amicably parted. Larry found a friendly companion ashore while Jay singlehanded the boat to Spain. She eventually returned to England. In thirteen years of meeting a wide mix of sailors, this is one of only two breakups I witnessed, despite the close-quarters pressure in which couples find themselves.

I moved on from Fethiye to Antalya, in the heart of the Turkish Riviera. Antalya is a popular spot for wintering, although quite different from Estepona. The city, with a population of 750,000, lies eight miles east of the marina. It contains the richness and the poverty of a big city. The minarets are there, but I did not hear the muezzins calling as I did in Fethiye. The area immediately west is mountainous with more woods and greenery than elsewhere along this coast. It is said that the Pamphylian coast to the east is flat, a major agricultural area since prehistoric times. Beaches are crowded in summer, and the weather is still clear and warm late in the year.

The marina in Antalya is well equipped and provides dockage for two hundred yachts. I noticed with interest the fishing caiques in the harbor. I like these Greek and Turkish double-ender boats with their outboard rudders and pronounced sheer. They are IQ's relatives.

I was met at the breakwater entrance by two marina employees in an outboard motorboat. They led me to my slip, took my lines, and tied me up. This was a unique welcome. I appreciated the escort for the marina was almost full. Martin and Elisabeth were here. Americans included Frank and Zoe on *Intuition*, Larry and Maxine on *Shingebiss II*, Bill and Gary on *Amadon Light*, and Ann and Fabe Saxe on *Heather*.

Shortly after my arrival, I dropped my only pair of eyeglasses overboard. The ten feet of water was too deep for me to dive down and scramble around in the mud trying to locate them. Preben, a Danish sailor, defied marina rules, dove down, and quickly retrieved them. His price was one bottle of wine. This was the second time a diver rescued me in an embarrassing situation and been repaid in wine.

I held my traditional morning coffee klatch in the marina restaurant even though it was not open for breakfast. By special dispensation, the management opened the bar and the sleepy cook served us. Martin and Elisabeth, Frank, Fabe, and Bill (*Nora*) were among the regulars. We discussed those affairs of the world that we considered serious: boat maintenance and navigational techniques.

One couple I became fond of did not join the coffee klatch. Ken and Clare on *Echo* were in their sixties. They are the only Irish couple I know where the husband is a teetotaler and the wife drinks. I had dinner on their boat several times. Ken is a retired boat surveyor, and I enjoyed stories from his working days. When I left Antalya, we agreed to keep in radio contact.

The marina was as close to an international village community as I can visualize. Frequent special events attracted crowds at the restaurant. The small upstairs club room was usually packed with dart players and beer drinkers. Weekly bus tours into the surrounding historic sights of Old Turkey always attracted an eager group. A German couple, Hans and Gisele, planned and organized the tours.

One Sunday a group of us went to the ruins of Perge. These are Roman, although Alexander the Great used the city as a headquarter during his march through the area. The construction of tunnels into the stadium, using huge blocks of granite, is remarkable. Perge was the home of the great Greek mathematician Apollonius, born 260 BC.

The guide book says his work on conic sections enabled Kepler to do his exposition of the motion of planets.

Another bus trip took us to the ruins of Aspendos, about 30 km east of Antalya. The ruins contain an amphitheater built by the Romans and still used in the summer for concerts. Some cement touch-up of broken corners is the only restoration. Acoustics are amazing. People in the higher tiers heard the click of my camera on the stage.

As we passed a hilly farmland, I saw an incredible sight: a Turk tilling his fields by hand with a wooden plow.

One day a cruise ship from Athens tied up in the port a kilometer from the marina.

Shortly thereafter, I heard, "Harry! Harry!" called from the pontoon.

I turned and recognized Nibs Brown, whom I had last seen on his boat in Daytona Beach. He saw my name posted in the marina list and sought me out. We had time for lunch before Nibs scurried off to board the cruise ship and set off once again. The poor souls on cruise ships learn little about a town beyond what their snapshots show.

By Thanksgiving, Chris and Wendy Weigman on *Spirit Of Delft* joined the fleet. That made eight American or Canadian boats in the harbor. We sailors decided to host a Thanksgiving dinner for the seventy people the restaurant could hold. It was quite a feast with informal empathetic company. For Christmas dinner those of us still in port, which turned out to be most of us, arranged a repeat performance and another rousing celebration. Several sailors handed out small token gifts—pens and candy and the like—which added to the festivities.

I spent the holidays, as I often do, reading Christmas presents. This year, I was given a biography, *Ataturk* by Kinross. I think Kemal Ataturk was one of the great men of the twentieth century. He wrenched Turkey out of the grip of the East and propelled it toward the West. He outlawed the fez, got the veil off women, deposed the Sultan, got the clerics out of government, changed to the Western calendar, secured the only equitable peace treaty after World War I and, by 1938 when he died, laid the foundation for a democracy. The book brought to mind a quote from N. Erbakan, quandum prime minister of Turkey: "The West learned everything it knows from the Muslims."

One day I sat reading, as heavy rain resounded on the cabin top. At 1808 I heard an express train bearing down with Casey Jones at the throttle. *Idle Queen* lurched, and the mooring lines squealed, as a tornado passed through. In less than a minute, the violent wind cut a hundred foot-wide path of destruction through the marina.

On "C" pontoon and the outer end of "B," broken masts lay scattered amid smashed dinghies, booms, and bow pulpits. Bits of awning, dodgers, and flags flew entangled in rigging. "C" pontoon, a concrete float, cracked in the middle. Surprisingly, the only injury was a woman scalded, as she cooked dinner. IQ was unscathed, *Navsika* was only ruffled, but *Spirit of Delft* was damaged by boats flung against her. Eight boats on land were blown off supports and wrecked. Nearby houses lost roofs, gaping holes appeared in aluminum-sided buildings, and fences were knocked down.

We Americans are familiar with tornadoes, but the other sailors were astonished at the storm's violence. No one ever heard of a tornado in this area.

My visa for Turkey ran out in early February 1997. Although the boat could stay, I had to leave the country. I flew to the United States out of the Antalya airport. At Customs before I boarded the plane, I was asked where I entered the country.

"Fethiye," I said.

I was pulled out of the line and waited twenty minutes while the officials puzzled over my case. "There is no airport in Fethiye," one said accusingly.

"I came by boat."

They looked incredulous. I finally convinced them that an elderly American could, indeed, arrive by boat.

Upon my return from the United States, I took a twelve-day bus trip around western Turkey. I particularly wanted to see the ruins of Ephesus and Troy. The bus route over the mountains from Antalya to Fethiye traverses one of the most desolate-looking areas in Turkey. This southwest part of the country is extremely rugged, mountainous and rocky, with snow along the road in mid-April. The lonely farmhouses on the high plateau add to, rather than relieve, the sense of isolation.

By local bus, I traveled to an area behind Fethiye where a deserted village sits. In the late 1920s Ataturk drove the Greeks out of Turkey. This village, atop a hill, was occupied by skilled Greek artisans. The Turks who moved into the area wanted to farm in the flatlands rather than occupy the ridge. The village and its church still stand, deserted, stripped, and deteriorating.

The town of Selcuk is situated on the main bus route and a mile from Ephesus. (It is called Efes in Turkish—also the name of the most popular Turkish beer.) I stayed in a hostel in Selcuk for ten dollars a night for a room with a private bath and shower. From the hostel, I walked to the ruins of the magnificent city of Ephesus. The city was once on the sea, but due to silting, now sits far inland. Archeological work is still being done. Some of the ruins, such as the Library of Celsus, are sufficiently preserved to show remarkable carving by the artists of that day. Large statues still occupy niches in the façade of the multistory library. These are not unusual considering the vast quantity of detailed stone carving that is scattered around this part of the world.

From Ephesus, I tramped back to Selcuk via a shortcut through fields and around a hill. A Turkish man on a bicycle overtook me and dismounted, ostensibly to chat. He worked with the excavation group digging on the hillside. He pulled from his pocket a handful of coins which looked dirty and corroded enough to have been authentically ancient. He offered to sell me one at a "good" price. I shook my head. I did not want to make my fortune that way.

Rain set in early the next day and poured steadily when I arrived at Canakkale on the shores of the Dardanelles. I noticed four English-speaking young men on the bus. They were Australians traveling around the world to celebrate their college graduations. In the Canakkale bus station, we drifted together and discussed where we might spend the night. The Australians had a list of youth hostels. We picked out the Yellow Rose, which specialized in arranging tours to Gallipoli. The five of us crowded into a taxi and were driven there for fifty cents each. Again I had a room with private bath and shower, including breakfast, for ten dollars.

In the morning, the Aussies and I regretfully parted, they to salute Australia's finest killed at Gallipoli, I to salute Homer's at Troy. Troy is twenty miles from Canakkale. It is well inland from the sea although the inhabitants once collected tolls from ships wanting to use the Dardanelles. The sloping walls of some of the nine layers of Troy (Homer's was number six) lie exposed and partially grass-covered on the low mound rising from the plain. The historical effect is diminished by the poorly designed and ugly twenty-foot high wooden horse which has been constructed in the foreyard.

Back in Canakkale, a two-mile ferry ride took me over into Europe and onto the road northeast. The Istanbul bus terminal is outside the crowded city. A courtesy car took me to a spot where I could catch a tram to the old part of Istanbul. At the tram line, I couldn't tell which way I should go. I asked a Turk who was selling pita bread and donuts from a mobile cart for the direction to Sultanahmet. He pointed the way, and I walked over to the rail line. Soon the vendor left his cart unguarded and jogged over to tell me that the tram did not stop there; I had to walk up the hill to a proper stop. I am continually amazed at how people anywhere in the world take the initiative to help strangers.

The old historical part of Istanbul is not a large area. A walk across Galata Bridge or a climb up Galata Tower will showcase the world-class skyline of Istanbul, dominated by the towers of its dozens of mosques and minarets. This skyline surely rivals that of any city in the world. Istanbul's seven hills, particularly those on the northeast side of the Golden Horn, are just as steep as those in San Francisco. Rome and Istanbul must vie for the title, "Most Exciting Old World City." History in Rome seems dormant; in Istanbul, history seems to still flow through the monuments and buildings.

Despite these aesthetics, Istanbul is crowded and as dirty as any city I saw. Hordes are disgorged every morning from the Sea of Marmara ferries near the Galata Bridge. They jam the tramline and buses on the way to work. Eleven million people are crowded into Istanbul. In 1600 it was the largest city in the world with a population of 700,000. Today the strains show.

The Sultanahmet (Blue Mosque) has a fat pillared, striking blue-tiled interior and a distinctive exterior sporting six minarets, two more than the usual. The Ottomans built it in the early seventeenth century. Hagia Sofia (Cathedral of Holy Wisdom) is more impressive. It is not beautiful, but is huge and cavernous. Inside, the dome is 184 feet high and 111 feet in diameter. For a thousand years, it was the world's largest man-made enclosed space. Constantine was consecrated here. It was converted to a mosque in 1453 and recently to a museum. Because of their size and close proximity, the mosque and cathedral struck me as symbols of the rivalry of these two major religions.

It takes a day to go through Topkapi palace. Construction was started in the fifteenth century and was the home of the Ottoman sultans until 1853. Most fascinating to me was the collection of early oriental pottery and the colored and beautifully embossed handwritten

Arabic manuscripts. A long line of people stretched back from the entrance to the harem. Since, as I understood, all the interesting inhabitants were gone, I did not bother to go in.

As I wandered about the Topkapi, I heard someone shout, "Ahoy, Captain!"

I turned around to be greeted by my four Aussie boys. Unfortunately, they were in a hurry to be somewhere else the next day.

The successor to Topkapi is the Dolmabahce Palace, a structure so magnificent it bankrupted the Ottomans. A nine thousand pound chandelier, the heaviest in the world, hangs over one of the reception rooms. In an entrance hall an identical pair of large carvings (in ebony?) depicts an elephant family grazing under a jungle cover. I dropped behind the tour group for a few minutes, mesmerized by this elephant tableau.

The magnificent palaces of the sultans confirm the wealth of the leaders of the Ottoman Empire. Weren't the rich richer and the poor poorer then, than now? Ironically, the last inhabitant of Dolmabahce was the dying Ataturk, the man who put an end to the sultans and the caliphs.

A huge archeological museum lies between Hagia Sofia and Topkapi. It contains material from the Anatolian Peninsula going back to neolithic times and many artifacts from Troy. One of the preserved sarcophagi is decorated with a carving showing Alexander in battle.

I was surprised to discover that Istanbul is not expensive. A good hotel costs thirty-five dollars a night. I preferred a particular French restaurant to the Turkish possibilities. This was due to style rather than substance. Because of a transport tie-up, I spent six days in Istanbul and finally got out on a bus. The glowing lights of the city faded after I crossed the Bosphorus Bridge. I dozed fitfully on into home at Antalya.

I remained in Antalya long enough to restock the boat before sailing for Cypress. The 235 mile trip to Larnica is an easy downwind run. In the Med in springtime the wind dies at sundown. Since I do not motor at night, the voyage took four days and was enlivened on the last day by a real downeaster fog from dawn until noon. Fog is not unusual in summer, but this fact did not leave me any less tired, as I strained to see.

Britain took over Cyprus from the Ottoman Turks in 1878. The island became an independent democratic republic in 1960. In 1979, fearing a takeover by Greece, the Turkish-speaking northern third of the island separated as a Turkey-supported cypnot state. They remain separated to this day.

There is still an active British base on Cyprus and most people are fluent in English. I am not sure how Greek the Cypriot Greeks are. For lunch, I ordered *souvlaki* and a small beer. What I got was a shish and a large beer. Someone was looking out for me.

In Larnica Marina, I saw for the first time yachts from Lebanon, Hungary, Bulgaria, and Russia. The marina is not as well kept as the Antalya marina, and I was glad I wintered in Turkey. Because of a prolonged drought, water in the marina is turned on only four days per week. Nevertheless the blooming jacaranda and bougainvillea in the town square glowed with splashes of color. The interior of the island, mostly wheat, hay, and olive trees, suffered.

I limited my sightseeing in Cyprus to a trip to Nicosia. Here most streets, even in the downtown area, are lined with shade trees. The archeological museum has an extensive collection of artifacts going back 9000 years. The Green Line, which separates Turkish north and Greek south, runs through the middle of town. When I came to a crossing point, an armed soldier made it plain I could go no farther. The country will not be reunited soon.

After only two weeks in Cypress, I sailed off toward the Israeli coast. I couldn't wait to explore the Middle East.

Chapter 17

The Hostile and the Hospitable

As it is impossible for us to foresee in what manner you will be received by these people, whether by hospitality or hostility, so it is impossible to prescribe the exact degree of perseverance with which you are to pursue your journey.
-Thomas Jefferson to Meriwether Lewis

Three sailing days and 200 miles took me from Cyprus to Ashkelon, Israel. As I approached within fifty miles of the Israeli coast, the Israeli navy radioed and asked my identity and my intentions. I could hear their questions, but they couldn't hear my answers. A passing ship acted as a relay station. When the Port of Ashkelon was in sight, an Israeli gunboat came out, circled me, and studied me through binoculars. In contrast, the marina welcome was hearty and sincere.

As I docked in my assigned slip, I inadvertently awakened American Janet Smith on *Apogee*. She came out and helped me tie up. Later that day, I was chagrinned to learn that she had been up all night as her husband, George, underwent emergency surgery. During their trip up the Red Sea, George became increasingly distressed. They realized an operation was necessary, but didn't want it done in Egypt. They hurried on to Israel. In Ashkelon, bleeding profusely, George was rushed to the hospital; an artery in his lower intestinal area had been perforated. If the surgeons had not quickly pin-pointed the location, George would have died.

I felt chagrinned a second time when I had trouble with my depth sounder. George brought over sophisticated testing equipment to diagnose the problem. I became aware that I was docked near a world-renowned scientist. While working at Bell Laboratories, George invented a device that is used today in all television and cell phone cameras. His sailing around the world was interrupted several times, as he received international science awards. In 2009, George Smith was one of three scientists who shared the Nobel Prize for Physics. Faido would have loved the irony of this world-famous scientist looking at my lowly depth sounder.

Ashkelon is an accommodating city able to supply most of the needs of the cruising yachtsman. A minibus runs into town twice a week from the marina to take the international set shopping. Major resort construction is in progress in the area. I am not sympathetic to those who shoot rockets from Gaza into Ashkelon.

I passed a hot, dry, Southern California-type summer in southern Israel. The coastal plain is farmland: citrus, peaches, grapes, vegetables, sunflowers, hay, and cattle. About halfway from the coast to the Jerusalem hills, sparse, scraggly pines begin to rise. The area around Jerusalem is steeply hilly, rocky and arid, with only a few patches of medium-sized pines. Red mimosa trees decorate streets in the towns.

On the cheap efficient bus system I visited Jerusalem and Tel Aviv. They are like any other large city except for the districts of the Old City of Jerusalem. I understand one of the reasons why the Israelis and Palestinians fight for Jerusalem: the old walled city is a moneymaker. Wherever one goes or whatever one stops to see, someone is there to collect a fee. The religious shrines are wedged into and surrounded by a huge covered bazaar where the narrow streets are lined with shops. A shopper can buy anything he can carry. I got lost in a maze of unmarked alleys. At one point, I thought I was in the Muslim quarter until a young lady, apparently Israeli, told me in perfect English that it was a mixed section.

Israelis are not happy people. Too high a percentage of the young are in khaki. The men and some of the women have heavy weapons slung across their backs. A group of women, boarding a bus for the Rafah border into Gaza, all carried sidearms. The saddest faced of all are the Moslem women in their white head scarves edging their way through the crowds in the Old City. These two peoples, both claiming to be descended from Abraham, are indistinguishable except for the head scarves on one and the skull caps on the other. Religion has much to answer for.

I explored other parts of the area with three sailing couples who had been in the marina in Antalya. Ray and Jean on *Toq Toq* were British. Ray, an ex-rugby player, looked too small to have played in the scrum. Larry and Maxine of *Shingebiss II* were hardy Americans who had sailed around Cape Horn. The Canadian couple on *Spurwing*, Dick and Debbie, were tall, slim and fashionable. When these three couples rented two cars for a trip to Jordan, they invited me to join them.

Since Larry and Dick are ex pilots (747s and 737s) our first stop was the Israeli Air Museum at Beersheba. On the way, we almost ended up in Gaza after taking a wrong turn. We were free to go there if we wished, according to the flak-jacketed, Uzi-carrying guard, but the massive barbed wire fence looked forbidding. The Israeli Air Museum has more than sixty planes on display. Most were used in wars with the Arabs, or are planes that were used *by* the Arabs. We spent the afternoon there, as Larry and Dick regaled us with their expertise.

Eilat is the southernmost city in Israel and provides an outlet to the Red Sea via the Gulf of Aqaba. It is an expensive town with a pack of large hotels. It contrasts sharply with the long dark tents of the Bedouin camps scattered across the barren hills of Israel and Jordan. The heat seemed not to bother these black-clothed people, as they tended their goat herds. But they railed at us, as we took their pictures.

Crossovers from Israel to Jordan by pedestrians present no problems, but vehicles are not allowed. We walked the few yards of no man's land and rented cars on the Jordan side. There is more knowledge and use of English in Jordan than in Israel. In Jordan, study of English is compulsory in elementary school.

When you meet a Jordanian, he will say, "Hello, where are you from? Welcome." I found Jordanians to be a gentle people. It was a pleasure to get away from the Israeli push, shove, and elbow routine. This method of operation is endemic in Mediterranean countries, not just Israel.

I went into a shop in Aqaba to get a Jordanian courtesy flag for the boat. The shopkeeper had none. Instead of telling me where to find a flag, he left me alone in the shop for five minutes. He went out, found one, and brought it back, the price tag intact.

After a night in an Aqaba hotel, we arose early to drive the fifty kilometers to Wadi Rum to catch the 0445 sunrise. I enjoy the fantastic desert landscapes of the southwestern United States, and marveled at the rugged stacks of colorful strata rising from the desert floor here.

The deserted and once-lost city of Petra provided the *raison d'etre* for this trip. *Indiana Jones and the Last Crusade* features Petra, so moviegoers worldwide know what it looks like. The Nabatians, nomads from Arabia, settled here a few hundred years BC and carved huge temples and tombs out of the vertical faces of solid rock which glowed in colors of rose, crimson and purple. How they did it none of us could decide. We saw evidence that scaffolding was used despite this being a treeless country. The city was a stopping point on the caravan route until the Romans moved in and shoved the caravans onto a northern track.

Our group of rugged sailors examined Petra in one day, a thirteen kilometer hike from 0600 to 1800. The low point in the valley and the narrow gorge is at 2700 feet; one high point is at 3400 feet, the other at 3300 feet with the valley between. We hiked to the top of both heights. At one point, when we thought we might be headed wrong, we came upon a girl tending goats. Maxine, speaking slowly and gesturing, asked the girl if we were going in the right direction. The girl, in English, replied that we were. I brought up the rear of our line of hikers—Debbie retraced her steps to find me—and was the last one to stagger into the hotel. This was as much walking as I could do. I prefer sailing. It's more fun, though at times more strenuous.

Farther north in Jordan near Mt. Nebo is the town of Madaba, famous for a remarkable mosaic map of Palestine prepared about 560 AD. I was astounded at its detailed accuracy. We continued on to the top of Mt. Nebo, the peak from which Moses saw the Promised Land. I hope that at his big moment, Moses's view was not obscured by smog and haze, as ours was.

Amman, contrary to some of the guide books, is a thriving, well-marked city. A good single hotel room goes for thirty dollars. We strolled into the Old Town in the evening for a look at the multitude of small shops selling almost anything. The apothecary and perfume mixers with row upon row of vials and bottles are things not seen in my part of the world.

Crossing back into Israel proved no chore, with only an X-ray scan of our baggage. Over the Jordan River, the famous Allenby Bridge shocked my preconceptions. The low truss bridge is only fifty yards long across a ten-to-twenty yard wide stream. The water flowed at a good clip. This area, not far from the Dead Sea and in direct line between Allenby Bridge and the outskirts of Jerusalem, is uninhabited and for good reason: it looks like the Badlands of South Dakota. We returned to Ashkelon by bus.

The following month, I saw more of the countryside. Judy, a schoolteacher friend of my granddaughter, Mollie, arrived to spend three weeks traveling through Israel and Egypt with me. Judy is an enthusiastic lady who laughs at problems and loves to haggle. We got along well. Her short brown hair, blonde highlighted, belied her forty-something years.

A bus took us from Israel through the Gaza Strip and on to Cairo. Because of terrorist activities in the area, the bus was preceded down the highway by a jeep loaded with armed guards. The bus and jeep, both traveling sixty miles an hour, were separated by only a few feet, which made an otherwise pleasant ride entirely nerve-wracking.

In the Cairo area we visited the usual tourist sites: the pyramids, the Sphinx, and Memphis. The Cairo Archeological Museum has an outstanding exhibit of artifacts excavated from the days of the Pharaohs. The view of Cairo from the top of its 180 meter-high tower located between two branches of the Nile is one of the more striking and less advertised sights to be found in this city.

Our land tour of Israel took us as far north as the Golan Heights, an odd area with seemingly deserted houses scattered over the landscape. The homes are actually occupied by Jewish settlers. The ubiquitous desert heat haze marred the view over the lowlands of Israel.

We walked the grounds of the religious relics at Capernaum, and Judy waded knee deep in the Sea of Galilee. We stumbled on an unusual place to spend the night in the agricultural kibbutz of Maegoa Ba'gilboa. This is located high in the mountain range between the Jordan Valley and Israel's coastal plain. These mountains would be a natural barrier between Israel and a Palestinian state. Continuing south, we found the Bethlehem area sealed off, disappointing Judy. We passed by Qumran, where the Dead Sea scrolls were found, and Judy waded in the salt-sticky waters of the Dead Sea. We paused only briefly at the entrance to the Israeli shrine, the high plateau of Masada. At Eilat, on the Gulf of Aqaba, the sea was too rough for snorkeling. We settled for a dive down seventy meters in the Yellow Submarine. The underwater view was spectacular, not for the reef, but for the variety and gaudiness of the fishes.

We traveled once again into Egypt, down the Sinai Peninsula and across a desert which is rough even by Utah standards. We spent the night in St. Catherine's Monastery, nestled at the foot of Mt. Sinai. In this quiet monastery, Judy unexpectedly squealed at the largest cockroach I've ever seen. The next morning our attempt to climb Mt. Sinai to see the sunrise went awry. At 0300 in the dark, we lost the trail. We stumbled our way back to the monastery.

Back in Jerusalem, we were in the Old City when a suicide bomber blew himself up in front of a café in Ben Yehuda Mall in the business district. We had lunched in this café on earlier visits. On our way back to the marina, we stopped to watch the authorities clean blood from the streets and buildings. Judy thought an injured girl pictured in the newspaper was our waitress.

After Judy flew home, I was ready to transit the Suez Canal. I sailed the 130 miles from Ashkelon to Port Said at the canal's north end. At Port Said, I asked one of the yacht club employees, twenty-five-year-old Hamada, the location of stores and a bank.

Instead of giving me directions, he said, "I'll take you."

I met Hamada in the parking lot and was unnerved to see that his transportation was a bicycle. He helped me onto the handle bars and then pedaled off across the canal bridge and through the heavy Port Said traffic. We must have been a comical sight, this white-haired man clinging to the handle bars while the fearless Hamada, tall and powerful, pedaled away. I paid Hamada well, but my bottom was definitely *unwell*. That was my last time on a bicycle.

Hamada is a fervent Muslim. He cut short a late lunch with me one day and hurried off to the mosque when the muezzin called for three o'clock prayers. He is convinced that all good women cover themselves; any woman who does not wear at least a headscarf or who allows her bosom to protrude is bad. He does not date. When he gets ready to marry, he will go to his home village in upper Egypt. His parents will find him a wife, and the couple will move into his father's house.

The Suez Canal, one hundred miles in length, is twice as long and half as interesting as the Panama Canal. It is a ditch without locks running through the dry Egyptian countryside. Only the pilots on my two-day trip provided diversion. My first pilot knew little English. He steered the boat all day long through the first fifty miles. Before leaving Port Said we agreed, through an interpreter, that the baksheesh would be twenty pounds ($6) plus another five pounds to distribute to friends at signal stations along the way. After dark we arrived at Ismailia, halfway down the canal. I gave the pilot the twenty pound note.

He stared at it. "Twenty dollars!" he cried.

"No, I said twenty pounds. If you don't want the twenty pounds, give it back." I put out my hand.

He laughed, shook my hand, and got off the boat.

My pilot for the second day, ending at Port Suez, was, by his own claim, a bad Muslim. He drank, smoked, and engaged in some practices frowned on even in the West. He told a story from his experiences working in Saudi Arabia. In Saudi Arabia, it is customary to leave your shoes outside the door when you enter a house. If a man returns home and sees a strange pair of women's shoes outside his door, he knows his wife has a female guest and he cannot enter. He goes elsewhere until the visitor leaves. Which is why, if a wife entertains a gentleman, the gentleman will leave a pair of women's shoes outside the door.

My agent in Port Suez, the self-named Prince of the Red Sea, proved a notable exception to the Egyptian devotion to baksheesh. The Prince is generous in spirit and in practice. He is short and rotund, smiling from his wrinkled face. Egotistical, he was proud that he helped recover a Norwegian yacht stolen in the Seychelles. When I arrived, the young Norwegian couple was there on their sail back to Norway. In honor of the Norwegians—the woman was a gorgeous blonde—the Prince hosted a "barbecue" for a dozen sailors. We sat on rugs in his large office and ate kebab, fried chicken, pita bread, and a few raw tomatoes, all with our fingers. No napkins were supplied. It was literally finger-licking good. Cake and coffee followed.

On several occasions, the Prince shouted at me from his boat to join him for morning coffee. During the coffee break, he lectured me on things nautical and political. Once he drove me to his downtown office to show off his collection of caged birds. While I was there, workmen pulled prayer rugs off the office wall and knelt to pray.

The Prince leaves the work to his two sons, Captain Heebi, who handles yachts, and Aseb, who handles British and Canadian naval vessels and is the Malta Consul in Suez. With Aseb, I sometimes discussed politics. He worried about the worsening situation in the Middle East.

Port Suez is a ragged dusty town with unkempt and unusually wide streets. Piles of sand and cracked concrete litter what should be the sidewalks. The town was destroyed by the Israelis in the 1967 war. There is no interesting old section and nothing imaginative about the recently constructed low concrete buildings. Many of the well-paid canal pilots live here. The town is not all bad; several establishments sell liquor and good cheap food. Morning coffee is $0.71. By comparison, in Turkey it was $0.84; in Israel, $1.42.

One morning a strange, 35 knot southerly, a *khamsin*, blew in. The wind picked up the tarry crude spilled from Red Sea operations and strewed it over boat hulls. My dinghy, tied astern of *Idle Queen*, was a sticky mess. I spent two days scrubbing it with kerosene and detergent.

The weather south from Port Suez was unwonted and unwanted. The usual northerlies blew up strongly, as I headed down the Gulf of Suez. Rounding the south end of the Sinai Peninsula, I thrashed my way a hundred miles to the head of the Gulf of Aqaba. This stretch of water has few anchorages that are technically and politically accommodating. Politically, Saudi Arabia is on one side with Egypt on the other. I couldn't anchor at Dhahab, Egypt, because the resort owners insist on keeping their waterfront clear. For two nights, I hove-to in mid-gulf to sleep while the wind pushed me back about half a knot.

The Royal Jordan Yacht Club in Aqaba had better facilities than I expected. With its short coastline and low per-capita income, I suspected the country could contain few yachts. But the yacht club had modern concrete docks, adequate tie-ups, and a guard at the street entrance. On the other side of a two-meter high privacy fence was the king's personal marina. There were only two other foreign yachts at dock. I became friendly with the couple on the Canadian boat *Trekker*. This late-forties couple was leaving the woman's native Iraq. Aleija tried to get her son, a medical doctor, and his family to sail off with them, but the son refused to leave his patients. I wonder if the family ever reunited.

The yacht club is in a picturesque part of town. At night, the lights of Eilat glow brightly across the bay. Behind the fence surrounding the club is a swimming beach backed by palm trees. On Friday, crowds of male bathers swam and sunned; not a woman was in sight. *If in doubt about morality, remove temptation*, I thought.

I continued to soak up the winter sun in Aqaba. I often ate long lunches in a little open-faced cafe at the edge of town. The businessmen, dressed in western-style shirts and pants, came in to chat and smoke, as much as eat. The waiter set up *hookahs*, filled the bowls with the smoker's choice of tobacco, and lit it. As the smoker inhaled, smoke flowed through the water trap and into his lungs. This left a tarry mess in the *hookah* pot. The waiter's job was to clean it.

I reflected on the peoples I met in this part of the world. The Egyptians are less likeable than other Mid-East peoples, primarily because one hand, palm up, seems eternally at the ready. Any help provided, regardless of how small, seems to merit a tip. Jordanians are a happier people, more self-confident. A Palestinian living in Aqaba willingly gave me directions to the shopping district even after we had exposed our differing viewpoints on Saddam Hussein. And I couldn't forget the Jordanian shopkeeper who went out and found a Jordanian courtesy flag for me which his shop did not carry.

In mid-February, with the tides right, I threw off docking lines and headed south on the Red Sea. I enjoyed this part of my trip, for the wind blew unremittingly from the north. I felt for those boats headed in the opposite direction, particularly when the northerly wind hit thirty knots. I was happy to have nature's help, for man's help was sorely lacking. I hoped that several ports along the Saudi Arabian coast would be welcoming, but I was a non-Muslim; the authorities wouldn't issue me a visa. Sudan, of course, was out of bounds for Americans. I spent several nights anchored off the shipping channel and slept well despite my inhospitable surroundings. During this passage I docked at only one port, Massawa in Eritrea.

Eritrea, with 600 miles of coastline, lies in Africa near the south end of the Red Sea. Ruled by the Ottomans, Ethiopians, Italians and British, it won independence in 1995 and has a constitutional form of government. Christianity is the dominant religion. Many people speak English.

At Massawa, a dozen foreign yachts were spread out in the anchorage. Usually three ships at a time unloaded at the wharf, mostly food aid for the interior. From one ship, grain was bucketed from the hold and dumped into a massive bin where it emerged into sewn bags. Waiting workers muscled the bags aboard a huge convoy of United Nations relief trucks.

Massawa appears prosperous in spite of the poverty in the country as a whole. The low sprawling architecture shows Italian influence, even though most buildings from the Italian occupation, including the governor's palace, are in ruins. I sat in the open bar on the waterfront and drank beer with the off-shift stevedores. They spoke English well. We made small talk about their jobs, my journeys, and boats. The cutely-uniformed waitresses were kept busy. A crowd of older women moved along the street with huge whisks sweeping up dust scattered by the parade of passing trucks.

As I left Massawa, I lost radio contact with Ken and Clare on *Echo*, the Irish couple I had met in Antalya. We had exchanged news and gossip once a week, as I proceeded down the Red Sea. Near the southern end, our contact became sporadic and then died altogether. This led to the rumor that I was lost at sea. I do get lost, but generally on land.

I ran on south from Massawa to Bab el Mandab, the narrow strait at the bottom of the Red Sea. In this Strait of Tears, the wind is predominantly southerly and up to gale force. To my surprise and delight, the north wind carried right on through and swung to the west in the Gulf of Aden. The wind pushed me eastward, with little hint of difficulties to come.

I felt apprehensive about the people of Yemen. They sided with Iraq during the Gulf War and are strongly anti-Israeli. But they treated me with much kindness and consideration. I think some of the treatment I receive in Middle Eastern countries simply shows the veneration of the East for the elderly. In one way this is unfortunate for it inhibits acceptance or even consideration of new ideas or innovations.

Aden, Yemen, was once a British port and protectorate, but the Arab influence is overwhelming. The port and surrounding enclaves are crowded and dirty. The dreary aspect of the encircling bare cliffs and sharp hills accentuates the discouraged feeling engendered by blowing papers, dust and trash around the streets. No one seems to take pride in improving the city. The park has few blades of grass; plastic bags coat the fences. What was once a church on a hilltop is a police station. The harbor is famous for its film of oil, a result of sloppy bunkering.

Omar, my taxi driver, has a British mother, so he is not typically Yemeni. He is Moslem, married with two small daughters, but he drinks beer and makes fun of the heavily covered Islamic women with slits in the veils. "Ninja ladies," he calls them. We drank beer together in a secluded hidden restaurant garden where, he said, all the liquor is smuggled in from Djibouti.

"The President is a dictator," Omar said, a statement that, if made openly, could land him in jail. Peoples of North and South Yemen are still far apart in political viewpoints.

When I complimented a group on how great I thought the people of Yemen, they replied, "Not the people of Yemen, the people of Aden."

I am often asked why I am traveling alone. I reply disingenuously, "I'm looking for a rich widow." But never again. Arish, one of the loiterers on the Aden wharf who always had a helping hand, showed up one day with a burqua-clad Muslim lady and a young male companion. Arish explained that they were prepared to go to sea with me. I almost fell off the seawall. Red-faced, I jumped into the dinghy and splashed out to *Idle Queen*.

The next morning, before daybreak, I sailed away.

Chapter 18

Wild Pirates, Wild Animals, Mad Bombers

A ship in harbor is safe, but that's not why ships are built.
-Chinese Fortune Cookie

On 20 March 1998, five days out of Aden, I sat in the cabin and stared at my inventory of food and supplies. They had to last well into May, but in five days I had sailed only 108 miles. I had another 487 miles to go before I could round Socotra and turn south. The northeast monsoon blew head-on at twenty knots, the current ran one knot against me, and breaking waves slammed the bow continuously. IQ and I were getting badly beaten, as I tacked back and forth from Yemen to Somalia to make easting. At this rate, it would be mid-April before I rounded Socotra. I would still be 1020 miles from the Seychelles.

I had plenty of water and hard tack. Dried mashed potatoes looked sufficient. Canned meat would last until 16 May, canned vegetables until 24 May. In case of an emergency, the problem would be in basic supply of meat and vegetables. Also on hand were two dozen cans of Oranjeboom beer, one bottle each of Scotch, Israeli brandy, Cyprus wine, and Eritrean gin; I would have to make do. Taken altogether, a possibly tight situation.

I considered returning to Aden to await the arrival of the southwest monsoon. This could hold me up until June and increase the possibility that I would run into severe weather later on. I charged ahead.

A few days later, the northeast monsoon lightened. The current became weaker near the Yemeni coast. Finally, I cleared the most easterly point of Somalia, the Horn of Africa. The strong Somali current from the south rushed through the gap with Socotra, spread out west and north, and lost some of its power. I rounded Socotra on 4 April.

The area around the coast of Somalia and the Yemeni island of Socotra is infested with pirates.

Omar, my favorite taxi driver in Aden, explained, "The Socotrans are not really pirates. They have AK-47s, souvenirs of their military days, and they just want to make use of them."

I stayed fifty miles off the Somali coast and traveled without lights at night. After passing Socotra I felt relieved and lucky in not being sighted. Just before I reached Kenya, the radio reported that a small cargo ship had been attacked twelve miles off Somalia. The radio operator was wounded but managed to get out a distress call. A large container ship steamed to the rescue. I recalled that the Barbary pirates were eliminated and I believe these pirates will be, too.

Winds were mild and favorable for my passage south from Socotra until I reached a point one degree north of the equator. One afternoon at 1600, as I sat reading in the cabin, a blast from an unexpected fifty-knot squall throttled *Idle Queen*. I hauled down the genoa before the sail ripped. The strain on the masthead fitting probably contributed to the calamity that occurred later. From then until I reached Victoria Harbor in the Seychelles 350 miles ahead, I fought one squall after another. The best system to keep the boat moving was to sail with genoa, staysail, and double-reefed main. When a squall threatened, I dropped the genoa, and IQ took care of herself.

Approaching Victoria from the north, I sailed for fifty miles in an area bordered with small islands and dangerous rocks. This stretch demanded careful piloting, particularly in squalls, and I spent hours at the helm religiously studying the water for any obstacles. Tired, but feeling triumphant, I arrived off Victoria's harbor only two weeks after rounding Socotra. Here my progress stalled. For the next two hours, I circled an offshore buoy while officials searched unsuccessfully for an Immigration officer to clear me in. At last, they allowed me to enter the harbor and anchor.

"We examine boats offshore to insure no disease is brought into the Seychelles," an official said.

The Seychelles consist of two island groups in the western Indian Ocean. The central group of forty islands is mountainous; the remaining group of ten is coralline. An independent republic, the country of 77,000 is comprised of French, black, and Asian ancestry.

The country is run by dedicated environmentalists. The town is remarkably clean. Always within sight is a trash bin labeled "Courtesy of the Environmental Fund." A panel truck labeled "Environment" in huge letters circles the area. A similarly labeled sixty-foot launch lies at anchor. With no trash in the harbor, not a single gull flies over.

Mahe Island, on which Victoria is situated, is a mountainous jungle. Individual houses and small villages are scattered on the heights. Buses grind up the slopes to give brief spectacular views of surrounding reefs, islands and a sea colored with all the blue-green shades ever visualized. I visited Victoria's outstanding botanical garden. It is not as large as the one in Mauritius, but beautifully organized. Some amazing tropical plants are here: the Traveler's Tree of Madagascar (like a huge fan) and the famous Coco de Mer, which produces the largest palm nut in the world. It is native only to the Seychelles. The nut of the Coco de Mer is double and shaped like a woman's midsection, leading to some bawdy decorations in the souvenir shops.

The country is expensive for much of the food is imported. Just after a ship arrives, the supermarket supply and variety are fine, but shelves tend to get bare before they are re-supplied. Despite the prices, I stocked up on fresh vegetables and bread. The solicitous group at the yacht club sells a cup of coffee for only a dollar. This is definitely a nonprofit group.

I took tours to four of the six marine parks that surround Mahe. To protect the coral, private anchoring and exploration is not allowed. The marine parks are unbelievable, oversized aquariums filled with a parade of the Indian Ocean's most colorful fish.

In spite of a spell of bad weather, I pushed on toward Tanzania. The problems that arose during this passage were due to my failure to routinely inspect the standing rigging. The accident occurred on 16 May. I was headed east, close-hauled with double-reefed main, contending with squalls and a rough sea. At 0330, I decided to drop the genoa and raise the staysail for more comfortable going. The wire of the headstay, perhaps weakened from the equatorial squalls, snapped at the masthead fitting. As the genoa started down, the whole set—sails, headstay and halyards—broke loose from the masthead and plummeted into the sea.

I clung to the lifeline and leaned as far over as I dared. I wasn't wearing my safety harness, and the waves rolled violently. They alternately pushed the sail into my hands and dragged it back. Over and over I grasped and heaved at the tangled detritus of cloth, rope, and wire. Once I considered just letting the whole mess go, but I kept at it. My arms ached and my back throbbed. I struggled for over two hours. When I had at last dragged it all aboard and no longer needed light, dawn broke.

I left the staysail and double-reefed main to control the boat. I lacked a head sail, but because *Idle Queen* is cutter-rigged, I still had a sail forward of the mast. Anxious to fix the problem, I scratched Tanzania off the itinerary and headed directly to Kenya for repairs.

I anchored in Kilifi Creek just north of Mombasa in an unofficial yacht club. The anchorage is below the residence of a generous South African/Rhodesian couple of English extraction, Daphne and Tony Britchford. Tony, a retired pilot for Rhodesian Air, runs a construction business with Daphne. Rather, the energetic and efficient Daphne runs it. Tony, diabetic and overweight, indulges his passion as a ham net operator. He is known to yachtsmen throughout the Indian Ocean for his wit and helpfulness. Later, when I again crossed the Indian Ocean, Tony kept in touch. On 5 October, from somewhere in the middle of the ocean, I remarked that it was my son's birthday. At his own expense, Tony called a thrilled Harry Third in Virginia to wish him happy birthday.

Idle Queen was one of a dozen boats anchored in Kilifi Creek. The shower stall on the waterfront and the Britchford house on the hill were open to all. We bought beer and kept it in the Britchford refrigerator. This collection of yachties was a unique experience.

Tony warned us: as he cleared the jungle for their house, atop the fifty-foot hill, he found a spitting cobra. He left it alone. Even the thought of this snake did not deter us from joining the late afternoon beer-drinking sessions in the Britchford living room. We discussed nautical matters and undertook chart corrections. One of the discussions remains with me, for its outcome is a mystery.

A couple left South Africa bound for Kilifi Creek. The boat owner and captain was a 60-year-old ex-navy Australian whose wife was back home. He took along a sailing novice, a young newlywed whose husband was delayed in South Africa. As they traveled up the coast, the pair kept in radio contact with Tony and other ham operators. One evening, the couple missed their scheduled radio contact. After several days of silence, ham operators alerted the BBC who reported the story and asked for any information. At the Britchfords we discussed their fate. Were they hit by a freighter? Did they run aground on Madagascar? Or, as I theorized, did the inexperienced newlywed, using the stove, cause a propane gas explosion? To this day, their disappearance is unsolved.

Whenever Daphne drove to town, she took a group of us with her. On one occasion, this included a Canadian couple: Hugh, a mild-mannered, retired doctor, and his wife, Christine, an assertive, take-charge woman. Christine helped with my shopping. I wheeled the cart and followed her about the store.

"You need this," Christine declared over and over as, without consultation, she picked up item after item and dropped them into my cart.

Another couple anchored in Kilifi Creek were Ian, a British police chief who retired from duty in Hong Kong, and his wife, Isabella. Hong Kong reverted to Chinese control in 1997 and they were sailing home. They left the boat in Kilifi Creek and flew to England to attend a wedding. Before they left, Ian asked if anyone wanted anything brought back.

"Yes, I would like a bottle of single malt Scotch whiskey," I said flippantly, knowing how expensive it is.

To my amazement, Ian brought me a bottle.

Tony and Daphne employed two black helpers. They chased other blacks away and kept their windows barred. Once I went into town with Daphne and her trusted black assistant, Johnny. While we sat in the back of the pickup and waited for Daphne to finish shopping, I noticed a sign for ice cream on a push cart.

"Is that really ice cream?" I asked Johnny.

He assured me it was.

I walked over to the vendor, ordered two, and was given two covered items on sticks. "This is ice cream?" I asked again.

The vendor said it was.

I uncovered the sticks and found popsicles. Irritated, I asked Johnny, "Why do they insist on calling this ice cream? It's not ice cream."

Johnny said simply, "Probably because we don't know it's not ice cream."

Another time out with Daphne, I sat with others in the bed of the pickup. Up ahead we spied a green mamba snake in a tree raiding a bird's nest. Just as we drove under the tree, the mamba fell. I think we all gasped. We were lucky the snake didn't land in the truck. Although not as aggressive as the black mamba, it's one of the most dangerous snakes in the world.

Although Kenya straddles the equator, much of it has a moderate climate. Mt. Kenya, 17,000 feet high, has permanent snow and glaciers. Nairobi, at 500 feet, has a fine climate, but the city is dirty and crime-ridden. The seacoast is subject to monsoon breezes; temperature was never a concern during my stay from May to August.

The coast from Lamu in the north to Mombasa in the south contains a series of historical sites which delineate life along this slave-marketing area beyond the days of the Portuguese occupation in the fifteenth century. The remains at Gedi are of a Moslem city which flourished from the thirteenth to seventeenth centuries. It differs from many historical sites in that a minimum of work has been done to bring it to light; only walls, low towers, and house outlines have been cleared of encroaching jungle. In Mombasa, the Old Town and the Portuguese fort are embellished and annotated in the usual way. One of the mysteries to me is why Kilifi, one of the best natural ports on the coast for dhow-sized vessels, was used by neither Arabs nor Portuguese in the early days.

The Kenyans, as almost all Africans, suffer from a poor corrupt government. The roads, even the main truck route from the port of Mombasa to Nairobi, are potholed to the point of being dangerous. The sizable petrol tax gets siphoned off by the politicians. There are over fifty tribes. The voter's interest is in whatever deal the tribal leader has made to keep the two largest tribes, Kikuyues and Luos, out of power.

For travelers, the big attraction is the inland game parks. With Daphne's efficient help, I booked an affordable safari. I took the bus to Mombasa, the train to Nairobi, and a small plane from Nairobi to the Maasai Mara. For three days I observed animals in the beautiful, tree-spotted, grassy plains, the extension into Kenya of the Serengeti in Tanzania. My hotel consisted of a canvas tent with a wood floor, a comfortable bed, and an enclosed porcelain toilet. Every morning coffee or hot chocolate was brought to my hut. By 0900 we dozen tourists were loaded into Land Rovers for the first of our two game drives of the day.

I saw the scariest animal in the world, a spotted hyena with its insane laugh. The high point was watching a cheetah stalk a Thompson's gazelle. The gazelle ran in among our Land Rovers and escaped. We watched a lioness eat a zebra. The pride included several lionesses, two large lions, and numerous cubs. We drove up beside a herd of Cape buffalo just after one gave birth to a calf. The green grass was soaked with a splotch of crimson. The mother trailed bloody tendrils as she pushed the calf away and glared at us. Huge dead snakes littered the roadways, making the scene macabre.

On the last day, I took a guided bird tour. I was the only one who did. I saw fifteen new birds. My outstanding sighting was of the huge and baroque marabou stork. I was impressed by my tour guide, John, a Maasai chief. He repeated the claim that the Maasai were the rightful owners of all the cattle in the world.

At the end of the safari, I flew back to Nairobi. I arrived in town at 1230 and hurried to the restaurant where I had arranged to meet friends for lunch: Laura, an American and the cousin of an old friend, her Kenyan husband, Reuben, and their baby. The couple are agriculturists working to improve the lives of those in northern Kenya's barren areas. When we met at the restaurant, I was surprised that they had brought four other adults. I discovered that in Kenya, when you invite someone to lunch, you also invite any relatives who wish to come. *Well, it's their party*, I thought. I let them pick up the check.

At lunch there was an air of excitement. At 1030 that morning a terrorist bomb had exploded at the American Embassy. I didn't realize that my taxi route to the train station after lunch went past the embassy. As the building came into view I stared nervously up at its empty windows. A huge crowd filled the streets. Their low murmurs sounded like a horde of bluebottle flies. Broken glass crunched under their feet. The taxi inched forward until the mob blocked our path. We had to abandon the taxi. The driver got out first. I hesitated. The driver grabbed my bag with one hand and pulled me out of the cab with the other. He shoved his way through the packed masses, dragging me along behind him. The crowd fell back against our onslaught. After fifteen stressful minutes we reached the train station. I didn't relax until I was safely aboard.

Through the window I watched my driver. For once, my tip made a taxi driver smile.

Back in Kilifi, I prepared to leave Kenya. Because I had spent so much time in this malaria-ridden country, Daphne insisted that I be tested. She drove me to the local clinic where the tests proved negative.

I made a final trip to the market for fuel and food. At a fruit stand, I told the vendor I needed four mangoes, one for each of the next four days. Taking his time, he thumped the fruit and selected four.

As he handed them to me, he said, "This one is for today, this one is for tomorrow, this one is for the day after...."

Daphne, Tony, and I had a final dinner together. Early the following morning, I sailed north. Before I turned east and again tackled the Indian Ocean, there was one out-of-the-ordinary stop I wanted to make.

Chapter 19

Of Sails and Sailors

*A tourist remains an outsider throughout his visit;
but a sailor is part of the local scene from the moment he arrives.*
-Anne Davison

One hundred miles north of Kilifi on a small island near the border of Kenya and Somalia is the ancient Arab town of Lamu. I anchored in the river and explored the locale over two days. The town gives an extraordinary look into the past for life has changed little over the centuries. The old stone houses, built in the seventeenth century when the Sultans of Oman ruled, are still inhabited. The open sewers in stone gutters still run freely through the town with surprisingly little odor. The island is without automobiles; except for one truck, donkeys provide transportation. The people are strictly Islamic, impoverished, and suffer from lack of wished-for tourism. Tourists can lie on the beach or take dhow trips into the mangrove swamps of the surrounding islands. I did neither. I preferred to wander by foot through the streets, looking and marveling at this piquant way of life. I ate several meals in the few quiet little diners created in hopes that tourists would drop in, but few foreigners walked the streets.

From Lamu, the wide breadth of the Indian Ocean faced me once more. I rode the Somali current north across the equator. Two days out, the main halyard broke loose from the sail at the masthead, plummeting the mainsail to the deck. Being well offshore, this occurred at an awkward time. The halyard is solid Dacron braid and hard to splice. I secured it to the sail shackle with a seizing only which, until this moment, lasted for years. I could have converted the topping lift to a substitute halyard, but I decided to climb the mast to recover the rope. Before leaving on this voyage, I installed triangular-shaped aluminum steps on either side of the mast. I crept up the steps, my arms clasped around the mast. I swayed wildly in the fifteen-knot wind and ten-foot ocean swell. I felt like the man on the flying trapeze. I reached the masthead, grabbed the halyard, and clambered down. On deck again, I reattached it with a massive, ugly, but secure knot, and hoisted the sail.

I wanted to stop in the Maldive Islands, but the water depth at the anchorages was at least a hundred feet, too deep for my anchor and chain. I continued on to Galle Harbor on the southwest corner of Sri Lanka. Sri Lanka is an island republic lying southeast of India. The population of 19 million consists of Sinhalese and Tamil. A bitter and bloody struggle of Tamils seeking separation from the Singhalese main government has gone on for many years.

I tied up to a mooring buoy and paid $175 to check in. Several naval vessels were in the harbor. Depth charges were set off approximately every hour all night long to deter would-be terrorists. The clang of the metal mooring buoys when the charges went off was enough to rouse any sailor.

Shopping in Galle was as annoying as trying to sleep. Whenever I went to shore, one of the many touts attached himself to me like a stray hound. This soured me on the Sri Lankans almost as much as the baksheesh-mad Egyptians soured me on Egypt.

A hired driver took me on a tour of the southern part of the island. It is a green hilly jungle with some entrancing sights of water buffalo kneading up rice paddies. Many tea plantations and rubber trees are spread on the hillsides.

My driver was a devoted Buddhist. Although I told him I had no interest, he drove me to see his conception of a great sight: the five-story high, pink and yellow meretricious statue of Buddha. The effect was leavened by the banks of brilliant purple lotus flowers spread before the idol.

After I left Sri Lanka, I was out of sight of land, reading below at the dinette table, when someone knocked on the boat. Shocked, imagining pirates, I dashed on deck. I found two men and a young boy in a heavy wooden fishing boat that thumped against the hull.

One man made smoking motions. "Cigarettes," he said.

I hurried below and returned with Turkish cigarettes. I bought the cigarettes to use as baksheesh on my trip down the Suez Canal, and I had two packs left. I handed a pack to each man. They pointed to the boy. I shook my head. Without another word, they started the boat's outboard motor and took off. I watched until they were out of sight.

A month after leaving Kilifi Creek, I tied up in Rebak Marina at the western end of the Malaysian island of Langkawi. Malaysia exists in two parts. The Malay Peninsula in the west is bordered on the north by Thailand and on the south by Singapore. The eastern part sits 400 miles across the South China Sea on the island of Borneo. Malaysia gained independence from Britain in 1957 and English is widespread.

Approaching Rebak Marina, I had trouble locating the entrance on the featureless south side of the island. I radioed in for help. In an Australian accent, Vic, on *Neliandrah*, answered the call and gave me directions. As I arrived, he met me on the wharf to help me into my slip.

Rebak Marina is well-protected and looked to be a good base. (Despite being well-protected, Rebak Marina was destroyed in the 2004 tsunami. It is being rebuilt.) I spent most of the next year here, with frequent stays in Phuket, Thailand.

Rebak Marina was the brainchild of Dr. Mahathir, the prime minister (dictator) of Malaysia. The landing strip for his helicopter was located on the bank above *Idle Queen*. I never saw him alight from the helicopter, only the limousine that whisked him the hundred yards to the marina restaurant. He was in conference as he ate in the dining room. I ate lunch at the same time to see him. He was dark: hair, eyes, suit, and demeanor.

The seascape scenery, on the sail between Langkawi and Phuket is different from anything I've seen. Mostly sheer-walled rocks, covered with green trees wherever vegetation can find a foothold, littered the area. These rocks are so distinctive in size and shape that after one passage it's possible to navigate a return trip just by remembering the shape sequence. Ko Phetra, for example, is 1200 feet high, two miles long, and only one-quarter mile wide. I anchored one night between two small islands, one a sheer 900 feet high, the other a sheer 400 feet. The light wind generally blew only at night and in the morning. This was my excuse to stop at noon. I sailed the 120 miles over seven days, anchoring each night in the shelter of one of the rocky islands.

The marina facilities at Boat Lagoon in western Thailand are outstanding. The staff is highly professional although few speak English. Thailand is a constitutional democracy, the only Southeast Asian country to avoid colonialism. But the self-important and pervasive bureaucracy shows the effects of the country's once having been under military dictatorship.

From the marina, the town of Phuket is only a bus ride away. Motorbikes, including one-passenger motorbike taxis, are popular. The town is not touristy. The outlying beaches carry the crowds and the honky-tonks. Unfortunately, the beaches suffered heavy damage from the 2004 tsunami. The area immediately around Phuket is thirty percent Muslim. In this tropical thermotank, I felt for the sweepers and gardeners who worked all day under their coolie hats, head scarves, long sleeves, and pants.

The country is famous for its variety of legitimate massages: "foot," "oil," or "Thai." The massage crew at Boat Lagoon was always busy. Some of the masseuses may be on the saucy side. One young lady, discovering I had no wife aboard, offered to come to the boat to provide her expertise there.

I had *Idle Queen* hauled out, and I went to work, painting her bottom and topsides. I contemplated replacing the rigging, but contemplating is as far as I got. I replaced it later in Rebak, with the help of the marina staff. After twenty years, I suppose it was due.

Spending a year in an area gave me the opportunity to observe my neighbors.

At times, the sailing community resembled Peyton Place. One couple, married with children, was having a rough time. The wife started sightseeing with a Scandinavian singlehander. I was on the couple's boat when the wife went off with her new friend.

The husband called gaily after her, "If you can't be good, be careful!"

One Australian woman exchanged her home on a small boat for a more glamorous catamaran, displacing a prettier, but slow-witted, blonde, in the process.

A seventy-year-old American kicked out his fifty-year-old British companion, converted to Islam, and married a beautiful young Malaysian. Several sailors attended the wedding. A year later, when I left, the couple appeared well-suited and happy.

One day a middle-aged Australian hippie and his seven-year-old grandson sailed in with a young South African woman aboard. When she became pregnant, the hippie kicked her off the boat. The sailing community was appalled. We collected enough money to send the woman home to her mother. Bob and Rose Selfridge visited the woman later in South Africa and reported that mother and baby were doing well.

Many sailing couples supported themselves with odd jobs. Berthed next to me on Aku Ankaa, Glenn and Erja specialized in bottom-scrubbing and sail repair. I hired them several times.

A Norwegian couple lived on a small boat with two babies, the youngest born at the Langkawi hospital. They sold their adventures to a Norwegian magazine to support themselves.

Karen was an English teacher in Brunei. She told me she quit her job because her students, the Sultan's children, were so inbred they were "too stupid to learn."

A retired orthopedic surgeon from California, Dr. Tom Enloe (*Tombatu*), performed impromptu surgery once. He and his wife, Bobbie, were in Fiji when a native fell and broke his hip. Learning that the man was awaiting an airlift and a long, pain-filled ride to a hospital in New Zealand, Tom volunteered to operate right there. After the successful operation, Dr. Tom's reputation spread throughout the island.

Other sailors pointed out the mortality of life. Bonney, an American, wandered the marina in Phuket confused and lost after her husband was killed falling off their mast. One of my sailing friends suffered a stroke. Taken to a small inadequate hospital, he waited hours before receiving attention.

One of the most popular figures in the Rebak community was Ines, a slight, vivacious German. She delighted in throwing parties in which the main dish was Ines-style Bloody Marys. Her husband died of a heart attack before I arrived. Ines died of cancer a few years after I left.

I met the English couple, Neville and Betty Root (*Wrangler*), when they followed me into the Boat Lagoon marina and docked on the same pontoon. Neville, retired from the directorship of several companies, was the wittiest man I've known. Before we met, Neville underwent a cancer operation in Malaysia.

When I was in port, I had gin and tonics in *Wrangler's* cockpit almost every night. Sailors on the same pontoon often joined us; the Roots were a popular couple. As time passed, Neville struggled with the pain of recurring cancer. Although our get-togethers lost some of their sparkle, Betty said the stream of visitors was a welcome distraction. Ultimately, Neville returned to England to die.

These sailors—the workers, the partiers, the ill—were a reminder of the transience of life despite an otherwise carefree year.

In July 1999 Carl and Dixie's daughter, Martha, arrived to celebrate her graduation from Penn State University. For four weeks, we toured Southeast Asia: Malaysia, Thailand, Burma, Laos, and Nepal. Martha's lucid account of what we saw and did follows in the next chapter.

Chapter 20

Exploring Southeast Asia with Capt'n
By Martha Heckel

Two of the greatest gifts we can give our children are roots and wings.
-Hodding Carter

My grandfather, a family legend, and I met up in Langkawi, Malaysia, to travel for a month through Southeast Asia: twenty-seven cities in twenty-nine days. He was a ripe slightly bent man of eighty-three. I was a strapping twenty-three, attempting to gain confidence in myself before tackling a career of some sort.

On the way to the ferry slip in Langkawi, we passed car dealerships from all over the world, shanty homes made of bamboo and tightly woven rods, rice paddies and water buffalo, rubber plantations with buckets attached to tree trunks to catch the latex, and more restaurants than I could count. Not so very different from home, less and more at the same time. Less stuff, more poverty.

We caught the 4:00 P.M. ferry across to Satun, Thailand. Satun is a small town, seemingly up-and-coming as a border town. I'm not used to being the minority color and being stared at, but I appreciated the experience. We hopped on the bus to Hat Yai. Once there, a man who spoke some English helped us jump immediately onto the bus to Bangkok.

That was truly a blessed moment because fifteen minutes later we would have had a long wait added to an already exhausting day. How does an 83-year-old manage all of this when a 23-year-old, who's been walking all over a sprawled campus for five years, is tiring already? He's made of the same stuff as a Pony Express Rider.

In Bangkok, we stayed at the Wendy House for about $15 a night. Two beds with pink blankets, a table, bureau and shower. I am slowly learning just how much America has.

After showers, we headed out to Siam Square to grab lunch and hunt down a travel agency. We found lunch at the Coffee House, where I enjoyed my first Thai curry and rice. Fantastic. There is something special to the spices in the Orient. They taste ancient in their freshness.

Capt'n ate slowly, drank some more coffee, and smiled across the table at me. "So, what did you learn at the Big University?"

"Probably about as much as I know now," I responded.

"I went to Berkeley during the depression. I got my doctorate during the Big War, so I didn't have to go to war."

"Why chemistry?"

"Well, it did come in handy. We would take a bottle of Beefeater, for example, and use our skills to replicate it exactly in the lab. It took some trial and error." The man twinkled.

I flashed back to a family story: Capt'n teaching a young Baptist neighbor to respond, when offered milk, by hitting one fist into his open palm while loudly proclaiming: "Whiskey is better!" Legendary.

After lunch, we walked through Bangkok. The smells are strong with pollutants. The streets are crowded. It's a big city. I've seen big cities before and I never want to stay long. Neither does Capt'n, but there are things to see here.

We headed off by *tuk-tuk* (three-wheeled motorized carts) to the Grand Palace. I saw some wonderful Chinese sculptures of dragon-dog hybrids with balls that rolled in their mouths and mosaics of gems and shiny pieces of earth made into dragons, telling the stories of the old country. I took bunches of photos, trying to capture some of the essence of the experience, of the deep tropical greens overgrowing with flowers, the golds and the turquoises, the smiling demons, the adorned heroes.

In the Wat Phra Kaew, I saw the Emerald Buddha, cut of solid jade. He has three outfits, one for each season: summer, rain, and winter. Tourists here were unlikely to be American. Most were Asian, British, Kiwis, or Australian. Clothing has become so homogenous these days, it seems everyone is from the same place.

After an early night's sleep, we headed out to breakfast. Amazingly, few shops were blazing neon "open" signs at 7:30 A.M. on a Sunday. We spotted McDonalds, home of the Samurai Pork Burger. Yes, it's a cliché for an American to eat at McDonalds overseas, but it's fun to see what the place offers.

Through the streets of Siam Square we passed the Hard Rock Bangkok. By phone we checked flights to Nepal. Monday 10:00 A.M. is available, but it is too soon. We need visas. Roundtrip fare could be $365.

We figured out with our guidebook how to get to the Chao Phraya Express River Taxi. For 28 baht total, Capt'n and I jetted up to the northern border of Bangkok, then back down to the high-rent district in the south. This took about two hours, and we saw a lot of the city. From the white riverboat, we passed more than a dozen wats (temples), all adorned with gold, including Wat Khien, the largest I've glimpsed since the Grand Palace.

The Chao Phraya is not a clean river, so I was most taken with the homes on stilts that lined a good stretch of it, and the children swimming in the water. This is a third-world country, and we drink water from the bottle always. Here people fished and washed their clothes and dove into the water. Meanwhile, tugboats carted barges of sand from place to place. Taxis went up and down the river with young monks in orange and inner peace.

The next day we got our tickets to Kathmandu, Nepal. We ate at the Wendy House restaurant after splitting three large Singha beer in the room. We ordered sandwiches. I chose my cup of hot tea, Capt'n his coffee. We started discussing probabilities.

"If I drop this saucer, what will happen to it?" asked Capt'n with his over-the-glasses eye twinkle.

"It would break into bits." Dear God, what is he up to?

"Are you sure about that? You know, there's a probability that it will shatter *before* it hits the linoleum." His slightly hunched frame seems to heighten when his mind works so rapidly to maneuver his adversary into position like a fine chess piece, perhaps the last rook on the board.

"Well, go ahead and drop it," I taunted, as he held the saucer above the hard, unrelenting floor. "But, I *believe* it won't shatter until it hits the ground."

Our waitress walked by, wondering what the crazy Americans were doing with her china.

"But you have to admit that the *probability* exists that it will break into a million particles before it comes close to hitting the ground, don't you?"

"No. That's not what I believe will happen at all."

"I'm not talking about belief here, I'm talking about scientific fact." Capt'n leaned back in his chair, adjusted his glasses, and continued to make his point, his hands folded before him. "There is a probability that this saucer will never hit the ground, but will completely vaporize in midair. It's not about what *would* actually happen, but what *could* happen. It's about the scientific theory, testing what you think *could* happen over what has actually happened in the past. Hypothesis, testing, theory. I hypothesize that this saucer will break into particles and not be broken by the floor itself."

I looked at him. Growing up, both my father and grandfather—lovingly pushy, stubborn men—wanted me to go into the sciences. I started college in Environmental Resource Management. But my strength and passion for languages overran their influence, and I studied a mixture of science and language arts. Sometimes, I thought they pushed me into the sciences because that's where the money was, in research and development. But now I think it was just so we'd have more to talk about. What is Capt'n trying to get at here? Is he testing my knowledge of how the scientific process works and the imaginative levels needed to pursue a career based in science? Is he questioning my vigor to explore the previously unimaginable? I honestly don't know, and he makes me nervous when he pursues categories I know little about, so I manipulate the playing board, switching the black squares to white when he's not looking.

"So, even though I don't *believe* that something is possible, you're trying to make me see and admit that there is a *possibility*," I responded, "though slight and insignificant statistically, that this saucer will shatter before it can hit the hard surface that would definitely create enough energy to break the atoms that hold the porcelain together. Correct?" I love trying to sound smart around him.

"Basically."

Uh, oh, short answers make me nervous. Am I missing his angle here, or am I really in control against his superior brain?

"So, you're asking me to *believe* in something I totally don't rationalize."

"Yes, accept the possibility that it could happen."

"Okay, then," I nibbled. "I accept that there is the slightest, the absolute *slightest* of potentialities that that saucer, once it's released from your hand, will not in fact be destroyed by the floor. It will instead break into atoms and disperse, almost like internal combustion, but with china."

"Good." He smiled.

"But in that case, Grandfather..." YES!! "*you* must admit the potential of something else. Mom told me about an argument you two had...something about how inconceivable it is that there is a God up there with his laptop pushing buttons, making the decisions of who wins what soccer game and who runs into whom when. Well, if I admit that there is the *potential* that the saucer can combust, you must admit that there is the slightest of probabilities, even against what you *believe*, that there is one God. There is one Being who makes all of the decisions and guides us in our actions. Go ahead; admit it. It's not probable, but it could happen."

I smiled and imagined my mother's face lighting up when I tell her later of my triumph in Capt'n's most prized philosophical realm— his agnosticism.

"Okay, I admit it." That is all.

We finished our warm drinks in relative silence, cooling down from the heat of conversation, and went to bed. I wondered what he thought of the exchange. I thought it was the greatest intellectual moment of my life.

Our Royal Nepal Airlines flight was just three hours. We looked out the window for a glimpse of the Himalayas, but the cloud cover was thick. We saw more of the mountains in the plane's video than I thought we were likely to see on this trip.

Landing at Tribhuvan International Airport was uneventful. We got our visas upon arrival for $30 each American and found our bags at baggage claim. Leaving the airport was another adventure. Several police were outside, and a horde of people awaited the arriving passengers. Everyone wanted to take us to their hotel, cards extended in dirty hands shoved in our faces. Suddenly, we were surrounded by hounding Nepali men and begging children. Capt'n started laughing. I stepped back and took in the scene. This little man, completely surrounded and laughing. I felt unnerved, as folks grabbed at my bags and pawed at me. The guards stepped in and pushed the people away.

In the end, we were suckered into going to the Dolpo Guest House instead of the one we'd picked out of the *Lonely Planet*. In the Thamel district, the older part of the city, the word "third-world" comes to life. The roads are narrow and shoddy, made of clay, as are the buildings. The streets are dirty and crowded, littered with debris and garbage from the households and the shops. Cows walk freely in the streets, eating the refuse. The people here do not smile openly although they will share one with you when prompted.

We took the cheaper, $8 a night, room. Capt'n complained about every aspect of the place, and we agreed not to let anyone take us for a ride (literally) again. The view from the roof was something else, though. We saw a large part of the city, and the ravens that towered above it. They were everywhere, these big black birds. The mountains, seen from the balcony, are beautiful; nature really knows how to paint a picture: deep greens with speckled, hill-top temples and housing in the distance.

Cows in the country are sacred; killing one meant jail for life. Dogs ran and barked freely and told a lot about the state of a town. If they are mangy and sore, then the people likely are. If they are well-kept and content, then there is a community. The dogs here looked hungry.

Pokhara was a shuttle jumper flight across Nepal, which is a bigger country than I imagined. The Himalayas towered beside our airplane, thousands of meters away, but majestic and solid. White capped, gray as a past president's hair, with deep tones of black and charcoal in the creases and crevices. The closest to God that one can get with his feet still upon the earth. I understood why people try to climb this peak. Awesome wasn't the word for it. I think Capt'n was pleased to have taken this trip inland to see Mount Everest.

In Pokhara, we took a cab (86 rupees) to the New Tourist Guest House and took the second room we looked at, priced at 500 rupees per night. Extremely well-kept establishment, twin beds, stoppers for the sink and showers, a classy joint with screens and a fan. The restaurant downstairs served real mint tea.

We've been talking a lot about what I'm going to do with myself after this journey ends. I've been out of school for a couple of months and have made no move to find a job. I'm not in the least motivated to create a resume, with two meager published articles, and to try to become something in the world. What if I'm not meant to work a real job? What if I'm miserable at it?

The next afternoon, we caught a flight back to Kathmandu and took a cab to a different town, Patan. Our room at the Café de Pan was wonderful and simple. We headed out to the Durbar Square by the marketplace. As stand-out tourists, we were offered tour guides, handbags, necklaces, and rarities. I had been so on my guard, watching for potential pickpockets and keeping my wits about me, that I lost a touch of humanity and was reminded of it.

A Nepali man made a move toward me with something in a plastic bag. I instinctively said, "No, thank you. *Namaste.*"

He called me on it, though. "No, Madame, this is not for you, and I wasn't speaking to you." Very polite, but with an obvious tone of disgust at my assumption. Everyone else with something in their hands wanted something from me, it seemed, but the experience drove home this point: Tourism can take people away from communicating with each other.

Early the next morning, we flew back to Bangkok and booked two spots on the 7:40 P.M. train to Chiang Mai, Thailand. The train rocked a bit, as I wrote in my journal.

"What kind of house do you want?" Capt'n asked.

"I don't know, a house with a little bit of land for privacy, I guess."

"You wouldn't want an apartment?"

"No, I think I'd like to own my own place."

"I wouldn't. An apartment would be fine. Less responsibility, someone else to fix things, not taking up too much space."

"That's easy for you to say, Capt'n. Look at your backyard. It stretches beyond the horizon."

Our own Orient Express carried us north, as I settled on the rack bed above our seats and looked down at Captain Harry Heckel, knowing how lucky I was to be in this place with him. Making sure the pictures my mind's eye took of the landscape will stick—the open fields of rice paddies next to temples, trees whizzing behind the rear of the train—and reflecting on the days ahead and behind.

We traveled by mini-bus to Mae Salong in the northern mountains. Climbing up through the mountains, Capt'n gave me a history lesson.

"These areas were settled by Chinese warriors who fled China when the Communists took over," he said.

I wondered what a town might be like that was settled by warrior refugees, and was surprised to find it quiet and charming: no swords hung on walls, no heads placed upon poles.

Capt'n continued his lesson about the KMT armies who fought the Communists. "Many of them have settled in these hillsides. The Thai government is still trying to integrate them into peaceful society and have even officially renamed this town 'Hillside of Peace.'"

I hadn't heard that name used here. I surmised that the two officials who stopped us were looking for illegal Burmese. We got closer and closer to the northern border of Thailand and Myanmar, formerly known as Burma, a country I had not heard of before this trip.

We arrived in Mai Sai before noon. Our 150 baht a night hotel is right across the river that runs as a border between Thailand and

Myanmar, country number four in our month's excursion. The hotel is actually made up of separate single-room huts scattered along the hillside.

Below the bridge in Myanmar, Capt'n and I saw things that I only saw in movies. This country is raw. It is a militant country, run by the militia, unsettled and uneasy. Peace is a foreign word here, I imagined, and the people don't smile much.

The bazaar under the bridge was plentiful with goods. Umbrellas, beach towels, pirated CDs, battery-powered fans, gold, antiques, knives, guns and animal parts from critters endangered or soon to be. The majority of the wares were spread beneath tarps, and people bartered loudly, unknown words falling from boisterous hungry mouths. I bought a wood carving of an ornate dog.

The roads are poor, mud-soaked and ill-kept. I had never felt so unwelcome. As we walked down the street, a Burmese man fell into step behind us. He started yelling, screaming God-knows-what at us. I imagined it was similar to "Get the Hell out of my country!" Whatever he said got the biggest smiles I'd seen from the natives.

"Well, Capt'n, at least we know what Burmese sounds like."

"And the alphabet looks similar to that of Sir Lanka."

We grinned at each other. Four hours was long enough to spend in this country.

We took a bus from Mai Sai to Chiang Khong, Thailand. The picturesque view of the Golden Triangle swirled by with the day's scenery. Here the Maekong River stretches out its huge tri-tentacles of water to create the border between Myanmar, Thailand and Laos. I wondered how much blood had been spilled in this river because of the opium trade.

Our slow boat down the Maekong River the next day had us up at 6:30 A.M. From the river, I was taken with how much of the landscape had nothing but nature in it. Acres upon miles of untouched wild lands stretching over hills and into valleys. My life would be different in one of the shacks we saw, surrounded by my small farm with endless terrain beyond to explore.

We finally stopped at Pak Beng about 5:00 P.M. We got the last room with two beds at the hotel we picked out from *Lonely Planet*. Capt'n and I dined on stir-fried rice, vegetables, egg, chicken, and Beer Lao.

The next day, only one slow boat moved down the river. The mountains, with their lush foliage and thatch-roofed houses, passed by. Children called to us. We passed some fantastic waterfalls covering cave entrances, enticing us towards Luang Prabang, Laos. As we got off the slow boat, Capt'n and I headed out to find dinner, walking to get the kinks out. After dinner, I laid down for a nap. I must leave Capt'n in five days. I felt our time winding down.

We went by *tuk-tuk* to the bus station and too soon were in our seats without breakfast, waiting for the bus to fill before leaving. By 9:10 A.M., the melons had all been loaded onto the roof, the rice had been strapped to the bumper, and the thirty-five person capacity of the interior exceeded forty bodies. Along the way we picked up another six people! Heat, nowhere to move, inability to stretch out our limbs or shift sideways. Fiery pain shot up my legs.

We traveled through the mountainous terrain, 238 km in eight hours. Up and down we climbed and descended, up and over the ragged blacks, whites, and greens of the mountainsides. Toddlers bathed naked by the side of the road where the water fell in its trek down the mountain. Men carried long curved knives to gather corn or rifles for hunting or protection. Old ladies passed by with loads of ginger root in potato-type sacks on their heads.

By Vang Vieng, our tender bottoms told us to go no farther. We hopped off the bus and got rooms at the Dok Khoun I Guest House. We slept that night on our sides, with our legs stretched out.

In the morning, Capt'n and I walked through Vang Vieng, pleased at our stop. The town is banked on a river, holds a small, wonderful, open-air market, and is surrounded by gorgeous cut-face mountains.

People in town noticed Capt'n and I, and we realized again what an odd couple we looked, sixty years between us and an obviously intimate relationship. Old women and children giggled, as we passed. Younger men looked at me like I was a hooker, and Capt'n like he was quite the lover.

"You know, Laos should pay us an entertainment fee just for the gossip we create," he said.

"Do you think that 'trophy wife' translates well in Laotian? I could get a really tight T-shirt."

In Vientiane, we settled into the Asia Pavilion, one of the most expensive and plush places we've stayed ($18 a night), with air-conditioning, cable television with CNN and MTV, and a mini bar.

I left Capt'n to relax and read and took off for a four-mile hike through town and beyond. I passed an ancient phallic monument called the Black Stupa. Stupas are holy structures said to house a part of the Buddha. I climbed the Laotional version of the Arch de Triumph, the Patuxai, which is adorned with the mythical figures of ancient Asian lore. The Patuxai is also known as the "Vertical Runway" because the concrete used to make this tourist trap was given to Laos by the United States to lay down a new airport runway. It was certainly a vertical salute to the U.S.

We approached our last day together. I have to leave him tomorrow.

We took a tuk-tuk to the Friendship Bridge between Vientiane and Nong Khai. We stood close together in line for Immigration and sat quietly, as we crossed the bridge, built by the Aussies and Thais. The shuttle was crammed with Asians. We entered and exited Laos through the only two border crossings between the country and Thailand.

Back in Thailand and settled in our hotel, we headed out to see the Sala Kaew Ku, which is a fascinating large park of concrete statues. Enormous and grotesque, one mythological figure towered above the entire park, surrounded by a throne of serpents a hundred feet in the air. One path took us to the story of Buddha, leaving his wife and child to quest for understanding and eventually reaching that higher plane through sacrifice and inner struggle. The park had been initiated by an Indian who wanted to depict Hindu and Buddhist folklore.

Our last day together had an anticlimactic finale. We left Nong Khai at 8:10 A.M. and arrived at the airport terminal at 7:53 P.M. We barely talked. Capt'n tried to teach me how to play bridge, but it was hard to learn. I couldn't think of anything but getting on a plane and going home. Back to the U.S., back to the real life of personal financial responsibility.

As we pulled into Don Muang station, Capt'n admitted, "I had a good time."

"Me, too, Capt'n. Thanks for letting me come along. I can't believe how easy it was to travel with you."

"Right-o, kid." He gave me one last look over his glasses.

It was emotional, jumping off that train and leaving him there to ride alone back to Hat Yai and on to Malaysia. I sat all night in the airport until my 6:00 A.M. flight, trying to memorize every moment. I desperately missed Capt'n Heckel and didn't want to go home. I thought of my resume and lined up the steps to find my first job out of college. Maybe it won't be so hard. If I survived a month alone with Capt'n....

I focused on the positive: I spent quality time with an icon, my hero and inspiration. This little old man made my heart dance whenever I thought about the connection we shared after bridging that generation gap to friendship. If I can gain half the insight, wit, charisma, compassion, and mystery that this guy has, I will have lived quite a thrilling life.

I can only dream of traveling with my granddaughter in sixty years.

Chapter 21

From Calming Waters to Killing Fields

One's destination is never a place, but a new way of seeing things.
-Henry Miller

I was saddened when Martha and I parted. I left her in Bangkok, she to fly home, I to take the Bangkok-Singapore train to Malaysia. Back on *Idle Queen*, I relaxed after our travels. I read Paul Johnson's *Intellectuals* and Wendy Kaminer's *Sleeping with Extraterrestrials*. I spent most mornings swimming in the resort pool. My exercising was often interrupted, as I preferred to watch the style and form of Dot Vidgen (*Neliandrah*). Dot was a champion swimmer in Australia. Her husband, Vic, was the sailor who guided me in when I arrived.

Other entertainment came from a boat in the marina that had a two-year-old gibbon aboard. She'll be a nasty mess in a couple of years, but her antics in the rigging provided much amusement. I often visited that side of the marina to watch her.

By chance my son, Carl, and colleague, Fran Reisman, with business interests in vegetable oils, arrived for a week of meetings in Kuala Lumpur, Malaysia's capital. I took a bus inland and 300 miles south of Langkawi Island, to join them. The bus passed through miles of palm tree plantations. These are short palms, shorter than most coconut palms, their small nuts the source of palm and palm kernel oils. The trees grow luxuriantly with large spreading fronds.

The first glimpse of the Kuala Lumpur skyline is revealing. Malaysia may have the reputation of a developing Southeast Asian country, but Kuala Lumpur is a cosmopolitan city, festooned with high-rises. A wealth of skyscrapers sets off the Twin Towers, at that time the world's tallest buildings. The heavy traffic is taking its toll on the environment. One day Carl, Fran, and I climbed to the top of the city's television tower for the view, but thick haze kept us from seeing the surrounding countryside.

While Carl and Fran struggled through business meetings, I explored the city's attractions. The light rail system is a smooth fast way to get around. I loitered in Chinatown, amazed at the merchandise; pirated movies cost $1.50 each. The Bird Park aviary is the best I have seen. The enveloping cage covers acres of ground with the net supported by 100-foot high poles. Viewers walk inside the cages. Many of the gaudy birds strutting about are imports; Malaysia has enough spectacular species that imports aren't necessary.

I toured the ancient town of Malaka, a two-hour bus ride from Kuala Lumpur. When the Portuguese arrived in the sixteenth century, this town was an important trading center. My interest in the history of this era was piqued by the excellent exhibits in the museum of the old Dutch Stadthuys.

When I returned to Langkawi, Carl and Fran came along for a few days of rest and relaxation. While they were here, the yachting community threw me a surprise birthday party. Rose Selfridge organized it. Rose knew how old I'd be, but not the exact date. Any excuse for a party. The restaurant provided a free cake and the bartender made a powerful punch. Sailors and hotel guests were invited.

I mingled and smiled and accepted congratulations. It was close enough to my turning eighty-four to count, but I was still surprised. Carl was surprised as well; he paid the bar bill.

As spring wore on, Richard Hovey's "The Sea Gypsy" ran through my head:

I am fevered with the sunset,
I am fretful with the bay,
For the wanderlust is on me,
And my soul is in Cathay.

One morning I dove into the polluted marina waters, chopped the barnacles off the propeller, and put to sea for a short cruise. A neighboring Australian yachtsman, Lex *(Pia)*, told me about the toucans that could be found in a secluded anchorage about nine miles from Rebak. A quick look in my bird book showed no toucans in this part of the world. When Lex looked at the book he soon found a picture of the "toucans"; they were hornbills. So I went searching for hornbills. In a lovely deep anchorage in a narrow passage between two big islands I heard, day and night, a cacophony of squawking birds. Numerous Brahminy kites floated by in their gorgeous chestnut, white, and black plumage. I didn't see a hornbill.

Twenty miles south of Langkawi is Pulau Paya, a small island designated as a national park because of the coral surrounding it. No anchoring is allowed, but several mooring buoys have been installed. I sailed there from the hornbill haven on a rare windy day. I bounced and pitched all night long on a groaning mooring. The coral was invisible under churning water. I sailed back to Langkawi on an even rarer two-in-a-row windy day.

A sunken estuary leads in from the northeast corner of Langkawi Island. It is a favorite hangout for those yachties who can get along without a city close by. The narrow channel, which comprises Hole-in-the-Wall, lies between high cliffs where trees cling to the weathered granite. The sun rises late and sets early behind mountain walls. I had no excuse not to do some varnishing, so I did a little over the course of several days of relaxation. To return to Rebak, I continued counterclockwise around Langkawi Island. I completed another circumnavigation. Not as exciting as some, but not as stressful as others.

The next month I flew to Cambodia. Cambodia is a strange country, its economy hardly touched by industrialization. The people are a smiling lot, certainly in no outward way xenophobic. Yet, only ten to fifteen years ago, one section of the community under Pol Pot brutally tortured and murdered two million people, twenty percent of the population. It chilled me to think that the teenage monsters who were the butchers then now walked the streets as accepted middle-aged members of society.

The capital city of Phnom Penh, with a population of about a million, is a shabby city, demonstrating the effects of thirty years of neglect. I saw no new construction and very little maintenance. Motorbikes and bicycles outnumber cars by twenty to one in the city; the ratio is much higher in the countryside. A pillion ride on a motorbike taxi anywhere in town costs a dollar. My guest house, Smiley's, of the backpacker variety, was a find: $3 per night for a room, meals $2 or less, and an obliging staff. Smiley's was full one night when a young female backpacker asked for a room. Hating to turn her away after dark, the manager mentioned that I had two beds in my room. She knocked on my door; I could never turn a young woman down.

In Phnom Penh, I often ate at the Foreign Correspondents Club, still a hangout for writers and the top spot in town for drinking and dining. Photos of Cambodian news scenes decorate the walls. I sat on the open balcony and admired the lovely view of the confluence of the Mekong and Tonle Sap rivers.

The Killing Fields monument is just outside Phnom Penh. The deep depressions in the grassy slopes mark the mass graves where thousands of bodies were exhumed. The monument itself, a transparent-sided silo stacked with about 3000 skulls, is actually tastefully done. The doctors, lawyers and intelligentsia of any sort were executed by the regime. The torture chambers in the heart of the city are even more depressing. Rows of pictures of the victims are displayed.

I took a six-hour boat ride north from Phnom Penh. Half the trip is along the winding Tonle Sap River with its nestled villages, many on stilts above the water. The second half is across a shallow lake where, at times, neither shore is visible.

The small town of Siem Riep is a bigger tourist draw than Phnom Penh. The famous clusters of temples of Angkor Thom and Angkor Wat lie a few miles north. These great architectural wonders of the world were built from about 900 to 1300 AD. I wandered through these monuments over the course of three days. The usual system for exploration was to hire a motorbike driver for the day for six dollars. He deposited me at one monument, picked me up at a designated time, and drove me on to the next. The two dozen close-in monuments are on a circuit of about sixteen miles. Another, Banteay Srei is twenty miles away.

Most of the monuments are multistoried sandstone structures erected to honor Buddhist or Hindu deities or the kings who built them. The steep stone steps up the towers can be hazardous; for some reason, I was specially warned. Inside the monuments, the corridors are narrow, because the Khmer architects knew only block-on-block false arches. The height of the towers is extraordinary. Most amazing to me was the extent and detail of the bas relief carvings in the hard sandstone. Acres of these carvings depict men, women, gods, soldiers, dancers, animals, birds, battles, wars, and Khmer and Sanscrit inscriptions. The detail is unbelievable. The temple at Banteay Srei is particularly attractive for it is constructed of pink sandstone. The color remains today even though other temples are stained dark by the aging processes of a millennium. Banteay Srei has been safe for visitors only since the Khmer Rouge were driven out in 1998. These ancient Cambodian monuments are as incredible as anything I saw in Italy, Greece, Turkey, Jordan or Egypt.

Returning to Phnom Penh, I made the mistake of going by road; nine hours of bouncing over potholes. The communist government continues to neglect its people and infrastructure. The twenty-knot boat ride I took to Siem Riep was a faster and more comfortable ride.

I took another side trip, a four-hour bus ride to Sihanoukville, Cambodia's only seaport. The ride was smooth, this road kept in good condition for truck transport from the port. I stayed only long enough to eat lunch. Several months earlier, before I decided to travel to Cambodia by air, I wrote for permission to sail here. I am still awaiting an answer. Perhaps I should have included bribe money with my request.

Having had enough of land and air travel, I returned to Langkawi and headed to sea once again.

Chapter 22

The Scrutable East

To reach a port we must sail, sometimes with the wind and sometimes against it.
But we must not drift or lie at anchor.
-Oliver Wendell Holmes, Jr.

The 450-mile trip down the western coast of Malaysia (the Strait of Malacca) from Langkawi to Singapore at the tip of the Malaysian peninsula was an exercise in ship-dodging on a twenty-four hour basis. It was exhausting. Like pieces on a chess board, ships and fishing boats clogged the waterway. I plotted an ever-changing course, maneuvering *Idle Queen* like a bishop, then a knight, as I weaved my way among them. I spent most of my time at the tiller and slept only in fifteen-minute increments. Several times, for longer rests, I stopped in harbors along the way: Pangkor Island, Port Klang, Port Dickson, Pulau Pisang.

After nine stressful days through the Strait, I berthed at the Republic of Singapore Yacht Club. Here the cost of one week's dockage would have paid for three weeks in Rebak. But Singapore is a consolation. It is an example of what can be done by a people dedicated to the work ethic. Having no natural resources, the island city nation makes its living in service industries, finance, and international trade. The place throbs with activity. Buses and light rail run smoothly, rapidly, and frequently. Much of the housing is government-built high-rise, with no sign of degeneration to slum class. The cost of living is similar to that of northern Europe. A private three-bedroom town house would cost a minimum of US$500,000. With over three million inhabitants, the port is one of the largest in the world.

In Singapore, I awaited delivery of an anchor windlass and 200 feet of chain from the U.S. My son Carl's employer deals with Stolt-Neilsen Shipping. Carl asked the shipper to deliver the items. The shipper's staff and some of their suppliers dedicated themselves to my welfare. Vincent Low, in charge of ship-leasing for Stolt-Neilsen, was my mainstay in Singapore. He kept me apprised of the shipment's progress.

While I waited, I explored the city. It is crammed with money, people, automobiles, high-rises, modern offices and apartments. Its prosperity contrasts with that of neighboring Malaysia where the Malays take life at a slower and less enterprising pace. It is not the Singapore of Joseph Conrad or the 1930s movies. Lee Kuan Yew's memoir, *The Singapore Story*, explains it all.

My most devoted tour guide and companion was Maryan Koehler, a slight brunette whose size belies a fearless explorer. Years earlier, after her college graduation, Maryan backpacked around the world. She was in Argentina headed to Chile when she discovered that the border between the two countries was closed. As she wondered what to do, a Norwegian sailboat arrived in Buenos Aires. The crew of four needed a cook and Maryan signed on. Her first sail was a rounding of Cape Horn, a terrible ordeal. Maryan left the sailboat in Chile and continued her trek. Steffen, one of the Norwegian sailors, kept track of her and surprised her in several countries. In Thailand, he told her this was the last time. If she wanted to see him again, she would have to marry him. She did.

Maryan and I met at a fancy lunch at the Raffles Hotel organized by the Stolt-Nielsen staff.

"I was expecting this tall Viking sort, imagining that only an abnormally giant-sized guy would be doing this sort of trip at eighty-four," Maryan wrote later. *"But there was Harry, no taller than myself. I was enchanted with him right away, and Steffen and I took every opportunity to be with him; however, Steffen left on a business trip for Europe, and that meant I had Harry to myself.*

"It became a great joke with my family and Steffen that every time he, or anyone else, tried to reach me, I was out with Harry. We usually ended up back at the Yacht Club bar for a drink or two and more conversation of places we'd been and people we'd met."

With Maryan as my tour guide, we did not leave many sights unseen. Singapore's architecture is outstanding. Raffles City is a huge complex comprised of two hotels and business offices with a water fountain of dancing jets in the lobby. The Colonial District is preserved from the days of British rule. The statue of Sir Stamford Raffles, the founder of modern Singapore, is near the famous old landmark, and exorbitantly expensive, Raffles Hotel.

The surrender of Australian and British troops to the Japanese in Singapore is a depressing story. An audio and visual show details the last hours before the Japanese overran the city in February 1942.

Changi Prison, used as POW camp by the Japanese, is a museum and contains pictures and diaries of the prisoners.

I could hardly pull myself away from the Singapore Zoological Gardens. This boasts being one of the world's few "open" zoos. Moats, rather than cages, contain most of the animals. A specialty of the zoo is a night safari where one can watch the animals' nocturnal activities.

Jurong Bird Park has more than 8000 species of birds. It's easy to believe it has one of the world's largest bird collections, a fascinating display from penguins to kiwis. I spent a day there. A live show, "King of the Skies," features speed-flying by trained eagles, hawks, and falcons.

We squeezed in all these sights before my shipment arrived. Murray Fulton of Stolt-Neilsen then took charge. He loaded the windlass and chain into a bumboat, delivered it to a truck ashore and carted it to Republic of Singapore Yacht Club. Here Raj, the Indian dockmaster, craned it into a launch and ran it out to *Idle Queen*. The gang hand-loaded it aboard, link by link. No wonder my stevedores complained about the weight; I was sent 300 feet of chain, not 200. Meanwhile, friendly Kjetel Gulliksen located other necessities for the installation.

Kjetel, a Norwegian, runs a business supplying ships with onboard requirements. He and his beautiful Malaysian wife, Hamadah, entertained me and a group of friends at the Raffles Hotel buffet and again at the posh Oaks Restaurant. I tried the local cuisine. The crocodile meat was tasteless, but the bright red meat of the kangaroo was tasty and novel.

Raj, the dockmaster, took me to his home for dinner. The two of us ate together. When we finished, his wife and young children ate. I found this strange social custom repeated later in Japan. I dined with Raj a second time when his father visited from India. His father is a faith healer and offered to cure my rheumatism. After consideration, I decided that I would rather have the rheumatism than the faith.

With the delivery of the windlass and chain, my excuse for continuing the plush life in Singapore ended. In early June 2000, I left in windless, motoring weather for the 450-mile run to Kuching on Borneo. Singapore actively expands its land area by cutting down hills and dumping them in the sea. As I passed one of these dumping areas, the milky water entered my engine, in spite of a strainer. It loaded the cooling jacket with fine sand and silt that clogged the water pump and overheated the engine. I could make only one to two knots as I headed east across the busy Singapore shipping lanes. Periodically, I had to stop to let the engine cool. My progress was an agonizingly slow, nail-biting experience for me and the ships dodging me. I finally made it across just as darkness set in. Once out of the channel, I dropped anchor for the night.

In the morning, I raised sail. Over the course of ten days, I sailed in light winds to the coast of Borneo off the Sarawak River. At the river entrance, the wind died. Two sailing vessels, the French boat *Oberon* and the German boat *Bushman,* came to my aid. First one and then the other towed me to a tie-up on the waterfront in Kuching. I ordered a new water pump from Norway.

Kuching, with a population of about 400,000, is modern in few aspects. It lives off the timber trade. It is not a yachting destination. During my weeks of stay, I saw only one French, one German, one Australian, and one American boat pass through. Those sailors who stayed could feast on natural wonders. I made three trips to national parks. I saw orangutans and hornbills in one, the Rafflesia flowers in another, and the Cultural Village in the third.

I haven't seen orangutans or hornbill birds in the wild, but the enjoyment of seeing them at all, even in the park enclosures, excited me. The male orangutan was not in evidence, only the mother and two youngsters; one was quite a ham. They are lovable rather than fearsome creatures. The rhinoceros hornbill, four feet long and with a huge red and yellow caste over his bill, is a more intimidating animal.

The search for the Rafflesia in Gunung Gadding National Park reminded me of the effort I put into climbing the towers of Petra. Seven of us, plus a guide, struggled for an hour up rocky jungle hillsides and across boulder-strewn streams to at last view three examples of the largest flower in the world. Two feet in diameter, the Rafflesia flowers are dull red with yellow spots. They lie low along the forest floor attached to creeping vines. Although large, they aren't otherwise outstanding. I was disappointed.

I usually don't bother with attractions like the Cultural Village. I enjoyed this visit because I was joined by Cindy Stewart, a cheerful knowledgeable Californian. Cindy came to Asia to visit her adventurous daughter who left to crew on a boat to India. Cindy was planning to sail west with Capt. Kirk and Cath McGeorge (*Polly Brooks*). When Cindy and I met at a July 4th party on *Polly Brooks*, we decided to visit the Cultural Village together. At the Village, we enjoyed traditional food, watched the native dances, and poked into the depictions of native life. A Dyak tribesman impressively demonstrated his accuracy with a blowpipe. He had no trouble consistently hitting a football-sized balloon at fifty feet.

Days later I cleared from Kuching bound for Labuan Island, expecting a trouble-free trip. But it is not only the skipper who is getting old; *Idle Queen* showed signs of increasing degeneration. First the bolts holding the shaft in place from engine to propeller worked loose. These could not be tightened because of worn threads. Then the masthead navigation light burned out. The substitute at deck level refused to come on. Without an engine and proper lights, I sailed in the daytime and hove-to with an anchor light on at night.

The southwest monsoon finally came into its own. I experienced several sixty-knot squalls with rain limiting visibility to fifty meters. Borneo has more lightning than any other place in the world. The lightning was more cloud-to-cloud than the cloud-to-ground lightning I'm used to. I enjoyed the displays.

My route took me the long way around the coast: outside the fishing boats and oil rigs but along the shipping lanes. I finally bumbled my way into the marina on Labuan Island under my own power and had the engine repaired first thing.

Labuan is part of the province of Sabah, Malaysia, and just off the coast of the sultanate of Brunei. In spite of its being a duty-free port, Labuan is a more expensive place than Langkawi. There are no beaches, sport fishing, or diving worthy of the name, but the place is replete with fancy hotels and blue-glass sheathed buildings the size of small mountains. Labuan is an offshore banking haven.

With the engine repaired, I sailed the short hop from Labuan Island to Kota Kinabalu farther down the coast of Sabah on North Borneo. Here I met Jacob Bakker and his pretty Filipina wife, Chris, who were on a sailing holiday from Coron Harbor, north of Palawan Island. Jacob is a burly, tough Dutchman. His sailing skills were developed during years dodging typhoons in the Philippines while running his charter business. We exchanged sea stories, and they invited me to visit them in Coron.

At the end of August, I sailed for the Philippines, the typhoon-swept group of islands lying southeast of Asia. Magellan discovered the Philippines and died there in 1521. The country remained Spanish until taken over by the U.S. in 1898. In 1946, the country became independent. This republic of 22 million people is still troubled by insurrections on Mindanao Island.

I felt uneasy about the passage to Bonbonon on Negros Island. The piratical Abu Sayaf was active in the area, and a sailor told me of his near-confrontation. But I had a quiet passage. I read Agnes Keith's *Land Below the Wind*. This classic, limning life in Borneo in the 1930s, is still popular in Borneo bookstores.

Bonbonon is a typhoon hole surrounded by jungle. The taller palms stick their heads above the green cover. The friendly Filipina, Dorothy, presides over a small snack bar and rustles up something to eat or drink at any time. She sells single cigarettes to those who cannot afford a pack.

Leaving Bonbonon I sailed for Hong Kong via Subic Bay. Along the way, I stopped at Puerto Princessa for unexpected repairs. While hove-to one night, I was awakened at 0300 by a loud banging on the hull. A stainless steel casting connecting the trim tab on the rudder to its control mechanism broke. This crucial component of my self-steering apparatus had to be fixed. Puerto Princessa on Palawan Island was the port of easiest access and, as it turned out, an entertaining stopover.

I hired a diver to take the trim tab off the boat. I could not make repairs to my self-steering system here—no expertise or materials available—but I could get to Subic Bay without self-steering. With this delay, I decided to skip Coron Harbor. I e-mailed the Bakkers about my change in plans.

Puerto Princessa is a busy prosperous town, unusual for the Philippines. The major supermarket is always crowded. Tricycles, 3-wheeled motorcycles with cab, take customers anywhere in town for eight cents. People don't walk farther than a block. The depth of the motorcycle exhaust fumes reminds me of the air pollution in Bangkok.

Sixty miles north of Puerto Princessa is Palawan Island's most interesting tourist attraction, the Underground River. I rode in a small paddle boat for five miles under the mountain through caverns sometimes as high as 200 meters. Colors are different from those I have seen in other caverns: little white, only red, orange, and tan. The prominent water-carved features show up well in the searchlight beams. They are all named: The Virgin, The Cathedral, etc.

I celebrated Christmas here with a new friend, Aimo, a short, lean, jovial Finnish sailor. The Trattoria in town has a suitably alcoholic atmosphere where we shared an Italian Christmas dinner.

Because diving season for tourists does not start until March, the three Filipino crew on the eighty-foot diving boat *Deepsea* had little to do. I hired them to do some work on *Idle Queen*. On New Millennium Eve, the Filipino crew invited Huang, a young Vietnamese boat-sitting a Canadian trimaran, Aimo and me to a party on *Deepsea*. The guests numbered about twenty, half men, half women, some mature couples. The rum, ninety-five cents per bottle, flowed. We yachties soon realized that three young Filipinas of suspect virtue had been invited to amuse the foreign guests.

But, as Aimo later wrote his son: "These Filipinas had little money. They could not afford our prices, so we did no business with them."

Also in Puerto Princessa, I met Peter and Becky on *Jonah*. Peter dropped his Seattle wife and was traveling with Becky, his secretary. At our regular morning coffee breaks on *Idle Queen*, Becky arrived with her own coffee in a glass. After much prodding, we learned that her "coffee" was rum and Coke.

With repairs completed, I sailed north to Olongapo on Subic Bay against wind and current. Except for the penultimate day of twelve, I was always close hauled, always tacking. Average wind was fifteen knots, generally fading at night. I carried main, staysail, and jib all the way without reefing. When the angle of heel reached thirty degrees, I dropped the staysail and proceeded with less strain and speed. I did not stop, even to heave-to. I slept in short spurts as often as the sea traffic allowed. The great number of ships in the West Cuyo Pass tended to keep me awake.

Olongapo, inland from the former U.S. Naval Base, is more modern than Puerto Princessa, with more cars and jeepneys, and fewer tricycles. The area close to the Base is a disaster with empty buildings and boarded-up shops. A strong effort is being made by the government to reignite the community in the Base area. This area, Subic Bay Metropolitan Authority, is still well-demarcated and is duty-free. The SBMA is green with trees on the hillsides; the surrounding countryside is barren.

This was another city with no bank able to handle credit cards. I followed someone's advice: I went to the Lengenda Casino in the Free Trade Zone and had no trouble withdrawing as much money on my credit card as I wished. I spent none of it on chips. With money in hand, I celebrated my eighty-fifth birthday quietly and alone.

Wanting to reach Hong Kong by the middle of March, I hired out much of the maintenance to be done on *Idle Queen*, including scraping off barnacles and painting her topsides. Underway again in early March, I reflected on the Philippines. I felt depressed, as I looked back on the friendly, lovable, and inept people. Prospects for their future look grim. Population is growing at a rapid rate in one of the most overpopulated countries of the world; no one seems to care. The people are highly religious, but corrupt officials take advantage of their own people as well as foreigners. At the Olongapo post office, my incoming mail was several weeks overdue. For hours a young postal worker searched futilely through scattered and neglected mail bags.

The work on my boat, particularly the engine, was done so incompetently that some of it had to be redone several times. How difficult is it to install a new gasket so it does not leak oil?

An American with a small labor-intensive business said, "The best Filipino men are the women." His staff is predominantly female.

Filipinas are ever ready to marry and leave the country. One day I was riding on a bus with two Filipinas seated across the aisle.

"Are you married?" asked one.

"No," I said.

"Then why don't you take my friend here?"

I met several solo sailors who had persuaded a Filipina to join him as crew.

The country is beautiful, well worth more exploration than I gave it. The drawbacks are the presence of communist guerillas and Muslim insurgents, and the country is hit by more tropical storms than any other region of the world.

I left Subic Bay for Hong Kong in a pleasant northeaster, shielded by the mountains of Luzon. When that wind died, I drifted for two days. I was below, out of sight of land, when I heard voices. Puzzled, I went on deck. Two men sat in a small fishing boat. They pointed to their mouths and made chewing motions. I scrounged through the cupboards and found bread and rolls which I handed down to them. They stuffed their mouths as they motored off. Their visit depressed me the rest of the day.

The 1730 Guam weather forecast on 11 March reported seas "eight feet and over" for that night. By 2330 I was down to double-reefed main and staysail. By noon the next day, the sea rose high and rough. I put a third reef in the main but made slow progress through the pounding waves. At 2100, I was forced to heave-to. I had waited too long. The rough seas loosened and raised the bowsprit platform and broke the stern stanchion supporting the VHF antenna.

The next morning, despite an occasional drenching, I stood on deck and watched IQ rise to the incoming seas. I calculate wave height by standing at the foot of the mast where my eye level is twelve feet above the sea. The seas were higher than twelve feet; the rising waves obliterated the horizon.

On the third day, the wind shifted, and I sailed 121 miles toward Hong Kong. When I arrived, I moored, as if I belonged there, at the exclusive Royal Hong Kong Yacht Club. Aimo had introduced me, via e-mail, to Simon Latham, an English admiralty lawyer. Latham smoothed my way into the prestigious club.

Hong Kong is a busy, crowded, energetic and flourishing city, a major trading and financial center. The largest density of high-rise buildings I've ever seen stretch for miles along the waterfront. Hong Kong is Singapore's cousin, but more mature, political and seasoned. Lying off China's southwest coast in the China Sea, Hong Kong was leased to Britain from 1898 to 1997, then returned to Chinese control. The seven million people are Chinese, but still British in many ways.

Shortly after I arrived, I joined a tour group to Beijing. Oddly, Hong Kong residents must have a visa to visit China. At the Beijing airport, our guide gave our seven-person group a warm reception. She answered our questions without spewing propaganda. The one question she couldn't answer was the name of the independence-minded leader of Taiwan.

Beijing is spread out widely—with only eleven million people I couldn't imagine where all the bicycles came from—but lacks the dynamics and high-rise buildings that characterize Hong Kong. The city is working steadily to modernize and convert to a free-market economy. Miles of old community housing are being bulldozed to give way for new construction. The older sections of the city are filled with one-story brick block housing, all painted a uniformly dreary gray. The better apartments consist of a tiny living room, kitchen, and bedroom. Four families share a bathroom. We talked for an hour through our interpreter with a resident older couple who were happy to show us their living quarters. We asked about everything but their politics.

The main attraction of the trip was the Great Wall, which is a two-hour drive from Beijing. The long straight stretch of road to the Wall was getting a face lift. Young trees were being planted at regular intervals along both sides of the highway. By the time of the Olympics, this will be a pleasant, rather than dreary, drive.

At the Wall, I climbed the steps cut into its broad top. I didn't walk far; it was too steep a climb. I leaned against the parapet and watched the tour group disappear high up the hill. As I rested, I recalled the story Ann Saxe (*Heather*) told me in Turkey of her and Fabe's visit to the Wall. Ann was forced to walk ahead and leave the broad and 6'4" tall Fabe behind. Fabe's progress was impeded by a surrounding crowd of small and excited Chinese children. They jumped around him in a frenzy, pointing and yelling, "Giant! Giant!"

The Wall snaked into the distance over the mountain ridges. The massive construction, started by Emperor Qin in 200 BC to keep out the barbarians, extended for 2000 miles. In the 1400s, it was strengthened and extended to 4000 miles. The wall wasn't enough. Centuries later, the communist barbarians moved in.

Tiananmen Square, in the heart of Beijing, is immense. Its other outstanding feature is the high ratio of police to pedestrians. The square lacks any pretense of attractiveness. The gigantic picture of Mao, keeping an eye on his subjects, stirred no excitement in our group.

Abutting Tiananmen Square is the Forbidden City, home of the emperors. The interior furnishings were hauled off to Taiwan when the defeated KMT left mainland China. I was sorry for I wondered how the opulence of the Chinese emperors compared with that of the sultans in Istanbul. The most striking object was the huge marble ship which floats in Lake Kunming at the Summer Palace.

On the tour I met Bryan, a relaxed middle-aged contractor from Australia, and his sister, Val. Back in Hong Kong I spent most of my time with them. Bryan's nephew lives in Hong Kong and is married to Lora, a beautiful and wealthy Chinese lady. Lora graduated from McGill University and is part-owner and chief financial officer for a string of Chinese restaurants. Knowing a lady restaurateur gave me a prime education in *dim sum*.

Lora has a box at the Happy Valley Race Track where we all spent an evening of free food and drinks while betting on the horses. Val, Bryan and I had a profitable evening until the seventh race. Lora's brother had a horse in the seventh, and we felt compelled to bet on it. Not a wise move; I think the horse is still running. Bryan, as usual, accompanied me back to the yacht club for a nightcap.

I enjoyed my life in Hong Kong. Every morning, I dodged heavy lanes of traffic, as I walked the half mile up the hill from the yacht club to the Seattle's Best Coffee house. For the price of a cup of coffee and my morning Danish, I used their computer to check my e-mails. Close by in the busy downtown area, I had my choice of Chinese laundries.

Hong Kong is separated from the mainland by a mile-wide stretch of water. Subways and car tunnels run under the strait to the Kowloon section on the mainland. I did most of my shopping in Kowloon. The famous Lee Sails shop is in a suburban area on Hong Kong island, over the hills out toward the ocean. I felt the thrill of successful exploration when I found my way there on a Chinese bus that had no English speakers aboard. At Lee Sails, I bought a staysail. As events unfolded, I should have bought a jib, mainsail, and genoa, too.

That evening in the yacht club bar I was introduced to Robin Knox-Johnson, winner of the first solo nonstop around-the-world race.

Shaking his hand I said, "I've read your book."

"Oh, you're the one!"

My socializing was shortened as the worst of the typhoon season approached. After only six weeks in Hong Kong, I sailed off to reach Japan before bad weather broke.

Chapter 23

My Year in Japan

It has been a bad habit of mine, generally,
to write an account of Journeys by land or by sea.
-H. W. Tilman, *Mischief Goes South*

The distance from Hong Kong to Kagoshima in southern Japan is 1200 miles. The recommended route is through the Taiwan Strait between China and Taiwan. This route is partially sheltered from typhoons, but it's a poor choice for the singlehander. The strait is saturated with pods of fifty to 100 Chinese fishing boats, always on the move. Sailing among them was a nightmare; in almost all cases, they have the right-of-way. For several days I used the kitchen timer to awaken me every fifteen minutes. I poked my head up, surveyed the boats around me, and went back to dozing. I avoided accidental contacts, but twice fell victim to deliberate ones.

A fishing boat does not have right-of-way when overtaking a sailboat. Just west of Taiwan Shoals and the Pescadore Islands, I barely made steerage way. A 60-foot wooden fishing boat came up behind on my lee side. I glanced over and saw the saturnine-looking crew lining the rail. As the boat passed, it swerved over and bumped me sharply. The crew grinned. I scowled back. The boat scraped my rails and twanged the rigging. The chain plate anchoring the mast was deeply grooved. A slightly deeper cut, and I could have lost the mast in the bad weather encountered later.

A second incident occurred when I was southwest of the northern tip of Taiwan. With full sail up in light air, I slowly made way. As I sat below at lunch, I heard the rumble of a large diesel roaring up on my lee side. I hurried on deck and watched with trepidation as a 100-foot steel trawler approached. Again the crew lined the deck. I was well aware that this heavy vessel could do serious damage to my topsides, even disable me if it caught the rigging. I gripped the tiller as I eyed the oncoming boat. I felt as if I were in a wild west showdown. I stared at the trawler's bow, like a gunfighter watching his opponent's eyes, waiting for the flicker that warned of impending action. When the bow moved in my direction, I was ready.

Seconds before impact, I pushed the tiller sharply and luffed the sail. *Idle Queen* moved just slightly into the wind and away from the attacker, but it was enough. Only the cable towing the trawl net scraped the bottom of my hull.

I had won this fight, but I was frightened. I was still among fishing boats. I wondered why I'd been attacked. These fishermen gained nothing by injuring me. Maybe they assumed I was American; I flew no flag. Was it China vs. America, poor vs. rich, xenophobia, or just puerile vandalism? I don't know, but it is axiomatic that a belligerent government with a controlled press will breed a belligerent citizenry.

On 23 May, without further confrontation, I neared the southeastern tip of Japan and motored into Kagoshima. This sheltered port is nestled in Kagoshima Bay between two peninsulas. It is at the southern end of Kyushu Island, one of the four main islands making up the archipelago of Japan.

Japan has limited space for marina docks. At Kagoshima Marine Service (KMS), yachts are stored on land. Because I was a visiting sailor, particularly an American, the staff found a secure spot along the canal bank for me. An honored guest, I was kept in the water with the privileged fishing boats.

KMS boatyard had no clubhouse or restaurant with bar, just a small office. The accommodating staff allowed me to use the workmen's shower and laundromat. Hideki Nakamura, the number two man, earned his helicopter pilot license in Riverside, California. He spoke English fluently, and was critically helpful in a country where few speak English. He not only answered my simple questions—*Where is the bank? The grocery store?*—he drove me to each place on my initial visit.

Land transportation was not a big problem. KMS is in the country but only two blocks from the bus stop and just a mile to the commuter rail line into downtown Kagoshima. A half hour's walk got me to the nearest supermarket. The prices weren't bad, either for groceries or fast food. At a nearby Kentucky Fried Chicken, the coffee is $1.50; the meal of one piece of chicken, one muffin, one side of cole slaw, and one drink is $5.25. At a little local restaurant, lunch cost $7.50. At this time, a dollar bought 130 yen.

I was up early every day and ate breakfast on the boat. Either lunch or dinner I ate out. The staff at KMS and I had dinner together occasionally. The owner, Hagiiwa san, picked the restaurant, and usually picked up the check. Hagiiwa was a short, solidly built man of fifty who knew little English. According to rumor, his business was financed by his father, an aristocrat of Old Japan, dignified, erect, carefully dressed. When I met his father, he formally shook my hand instead of bowing. I wondered what he thought of Americans, then and now.

Shortly after I arrived in Kagoshima, I was interviewed by the local paper. As an octogenarian singlehander, I was news. Japan reveres solo sailors. The interviewer asked if I was lonely sailing long distances by myself. I knew the answer he expected. Dutifully, I said I got lonely. Actually, I rarely feel lonely. I keep too busy. I read, write up the log daily, and routinely clean and check the boat's equipment.

After the interview, I took a two-week rail tour of Japan. The Japanese know how to build railroads and how to run them. The high-speed trains have their own dedicated tracks. The fastest bullet train, Nozomi, runs at 186 mph. The trains are expensive, but they run frequently, are always on schedule to the minute, and are the popular way to travel in Japan.

On my first day, I traveled from Kagoshima to Fukuoka and arrived in late afternoon. The nearby hotel was full. I stood on the sidewalk and looked about, wondering which way to go to find lodging. A car stopped beside me.

The Japanese driver asked in English, "Can I help you?"

"I'm looking for a hotel," I said. "This one is full."

"Get in, and we'll find one."

I got in and we drove around, talking all the while, until we found a hotel. I thanked Ogawa san for his help. We still "talk" via e-mails.

The next evening, I met and dined with friends of friends, a charming Dutch couple named Jaap and Marijke. They live on a boat and teach English in the local schools. They were "warned" by mutual friends in the Malaysia/Thailand area that I was headed their way. Over dinner, we discovered we were in Whangarei at the same time. With so many boats in the marina, we had not met.

I continued by rail across Honshu to the north island of Hokkaido. Japan is a green mountainous country, seamed with rivers. The rail lines don't go around or over the mountains, they go through them. Japan must have as many tunnels as Norway. The longest tunnel in the world is thirty-three miles long and goes under Tsugaru Strait.

The population of Japan, half that of the U.S., is crowded into a country the size of Montana. The effect shows in deforested areas and the extreme sprawl of cities and villages. This is a country of low buildings. This is earthquake country.

Sopporo, Hokkaido's major city, is bright with neon lights, but with little else to recommend it. I headed on to Kushiro. Outside Kushio is the largest wildlife refuge in Japan, the Shitsugen National Park.

Shitsugen is huge. The observation building is on a hill overlooking a wide area of marshland that spreads into the distance of the Kushiro River valley. The building, with its fine exhibits, reminded me of the Don Edwards Refuge building in California. Miles of well-engineered wooden walkways lead into the wilderness. All day I hiked these trails. I particularly wanted to see the famous red-crested white cranes of Japan. I couldn't find one.

From Kushiro, I headed north. As the train ran along the edge of the marshlands, I sat mesmerized. I saw more waterfowl from the train window than I had in Shitsugen. Farther north, through Akan National Park, clouds of steam rose from hot springs. Sadly, logging is a major industry in this northeastern corner of Hokkaido. The city of Abashiri is an outpost-looking harbor town on the north coast; people come here in winter to see ice floes floating down from Russia.

Back on Honshu, I visited the first of the designated "Three Great Sights" of Japan: the islands in the Bay of Matsushima. These small tree-covered islands are reminiscent of South Sea Islands. A good vantage point to view them is from the railroad that hangs over the cliffs above the bay. These islands are on the east coast of Honshu, not far from the major city of Sendai. Sendai was destroyed by bombs during the war. Although rebuilt and blessed with wide, tree-lined boulevards, the city is no longer Old Japan.

Heading south, I arrived in Japan's most popular tourist city, Kyoto. An efficient woman in the tourist office scrambled to find me a place to stay. I ended up in a *minshuku*, a Japanese bed and breakfast, without the breakfast, in a *tatami* room, where the floor is covered with finely woven *tatami* mats. Neither shoes nor slippers are worn. There are no chairs, just a sixteen-inch high table. The bed is on the floor. It's hard to relax for long in any position except prone.

The young landlady spoke English. Separated from her husband, she had two preteen boys. On my last night, she invited me to join her family in the communal bath. I flashed back to the first time I used a Japanese bathhouse. The facility was a combination restaurant/bathhouse. I had viewed the operation warily. The instructions on the automatic ticket dispenser were in Japanese. A young lady came to my aid, took my 500 yen, and purchased my ticket.

"I will show you where to go," she said.

I followed her upstairs and into the men's locker room. She stood behind me while I undressed. When I was nude, she took my hand and led me to a stool in front of a shower head.

"This soap, this shampoo, this hot water, this cold," she said, pointing to the knobs.

She left me to do my own scrubbing. An older woman came by and handed me a towel. I toweled off quickly and got dressed, passing up the final soak in a hot tub filled with old men.

Now I looked at my landlady, as she awaited my answer. Questions of proper etiquette overwhelmed me. I made my excuses and spent the evening elsewhere.

Kyoto is filled with the crush of humanity, foreign and domestic. I located one quiet street, the Philosophers Path, which winds along a shaded stream for a couple of miles in the midst of the city. Along this way, I paused to look at the sights of Old Japan: temples, shrines and gardens. It is my favorite spot in Kyoto. In another area, a temple I will remember is Kinkaku-ji with its three-story pavilion coated with gold leaf. It fronts a small lake with tiny islands. I wandered downtown Kyoto and toured the huge Gion shopping center where I spent no money, a difficult feat.

A day trip out of Kyoto to the northwestern edge of Honshu Island brought me to the second of the "Three Great Sights" of Japan. A thin, flat, wooded sand spit cuts off an arm of the sea to make a near-lake. I walked the two-mile length of the spit and climbed the mountain on the far side—with the aid of a cable car. I saw the novel configuration of sea, sky, woods and villages. It is a peaceful view, perhaps best appreciated when one is in a pensive mood. It's a popular spot for Japanese. I was the only *gaijin* there.

Located on the Inland Sea a few miles west of Osaka and Kobe, is Himeji, the putative finest castle remaining in Japan. Himeji looks more like a white pagoda than a European castle. It is a well-maintained, not reconstructed, fortress put together with massive stone blocks. Perched on a high hill and surrounded by gardens, it dominates the landscape as no other man-made structure I saw in Japan.

I was curious about Hiroshima and stopped for a look. I was glad I did. Near the center of this bustling city is the A-bomb Dome. The center of the bomb blast, a five-story shell surrounded by a pile of brick and concrete rubble, stands as a memorial. The Peace Memorial Park is across a small river from the dome. Like our Vietnam Wall, a cenotaph contains the names of the blast's victims. An eternal flame there will be extinguished when the last nuclear weapon is destroyed. Nearby, an odd T-bridge, thought to be the *Enola Gay* bombardier's target, crosses the river.

Hiroshima, like many Japanese cities, has an efficient tramline. I rode a tram out of town to the landing where ferries leave for a short trip to the island of Miyajima and the site of the final "Three Great Sights" of Japan: the Floating Torii of Miyajima. A *torii* is an entrance arch to a Shinto shrine. When I arrived that afternoon, the tide was out and the *torii* was not "floating," it was standing on a mud flat. This *torii* is an enormous red arch in the familiar Japanese shape and quite photogenic with sea and mountains behind it.

My two-week rail pass was coming to an end as I hurried back to Kagoshima. I passed through Beppu and the Aso National Park. The only rainy weather of the trip set in, and Aso's peaks and volcanoes were blanketed with fog and mist. Beppu has a famous sex museum, but I hadn't the time to visit.

My final day of train riding took me south along the east coast of Kyushu. The many indentations on this coast sport concrete breakwaters and small fishing harbors. I wondered if the fishermen would survive the decline in fisheries around the world.

Back in Kagoshima, it was cool in November. I lit my kerosene heater and read in the evenings. Few foreign boats stop in Kagoshima. In December 2001, the small Korean sloop *Isaac* motored in. I went on deck to help the couple tie up. Myungchul Lee, a slightly-built man with a ready smile, is a retired engineer who built his 28-foot boat. His placid wife, Hwang, nodded at our introduction, but never spoke. They were on their maiden voyage from Pusan.

In Faido's tradition, I invited the couple aboard for Happy Hour. Hwang quietly sipped her drink while Lee and I talked.

"There are only two dozen yachts in all of Korea," Lee said.

Because there were so few boats, Lee was determined to prove that a Korean could be a world traveler.

"Where are you heading?" I asked.

"Bonbonon, Philippines," Lee said proudly.

"Do you have charts for the area?"

"No."

The next day I emptied my chart bin. I would not be back this way again. I piled up about a hundred charts for Okinawa, Taiwan, the Philippines, Borneo, Singapore, Malaysia, and points west. I called Lee over and handed them to him. Stunned, he silently bowed his gratitude. As he sailed to these now-charted countries, he kept in touch via e-mail. In one e-mail he wrote that a friend lists news of "Sir Heckel" on a website viewed by Korean sailors.

That same month, I met James K. When I had been in Virginia in the fall, James called me at Harry Third's and asked if he could visit when I returned. In December, James and his girlfriend took me to dinner. The dinner, I realized, was a "thank you." James, a yacht sailor, was sixty, with a weathered face that reflected hard times. During dinner, he described how his business and marriage failed. He became depressed, he said matter-of-factly, and planned to kill himself. Then he read the article in the *Yomiuri Shimbun* about what I was doing as an octogenarian. He was inspired. He bought an older 36-foot sailboat and is fixing her up.

"I plan to go to sea," he said.

I was happy that I inspired one person. I retell this story only to impress my children.

I returned from the market one day and found a Japanese woman awaiting me at the boat. She was perhaps thirty years old, less than five feet tall, with a lively expression. I looked at her suspiciously, wondering what she was selling. In hesitant English, Toyomi introduced herself. She wanted to get a job with an import/export company, but needed to improve her English.

"Could I talk with you?" she asked.

We talked often, either on the boat or in restaurants. Our conversations were made easier because we share a common interest: she races a Lazer-class sailing dinghy. I felt parental pride when Toyomi landed a job with an import/export company.

Around Christmas, I was invited to what I thought was a KMS office party. Instead, Sosh of KMS took me to the home of Kyouko Imakiire. In the early nineties, Kyouko became the first Japanese woman to sail solo nonstop around the world. She showed me her book; it contains some fine pictures, but is available only in Japanese.

Kyouko is a buoyant outgoing woman and seemed thoroughly Western. Except for difficulty with English, she could have been presiding over a dinner in San Francisco. When I asked if she planned to repeat her trip, she replied, "No, too lonely." Today she seldom sails her boat *Kairen*, which is in the yard at KMS.

Christmas Day announced itself with thunder, lightning, and hail. The mooring lines complained about the wind. At such times, it's nice to be in a quiet canal. I thought of Christmases past. Every Christmas Eve Faido brought out the accumulated, unopened Christmas cards. As the four children sipped hot chocolate, Faido opened and read each card before passing it around. On Christmas Day I passed around, one by one, the presents. We waited while each gift was opened and exclaimed over. The anticipation and excitement lasted for hours. This year I spent the holiday alone.

Days later, I was roused from my solitude to join in New Year's celebrations. The New Year in Japan is a time for families to gather at the parental home to celebrate a traditional homecoming. Nakamura invited me to go with his wife, Momy, and baby to his parents' home in Makurazaki, where he was born. The little town is on the coast about an hour's drive southwest of Kagoshima. Nakamura's father, mother, and relatives welcomed me. Inside the house two open closets, side by side, held Buddhist and Shinto shrines.

When we arrived, everyone was hard at work. Rice was being steamed in a wooden box over a wood-fired boiler in the shed. After steaming for several hours, the damp rice, a few pounds at a time, was put into a mortar made from the hollowed-out end of a big pine log. It was then pounded with a heavy wooden mallet to a smooth pulp. This was a two-person operation, one putting the rice into the mortar and turning it by hand, while the other swung the mallet. Nobody got a mangled hand even when I did the pounding. The rice was then formed into patties and set aside to dry. Meanwhile, the wine flowed freely.

At lunchtime, the rice patties, buttered with a sugary bean paste I found repelling, were served with a salad, green tea, and beer. We sat on floor mats to eat. After the rice course, the party moved to the open fire outside where squid, sardines, and fish fillets were roasted.

The Japanese also celebrate Valentine's Day. The recognized system is that the woman gives the man of her choice a gift on 14 February. One month later, the man is obligated to reciprocate. It is a great system; I learned I have two aspiring girlfriends. One is the fifteen-year-old daughter of a workman in a nearby boatyard. At Christmas, she proudly gave me homemade cookies. On Valentine's Day, she gave me homemade fudge.

The second lady is a stocking clerk at the local supermarket, a friendly woman of indeterminate but mature age, wife of a professor at Kagoshima University. She learned her English, such as it is, when her husband taught at Rutgers University. When I bought prepared Japanese dinners, she translated the cooking instructions for me. On Valentine's Day she gave me a box of chocolates. A month later, I gave macadamia nuts to both ladies.

The second of February was the season's coldest day, but bright and clear. I skidded on frost, as I crossed the deck on my way off the boat. At the railway station in Kagoshima, I told the ticket clerk, "*Izumi yuki no oofukukippu o, kudasai.*"

He was not fooled; he did not come back at me with a stream of enigmatic Japanese. He simply smiled, as he handed me the round-trip ticket, took my 5000 yen, and said in English, "Track 4, 8:35."

At 1030, I was looking at an almost boundless mass of 7000 cranes from the Arasaki observation tower. I was forty miles west of Kagoshima where the town of Izumi and the village of Arasaki are hosts to the largest concentration of cranes in Asia. The government supports the winter feeding of these birds on 600 acres of rice flats.

The birds were fifty yards from the viewpoint. The sight held me spellbound. For two hours through binoculars, I watched the cranes probe for food in the mud, take off for short flights and sail back in. They looked elegant even splashing in the mud. Flocks of pintails, grey herons, and little egrets were visible in the shallow ponds. Black kites circled overhead. I saw my first Eurasian widgeons. The Japanese crane with its bright red cap eluded me again; this area is outside its habitat.

I decided to look for a Japanese crane at Mi-ike, a lake famous for its birdlife. Getting to Mi-ike in the off-season is problematic. Local advice made it a long day by bus or train with a couple of taxi rides thrown in. The afternoon before I planned to go, Hagiiwa, the owner of the boatyard, hopped aboard IQ with a note from Nakamura: "Don't leave early in the morning. We are going to take the day off and drive you to Mi-ike."

The drive took us two hours north from Kagoshima to Kirishima National Park where the small circular lake of Mi-ike is almost hidden in the ruck of the surrounding volcanic peaks.

The flocks of ducks that winter on Mi-ike were gone. Only a few dozen Eurasian widgeons and mallards had not migrated. My companions located a new bird for me, the easily distinguishable daumian redstart.

The scenery made up for an otherwise disappointing day. No logging is allowed in this area, and old trees show what a wild wilderness Japan was in an earlier age. Of the string of volcanoes making up these mountains, only Sakurajima, across the bay from downtown Kagoshima, is active. When the wind is right, ash falls on the boats at KMS.

When Hagiiwa had to travel to Yakushima Island to repair a small yacht, he invited me along. We traveled in style. He rented a helicopter, picked up co-pilot Nakamura, and off we flew. Once on Yakushima, Hagiiwa spent little time working on the boat. I suspect this was his excuse to show me the island.

Yakushima lies seventy miles south of Kagoshima. It was designated a UNESCO World Heritage Site in 1993, the first in Japan. It is fifteen miles in diameter, but rises to 6,000 feet and is well-forested. Snow covers the peaks in winter while the narrow coastal plain is subtropical with oranges and bananas. On a rare clear day in one of the wettest spots in a wet country, we flew over the top of the island. We looked down on rocky grass-covered peaks, deep-forested ravines, rivers, and a seashore dotted with typical Japanese small boat harbors.

One last exploration remained before I left the city and the people who had been so kind to me. From Kagoshima, I took the red-eye train to Fukuoka and caught the early morning ferry to Pusan in South Korea. The catamaran covers the 115 nautical miles in just under three hours. It is a fun fast ride. The sea was calm. After we landed, I had no trouble locating myself in town for, as usual, people are helpful to strangers. English speakers are easier to come by in Pusan than in Japan.

They told me in Japan that the people of Korea are different, and so they are. I rode crowded subways in Pusan several times and never had to stand. As soon as I jammed myself into a subway car, the nearest person, young or middle-aged, man or woman, jumped up and insisted that I sit down. I have seen that nowhere else in the world.

Pusan, a city of four million, is not a popular tourist destination. The outstanding feature for me was the 100-meter high tower perched on a hill which gave a picturesque view of the harbor spread out below. As a bonus, in the surrounding park I spotted a pica pica, the magpie with the extraordinarily long tail.

At the information office, I asked for directions to an area south of Pusan that is a major stop for migrating birds in Asia.

The information lady said, "You don't need to go. No birds."

I went anyway. Sure enough, no birds. A dam built on the estuary and poor agricultural practices destroyed this sanctuary.

The night before I left Pusan it rained and a strong cold front moved in. The north wind raged at thirty knots. On the return trip, the weather pushed us along, as the big catamaran pounded and shuddered, weaved and twisted. Every so often, the vessel slammed into a sea. Water cascaded over the top and gave the second floor windows a salt wash. I was ebullient; it wasn't my boat getting her rivets rattled. I staggered out to the open stern to watch the spray and seabirds. The stewardess dragged me back inside the cabin.

Back in Kagoshima, I prepared to leave Japan. I needed to sail from Beppu, on the east coast, by 1 June to cross the Pacific Ocean in optimum weather. I hired the KMS crew to paint *Idle Queen's* bottom. Nakamura painted the deck. I was charged much less than a native.

Before I left, a Japanese sailor I met at KMS approached me. Sako san was a brisk active man in his late forties, articulate in English, and a fellow solo circumnavigator. He invited me to stop in his village of Nomaike, which was on my way up the west side of Kyushu. His sailboat was in the museum there. I liked Sako who was well-respected by the KMS staff. I promised to stop, unaware of Sako's plans.

In the sail up the coast, I passed rocky islands and green-covered hills with patches of houses. I shared the water with other sailboats and fishermen. I stopped that first night in a small inlet. Shortly after I dropped anchor, I heard a yell from the shore. Sako and his friend, Shinichi, waved and invited me out to dinner. At the restaurant, I was taken aback when the manager greeted Sako effusively. We had a couple drinks in the bar, which we did not pay for, and afterward were escorted to a private booth already set up with dinner. Sako, I realized, was an important man. Over dinner, Sako told me he had a son with him in Japan. He was divorced from his South African wife.

"It's hard to keep an interracial marriage going," I said.

"Oh, no," he said, "it wasn't interracial. She's a white woman."

Before we parted, Sako asked when I would reach Nomaike. I was a little annoyed at the question. *What difference does it make?*

The next afternoon, soon after I anchored, Sako and Shinichi hailed me from shore. They again treated me to dinner. I realized that they were keeping track of my progress. The next day, I assured Sako, I would reach his village.

In the morning, as I neared Nomaike, Sako and Shinichi met me in a boat and guided me in. Shinichi videotaped my arrival. As I came up to the dock, I was astounded at the sight: schoolchildren, given the day off, held a banner inscribed in Japanese and English, "Welcome Harry Heckel." Rows of folding chairs held village dignitaries. Sako, Shinichi, and Nomaike's mayor, Ichiro Hamaguchi, had arranged a reception in my honor. This small village welcomed me as one would welcome a hero.

I was met with an ovation as I stepped onto the dock. I was seated near a pulpit and listened to several short speeches in Japanese. Between speeches, I was given the banner and a gigantic bouquet of flowers. I bowed after each presentation while the crowd clapped their approval.

At the end, Mayor Ichiro presented me with a plaque. In English he said, "When he will arrive in the United States, he will be the record holder of the most advanced yacht sailor."

I kept my remarks short. "At no time around the world, alone, have I ever had a reception such as this that I am getting in Nomaike," I said. "Certainly I will never forget Nomaike and all you wonderful people. I hope to come back."

I stayed in Nomaike for three days. Ichiro and Shinichi took me on tour of the Shochu brewery where I was given two bottles of this popular whiskey-like liquor. At the Kamikaze Museum, a Japanese Zero fighter plane, fished from the local bay, was on display. I was amazed at how small it was. Ichiro explained that Kamikaze pilots did not volunteer but were forced to fly. They had only enough fuel for a one-way flight to the nearest American fleet.

When I visited the Nomaike museum, I looked for Sako's boat. It wasn't on display. A friend had taken it out for a sail.

As I left Nomaike, I became depressed by the thought that a small town in America would never throw such a reception for an unknown Japanese circumnavigator.

I headed up the coast to Nagasaki, a city of half a million. The most visited spot is the hypocenter of the explosion of the second atomic bomb. This is an open tiled, circular area, about 100 meters in diameter. A large prayer monument sits on the edge, with other monuments scattered about. The most touching is the one dedicated to the 10,000 Korean slave laborers who died. The total dead numbered 75,000. It saddened me that, because of the weather, the bomb was dropped on lovely Nagasaki rather than the heavily industrialized area at the north end of Kyushu Island.

From Nagasaki, I sailed to Fukuoka Marina. Marijke and Jaap drove me to the supermarket to restock the boat for my sail home.

"I don't eat so much any more," I told Marijke, "so I don't need much."

Months later, Marijke e-mailed my children: "If we'd known what would be in the future, we would have shopped for many more supplies."

I took a final side trip by train and ferry to Shikoku Island. Maggie and Ichiro Suzuki are active Japanese environmentalists and friends of my sister, Florence Mary LaRiviere. I wanted to meet the American-born Maggie. She enthusiastically welcomed Florence Mary's environmental efforts in the San Francisco Bay area and arranged her environmental lecture series in Japan.

I arrived in Shikoku in late afternoon. The first thing Maggie asked was whether I'd like a nap or a sightseeing tour.

"Let's go, let's go," I said. I was excited to be there.

The most memorable experience of our tour was standing on the high glass-bottomed bridge that connects Shikoku and Honshu islands and looking down at the huge whirlpools created by the tide racing through the strait.

At dinner, I met Ichiro, a handsome, polite, and cultured man. He owns a ball-bearing factory on Shikoku but is moving his operations to China. He was busy finding replacement jobs for all his local employees.

After dinner, I heard how Maggie and Ichiro met. Maggie, a young and exuberant back-packer, noticed Ichiro in the Orient Express terminal in Istanbul. Ichiro was sitting on a bench, alone and discouraged. Maggie joined him, cheered him up, and traveled on with him. Ichiro's parents were initially unhappy that their son had chosen an irreverent American bride. They have since changed their minds.

My last stop was Beppu where once again I had no time to visit the sex museum. I cleared out of Japan with Customs and Immigration. I called Sako in Tokyo to say good-bye and express how much pleasure the visit to his country had given me.

In a cyber cafe, I e-mailed family and friends: "Tomorrow, 1 June, I take departure from Beppu, NE Kyushu, bound across the North

Pacific. I will miss this lovely country of Japan and its matching people. See you all somewhere down the line."

As my voyage unfolded, "somewhere down the line" came dangerously close to "the end of the line."

Chapter 24

Anatomy of a Rescue

Better pass boldly into that otherworld in the full glory of some passion than fade and wither dismally with age.
-James Joyce, *The Dead*

I provisioned *Idle Queen* for ninety days. I estimated the trip to Neah Bay, Washington State, where my brother John lived, would take no more than sixty days, at a conservative eighty miles per day. I was overly optimistic.

Cornell, in *Ocean Routes of the World,* writes, "Fair winds can be expected right across the North Pacific." He adds, "The percentage of gales in the summer months is low, although the occasional depression can pass over bringing stronger winds." I never found any consistent westerlies. Nine times I encountered winds of thirty knots or more.

In the first eleven days at sea, I experienced two headwind gales. Both came on strongly at dusk. Each gale lasted less than twenty-four hours, but I recovered from one only to be hit by the other. I considered returning to Japan.

On the morning of 19 June 2002, 700 miles east of Honshu, *Idle Queen* was running northeast before an increasing south-southwest wind. The early morning weather report from Guam warned of gale winds. At 0830, I tied off the tiller and streamed a drogue to slow the boat and help keep her on course. The drogue was commercially made and one size larger than necessary. The afternoon broadcast from Guam reported winds at forty-five knots, seas at nineteen feet. IQ ran smoothly under storm jib, quartering the seas and making about two knots. I stood in the companionway marveling at the way the stern rose to the challenge of the steep oncoming seas. I went to bed in early evening feeling comfortable and pleased to be making reasonable speed on course.

Sometime after midnight, the boat suddenly shot up in the trough and rolled down close to ninety degrees. The lurch of the boat awoke me abruptly. I had lain down fully clothed. I threw back the covers, stumbled into shoes, and hurried up the companionway. A breaking sea had slam-dunked the boat, driven the nested main boom down through the splintered boom gallows and smashed the dodger en route to a crash landing on the fantail. Most of the wooden caprails, port and starboard, were ripped loose. The winch handle was lost overboard. IQ righted herself, but the rest of the night was a rough, rolling, uneasy period. I spent it alternately braced in the companionway staring out at the waves, or lying fitfully on the settee trying to rest.

I thought the drogue was lost. I suspected that the towline chafed through at the hawse hole on the quarter bulwark. But in the morning, I saw that the towline was intact, and I pulled it in. The drogue, which consisted of a canvas parachute, was gone. The heavy nylon straps that secured the drogue to the towline broke, chafed or were cut through. Since the nylon straps were too heavy to break, one theory proposed later was that a sea animal attacked it.

The most distressing damage was the loss of the boom gallows. This left the tall stanchions, one on each side of the cockpit, without adequate bracing. These stanchions anchor the lifelines and support the steering vane control line and the topping lift. I could not afford to have them damaged, but they were endangered whenever I raised or lowered the main boom. To keep the boom from swinging wildly, I needed to run guy lines from the aft end of the boom to the bow on port and starboard. The waves were high as I leaned on a stanchion and stood precariously on a cockpit seat. I reached overhead and tied a line around the boom. I did this on both port and starboard. I ran the two lines forward outside the stays, and secured them to the Samson posts on the bow. Raising or lowering sails remained an awkward, stressful task. Eventually, I put a triple reef in the main and left it up permanently.

I was now too far off Japan to turn back.

The weather was a frustrating mixture of light headwinds, gales from any direction, and calms. I traveled the alley along 45° north, plus or minus a few degrees. Highs were consistently north of my position, lows to the south. Once, I tried unsuccessfully to get above the high by going as far north as 50°. I did not want to stop in the Aleutians; repair facilities there would be minimal. I didn't try to get south of the lows for fear of being stuck in the stable high-pressure zone and running out of wind. Even so, twice I was becalmed for several days.

I averaged closer to forty miles per day rather than the expected eighty. As the days slowly passed, I found running through my mind some lines from John Burroughs (*Waiting*):

Serene I fold my hands and wait,
Nor care for wind or tide or sea;
I rave no more 'gainst time or fate,
For, lo! my own shall come to me.

And frequently, some lines from Joaquin Miller's *Columbus*:

Brave Admiral say what shall we say
If we sight naught but seas at dawn?
Why you shall say at break of day
Sail on, sail on, sail on and on.

As I sailed on, many sights gave me pleasure. In the northern reaches, sea otters often congregated around me, staring up at the boat, pirouetting, and showing off their white bellies. One large whale steamed across my bow, puffing and blowing. Dolphins flashed by in a series of jumps and dives. For the first time, I identified Laysans, short-tailed albatrosses, and short-tailed shearwaters. Later, I noted a pair of tropic birds as far north as 40°.

Some absorbing books kept me company. E. Annie Proulx gets my vote as the best wordsmith of this generation for the novel *The Shipping News*. *Dave Barry Does Japan* is highly amusing and knowledgeable, a true mirror of what I saw of the culture. One of the original novels of the Napoleonic sea wars is *Peter Simple*, written by Frederick Marryat, a British captain who was there.

Reading kept my mind occupied. When unoccupied, my thoughts were anxious:

These toothy breaking waves embitter me,
The gods do howl and spit.
My doubtful courage struggles with adversity
And Aleut islands lure my tiny ship.
I will desert this lonely sea and sail on homeward bound.
My failing skills may not prevail
And strength to carry on may not be found
So, will this be my final sail?

In quiet moments I thought of my family. With no word from me, they would be worried.

In mid-July, family members phoned each other to check Dad's projected arrival date. Estimates ran from the end of July to early August. My brother, Carl, reminded everyone that Dad had an Emergency Position Indicating Radio Beacon (EPIRB) on board. If Idle Queen *sank, the EPIRB would send out a radio signal which would be picked up by passing airplanes.*

At the end of July, Dad's brother-in-law, Philip LaRiviere, a World War II navigator, got on the internet and studied the currents in the Pacific Ocean. After calculating Idle Queen's *speed and possible route, Philip concluded that Dad should have made land. With the family's approval, Philip and Florence Mary, on 7 August, contacted the U.S. Coast Guard at Alameda, California.*

Within days, the U.S. Coast Guard contacted the Japanese Coast Guard. The latter interviewed people who might know Dad's plans. Their conclusion: Dad would arrive in the States between 1 August and 1 September.

On 31 July, my projected passage time was running out and I was still over 2000 miles from Neah Bay. I tried to contact the U.S. Coast Guard by SSB radio, but the transmit distance was too great. One night I left the antenna upright on the deck and the top half was lost in bad weather. That left me with only short-range VHF radio to contact the outside world.

In mid-August, Carl accessed Dad's e-mail list and contacted Dad's fellow sailors:

"My father left Japan June 1 with a potential arrival date at Neah Bay, Washington, USA, of August 1. We thought we would try to reach him by ham radio. The question arises as to what frequency he might be monitoring. Do any of you know if he is monitoring the radio, and if so, what frequency, or time, we might be able to contact him? Actually, if any of you have heard from him recently, let us know."

Barbara Enloe (Tombatu), in Malaysia, e-mailed back: "Your dad is a good sailor and it might take longer than he planned. He also has a great boat…I think Harry is familiar with Rowdy's net and may be listening to it on his trip although don't know if he would talk without a license unless an emergency. It is at 2400 zulu at 14320. I will try to put out a message for Harry. Will let you know if I have any success."

Meanwhile, Florence Mary LaRiviere found an old note with a radio telephone number on it. Someone else recalled a conversation in which Dad would monitor the radio on Sundays. This information was passed along to David Hope, a family friend and ham radio operator in Virginia. David started working his ham radio network to see if Dad could be raised.

In Japan, Maggie Suzuki on Shikoku became distraught when she learned that Dad had not arrived and had not been heard from.

"I don't want to be the last one to have seen him alive," she told Florence Mary.

Several weeks before my ninety days of supplies ran out, I began to ration food and water. I no longer drank coffee, bathed, or even washed my face. I only sparingly sprinkled water over my hands. Breakfast was a handful of dried fruit. For lunch I opened a can of soup and ate half of it, undiluted, straight from the container. The remaining half I ate for dinner.

I was hungry. At night I dreamt of food. I was weakening. I no longer had the strength to walk the decks, I crawled. I desperately wanted to contact the U.S. Coast Guard for help, but I needed a ship, and a ship's radio, to transmit a message. I hadn't seen a ship for weeks. The days passed, one after another, in monotonous succession. I worried about my family. By now they would be frantic.

On 20 August, Florence Mary and Philip LaRiviere suggested that an immediate family member work with the U. S. Coast Guard to lend urgency to the situation. Carl stepped in and called Commander Hicks at the Alameda, California, post. Commander Hicks explained in detail what the U.S. Coast Guard was doing. This included Naval Tech Messages to all shipping, and Safety Net messages on an Automated Mutual Assistance Vessel Rescue System.

"The Coast Guard's computer system plots all known ships in the North Pacific," Commander Hicks said, "so that in an emergency, the computer system can plot the optimum search pattern."

With these assurances, Carl e-mailed the family on 29 August: "If any unknown EPIRB signals are received, the USCG will know exactly which vessels are in position to assist. The U.S. Coast Guard is very ready to act when it seems appropriate."

I began putting out VHF calls at random times at night: "This is sailing vessel *Idle Queen, Idle Queen.* Anyone within the sound of my voice who can transmit a message for me to the U.S. Coast Guard, please come back."

At 0245, on the morning of 31 August, a voice came back. "This is *BBC Sealand*. We can transmit a message for you."

I was momentarily speechless. Then I rallied and continued with the words I had rehearsed for this eventuality.

Later that day, Carl received an e-mail from Lt. Dubay of the U.S. Coast Guard: URGENT RELAY MESSAGE 31 AUG. 1230Z FM. SAILING VESSEL IDLE QUEEN. SAILING FM. JAPAN TO SAN FRANCISCO, 1 PERSON ON BOARD, 91 DAYS AT SEA IN POS. LAT. 4515N LON. 15315W, RUNNING 50 NM/DAY. ETA SAN FRANCISCO ON 26TH SEPT. REQUEST:

TO INFORM HIS CHILDREN ETA SAN FRANCISCO 26TH SEPT.

REQUEST TO ARRANGE SOME SHIP TO MEET HER BECAUSE SHE IS RUNNING OUT OF FOOD AND WATER FOR FEW DAYS TO COME.

Carl was also called directly and given the news. Dad's position, as Carl put it, was "right smack in the middle of nowhere." There were no indications of health or mechanical problems. As indicated, Dad had abandoned Neah Bay and was headed for San Francisco.

In the afternoon, Carl received another e-mail from the Coast Guard. The BBC Sealand, which continued on course for fifty miles, was turning back to supply Idle Queen with food and water.

At 0800 on 31 August, the VHF came alive. "This is *BBC Sealand*. We propose to supply you with a month's worth of food and water. What is your position?"

We were twelve miles apart in thick fog. As she appeared out of the fog, *BBC Sealand* proved to be a small German container ship.

Captain Hoerst Kuenzel had assembled the supplies on the deck in a crate with flotation. The supplies consisted of forty liters of water, four huge-size sausages of cold cuts, eight loaves of bread, 750 grams of butter, six packages of Ramen noodles, six cans of sweetened condensed milk, fourteen large cans of fruit, and one large jar of dehydrated asparagus soup. The load must have weighed 100kg. I could see the supplies, but getting them to me was a problem. I couldn't help. The wind was too light for me to maneuver under sail. The engine batteries were too low to start the engine. I was too weak to crank the engine over by hand.

Captain Kuenzel's crew lowered the crate into the water to float it across to me, but the current pushed it away. They tried over and over.

Captain Kuenzel nudged his ship into different positions. They tried to float the crate from different angles. Nothing worked. The crate floated tantalizingly close, but not close enough. Once I grabbed the boat hook, thinking I could snare the crate, but I was so weak I couldn't hold the boat hook steady. I watched the crate of food drift away.

In early afternoon, Captain Kuenzel tried a different tactic. Crewmembers tried to connect our ships by shooting a line across my bow. The line had a monkey fist, a hard ball, at the end. Crewmembers shot a line over and over with no success. When I had given up hope, the monkey fist landed on the bow. I lunged and grabbed it. I knotted it to a line and threw the line around the cleat. When I looked up in triumph, I saw the other end of the line trailing in the water. The crewmember had either forgotten to secure his end, or had dropped it.

Several times during the day, as first one strategy and then another failed, Captain Kuenzel called me on the radio and asked me to come aboard his ship. He reminded me of the captain at the end of my first voyage who implored me to come aboard for medical attention. A captain faced with a recalcitrant sailor is in a dilemma. But now, as then, I could not sink *Idle Queen,* even to save myself.

Late in the afternoon, Captain Kuenzel came on the radio once again. He said, "I have done all I could. I must leave you now."

I was shocked. "I'm desperate to get those supplies," I said. I hesitated, then suggested, "Please bring your ship up to mine and dump the package on my deck."

We both realized the danger. Big ships often damaged, or even sank, small boats when attempting a rescue operation. "You are sure?" Captain Kuenzel asked.

As I watched apprehensively, Captain Kuenzel, in a magnificent display of ship handling, brought *BBC Sealand* so close alongside *Idle Queen* that the food package could be dangled over my fantail. I hauled myself to my knees, but I was not strong enough to pull the crate to the deck. Two crewmembers watched me struggle, then shimmied down a rope ladder. They deposited the rescue package on the deck and scurried back aboard their ship. Captain Kuenzel raised his arm in a final farewell. *BBC Sealand* steamed off back on her course.

I sat on the fantail, ripped open the cold cuts, and ate several pieces. I drank a bottle of water. I felt refreshed and full, something I had not felt for weeks. Over the course of the evening, I dragged the supplies below, little by little. With the new provisions, I slowly gained weight and strength. In a few days I walked the decks again instead of crawling. The food lasted to the end of the voyage.

After Idle Queen *was re-provisioned, the Coast Guard contacted Carl.*

"USCG considers the case closed on this one," Carl e-mailed the family. "One can view it as the beginning of a 1345 nautical mile cruise from the middle of nowhere to SF with an ETA of September 26, give or take a few days, depending on weather.

"A fine, professional job by the Alameda crew.—Thanks.

"PS: If, however, any of you bump into the BBC Sealand, *I hope you'll buy the Captain a measure of grog, and send the bill to Dad. Ditto the USCG gang at Alameda."*

A thank you letter was mailed to Captain Kuenzel at his base in Emden, Germany. A 5-lb box of See's chocolates was sent to the coastguardsmen in Alameda. The accompanying note read, in part: "Please accept our deepest thanks for the competence, persistence, and caring you showed for Idle Queen *and her captain, Harry L. Heckel, Jr."*

Believing that the crisis with Dad was over, family members went about their normal activities. In California, Florence Mary and Philip met with their conservation group, The Committee to Complete the Refuge. One meeting was covered by Douglas Fischer, a reporter from The Oakland Tribune. *During the meeting, an old friend of the LaRivieres—"completely out of order," Florence Mary pointed out—leaned over to the reporter and confided, "Doug, Florence's brother is eighty-six years old and he is…"*

Intrigued, Douglas Fischer made some phone calls, researched sailing across the Pacific, and wrote a feature article about Dad.

The help from *BBC Sealand* did not mark the end of my troubles. As early as 26 June, I had repaired small rips in the mainsail and jib. On 5 September, in one of the ubiquitous squalls, the jib was ripped beyond repair. This was not an overwhelming loss since I could get along, albeit more slowly, with the staysail. A little after midnight on 17 September, 780 miles from San Francisco, I jibed the boat in a strong wind and big seas. Although it was a normal jibe, it was one too many. The mainsail exploded; "shredded" may be a better word. I was stunned. How was I to get IQ into any port without a sail aft of the mast? Worried, I lay awake the rest of the night wondering what to do. Then I remembered that I had stowed away up in the forepeak a spare staysail. This sail, repaired in Jamaica on my first voyage, had not been used for ten years. In the morning, I cut some slides from the mainsail, attached the staysail hanks, and had a sail of sorts aft of the mast. It provided much help in going to weather, enough to get me into a port, but not enough to reach San Francisco.

On 25 September, 715 miles from San Francisco, I knew I could not stay sufficiently north to reach this port. Northerly winds could be expected from then on. I feared I'd be blown south and driven away from the coast. Hawaii was 1610 miles away, all down wind. Heading to Hawaii seemed the prudent course, even though winds are notoriously light around the Islands in October. Although my family wouldn't know about my change in plans, I turned south.

On 27 September, U.S. Coast Guard Commander Hicks contacted Carl. The Coast Guard had overheard a conversation between Idle Queen *and a freighter named* Joyous Land. *The transmission was not clear, and Commander Hicks could not contact either vessel, but Dad was headed to Hawaii. His estimated ETA into Honolulu was 15 October. Commander Hicks thought the estimate optimistic.*

On 10 October, as we waited to hear from Dad, an e-mail flashed across the country.

"They say it is a small world," Carl wrote. "I just met the captain of the BBC Sealand.*"*

Carl was on his way to work in New Jersey, driving along an estuary, when he glanced at the ships at the docks. To his astonishment, one was the BBC Sealand. *Carl immediately changed direction and headed for the harbor. In the car was a copy of* The Oakland Tribune *folded to the article by Douglas Fischer with its accompanying picture of Dad and* Idle Queen. *Newspaper in hand, Carl strode purposely up the dock to the* BBC Sealand. *At the gangplank, he shouted for permission to see the captain. Shortly, he was face to face with the man who had saved Dad's life. Carl pointed to the newspaper and asked Captain Kuenzel if the sailboat looked familiar. Realization dawned in Captain Kuenzel's eyes.*

"The 'Old Man,'" Carl said, referring to the picture caption, "is my father."

The two sat down and had coffee. Captain Kuenzel said Dad looked well and appeared mentally alert. He knew, having been in contact with the Alameda Coast Guard, that Dad was headed for Hawaii.

The next morning, Carl returned with four dozen doughnuts and a bottle of Auborg Schnapps. He asked the man on watch if he was aboard when they helped the sailor in the Pacific.

"It was your father?" the crew member asked. "I was one of the guys that went on board the sailboat to help him with the food. It was too heavy for an old man. We thought we'd better help him."

Before the man headed off to find Captain Kuenzel, he stepped into the crews' mess and rattled off in Tagalog. Heads appeared around the corner. Carl went over and shook hands all around.

Captain Kuenzel asked Carl to give his regards to Dad when he sees him. Then he smiled and added, "Of course, I may see him before you do!"

I did not have Hawaii charts aboard. I studied *Reed's Almanac.* Using information in the almanac, I managed to make a rough chart. I passed down the channel between Oahu and Molokai. I rounded the island of Oahu, even though I couldn't find the buoy off Diamond Head. At 2130, I hove-to with the lights of Waikiki beckoning me from a mile away. I needed to start the engine, but it had to be hand-cranked. I needed to locate the channel entrance that led through the reef. These seemed impossible tasks. I couldn't do either. I was exhausted. I stumbled below to the radio.

"Honolulu Coast Guard, Honolulu Coast Guard," I croaked. "Sailing vessel *Idle Queen.*"

The reply came back immediately. "*Idle Queen*, what is your position?"

I was not asked the usual questions: *How big a boat? What color? How many masts? How many people aboard?* An All Points Bulletin had been sent out, and the coastguardsman recognized the boat's name. They had expected me and arrived within minutes. I clawed down the sails as a coastguardsman jumped aboard. He attached a line to the bow and took the tiller. After looking me over, he said, "Put on your life jacket."

As I was being tied up to a dock at the Hawaii Yacht Club, the coastguardsman used his personal cell phone to call Harry Third in Virginia. He handed me the phone, but my hand shook and I had trouble hearing. He took over and told Third that I had arrived and that I was well.

The date was 21 October 2002. I had been at sea for 142 days.

I felt strange on land.

Chapter 25

Older But No Wiser: Forging On

A good traveler has no fixed plans and is not intent on arriving.
-Lao Tzu

I felt lost and a little dizzy as I stood on the dock. I had not showered in four and a half months, but I didn't have the energy to face that task. I stepped back onto the boat, went below, and flopped onto the berth. That night I had my first restful sleep since leaving Japan.

In the morning I trudged fifty feet up the dock to the yacht club shower. Emerging refreshed, I found a pleasant surprise. The yacht club restaurant is not open in the morning, but several ladies had come in early to prepare me a welcoming breakfast.

This gesture was typical of the Hawaii Yacht Club hospitality I enjoyed during my winter stay. Even after I moved *Idle Queen* next door to the Ala Wai Marina, due to lack of space, the yacht club became my social home. Whenever I walked into the bar in the early evening, Commodore Al Bento stood me a drink. When he was not present, the bartender said, "The Commodore will be here soon."

Every Thursday I ate lunch at the club with a small contingency reminiscent of my coffee klatches in other ports. The group consisted of Nick, a local sailor; a visiting Norwegian sailor; and Henk Duelde, a Dutch singlehander. Henk's big steel boat, *Campana*, was berthed next to me. From his boat, Henk broadcast weekly on Dutch television. His broadcasts, as he had sailed in a solo nonstop around-the-world race, had made him a celebrity. He planned to sail home via the Northeast Passage, around the top of Siberia. Much to Henk's disgust, the Russians insisted that he have two Russians aboard while he was in Russian waters. I learned later that Henk's trip back to The Netherlands through the Siberian ice floes was an outstanding success.

One day at lunch at the yacht club, a woman walked in and asked a man seated near me if he knew a Harry Heckel. I took a quick look—she was a handsome, mature woman, well dressed, wearing a hat—and promptly spoke up. She came to the table, introduced herself as Carol, and handed me a large box.

"This is a care package from Bob and Rose Selfridge," she said. The Selfridges, who were in Australia, learned of my arrival and arranged the package with Carol's help.

Carol and I unwrapped the gift together. It contained everything a shipwrecked sailor on an uninhabited island would hope to find. Carol sailed the Pacific extensively, so she knew what toiletries and food items to buy. I enjoyed Carol's company on a number of occasions. I was never able to take her out to dinner; as I discovered, she was too good a vegetarian cook.

Repairing *Idle Queen* was a high priority. I carted some 2x6s from the other side of Honolulu and remade the boom crutch. I replaced and painted caprails, as needed. While a sailmaker in Kahului made a sail cover and dodger, I ordered a jib and mainsail from Hong Kong's Lee Sails, the same shop I visited when I was in Hong Kong.

When I called, the woman taking my order asked, "Are you the Mr. Heckel who came in to see us two years ago?"

As I worked on *Idle Queen*, I recharged my own batteries in preparation for my final ocean crossing and the end of my circumnavigation. The following May, with new sails and most of *Idle Queen's* repairs completed, I left Hawaii.

It took twenty-seven days for this slow boat and lazy skipper to sail to the mainland. When I arrived through the Golden Gate after dark, I couldn't find a place to tie-up. I hove-to off the Embarcadero one night and anchored in high wind off Coyote Cove a few miles down the peninsula the next. Florence Mary and Philip LaRiviere used their influence to get me a slip at Pete's Harbor in Redwood City. Normally, the dockage does not allow transient boats. Florence Mary told me what to say.

"Mark Sanders said you probably had a place for me," I said at the harbor office. Sanders was an important figure in the yachting community.

When I went in to pay my rent the next month, the substitute dockmaster said sourly, "I see you're a transient. You must have some pull to get in here."

Florence Mary and Philip arranged a visit to the Eleventh Coast Guard District station in Alameda. We were joined by Douglas Fischer, *The Oakland Tribune* reporter, whom I enjoyed meeting. At the station, I greeted the men who had been so helpful to me and my family: Commanders David Swatland and Mike Hicks, Lt. Jerry

Dubay, and Petty Officers Dennis McNamara and Kevin Denicher. I greatly admire this group.

In October 2003, I left Pete's Harbor and slowly sailed down the coast. I was in no hurry. When this circumnavigation ended, I knew I would never sail alone again. After the traumatic passage from Japan, I expected this final leg to be trouble-free.

As usual, I was wrong.

The trip south was made through a mixture of light airs and near-gale force winds. When I reached the area between Catalina Island and Point Fermin on the mainland, the wind died—and so did my engine starter. For two nights and a day, I struggled to keep IQ from drifting onto one shore or the other. I finally called for a tow from Vessel Assist and was taken into Dana Point Shipyard, just north of San Diego. The tow boat captain took me to breakfast afterward; he could well afford to.

After leaving San Diego, I planned to skip Mexican ports and head directly for Guatemala. As I approached the Gulf of Tehuantepec, south of Acapulco, water and steam started to spurt from a ruptured water jacket gasket. This ended my motoring. In this area of prevailing calms, I sailed as best I could back to Acapulco, but was unable to make it into the harbor. When I was close to the narrow harbor entrance, a mid-day squall drove me back to sea. On VHF, I couldn't raise the Port Captain or the marina to arrange a tow. *Idle Queen* drifted under a flapping sail. I lay below considering my options when a couple of toots brought me on deck. *My Pastime*, a sleek, modern maxi-motor yacht, lay fifty meters off.

A woman shouted over, "Are you all right?"

I explained my situation. Alan and Marla Palash were headed for Costa Rica. They hadn't planned to go into Acapulco, but they decided to tow me in. Nine miles and two hours later, at 2000, I was anchored in seventy feet of water off Acapulco Yacht Club. The Palashes called their good-byes and headed back out to sea.

Over the next week, the engine was repaired by two able mechanics from the yacht club. Word of my mechanical problems spread among family and friends. Maggie Suzuki in Japan e-mailed my son Carl: "Thank you for the update. Have you ever been to Mexico? They are driving cars much older than thirty years, and presumably the mechanics will be good at fixing motors that really ought to be replaced…The boat is certainly being true to its name."

Shortly after I reached Acapulco, my daughter Faith flew out from Virginia to visit. When I was in San Diego, I bought a new dinghy and I needed a dinghy motor. I asked Faith to buy one and bring it with her. She bought the motor at a store an hour's drive from her house during an ice storm. Two days before her flight, she hauled the motor to the airport to be inspected for shipment. Because the box had been opened, the motor was rejected. Faith drove an hour back to the store, this time during a snowstorm, and exchanged the motor for one in its original unopened box. The day before her flight, she returned to the airport for a second, successful inspection.

In Acapulco, Faith presented herself and the motor at Customs. The inspector asked her, "Is this item worth $300?"

Thinking of the hazardous winter driving she'd done to get the motor, her two trips to the airport, and the hassle of hauling the heavy box around, Faith replied firmly, "No, this is *not* worth $300!"

She was waved through Customs. The motor cost $700. The same model sells in Acapulco for $1300.

When I left Acapulco, I endured a frustratingly slow light-wind passage south. However, there were some compensations. The sunsets along the Central American coast are the most spectacular I have seen. Some were blood red, but bright colors, no pastels, from yellow to mauve were present.

Sea life was entrancing. On some calm nights, darting fish stirred the phosphorescence into brilliant, bright white flashes, so that the surrounding sea looked like an underwater Fourth of July display. Four large turtles crossed my path. Sharks and mahi-mahi chased schools of small fish. Two large whales passed close by on the way south. A small whale swam back and forth under the boat several times, an activity which left me too uneasy to fully appreciate. Athletic dolphins showed off their jumping ability. I often shooed brown, red-footed, and masked boobies off my bowsprit where they delighted in making a mess. A rare least petrel spent one foggy night in the cockpit. Forster's terns and red-necked phalaropes were part of the scene.

Guatemala is building a marina in Puerto Quetzal. I don't recommend this rudimentary, expensive, poorly-designed project. The marina had no water or electricity, and I was still charged $1/ foot of boat length per night to tie up. It is near the town of San Jose, a slovenly place hardly meeting standards of a Middle Eastern city. I stayed only a few nights and did no exploring of the countryside.

When I reached Costa Rica, I tied up at the Flamingo Marina, even though it was officially closed. The marina owners were fighting the government's closure edict, believing it was politically motivated. They defiantly rented me a slip. I was the only foreigner among the local fishing boats.

I hired a taxi to take me to the airport in San Jose when I flew to Virginia for my annual visit. Although the eight-hour drive cost four hundred dollars, I deemed the charge worthwhile considering the extent of my baggage. When I returned to Costa Rica, I arrived late in the day. By pre-arrangement, the same driver met my plane. Because of the late hour, he took me to his home where I was given dinner and a room for the night. The next morning he drove me back to the marina.

One of the famous inland nature areas of Costa Rica is Monteverde. The bus ride there was uncomfortable, over an unpaved, rough, and potholed road. In Monteverde I hiked through deep jungle on well-designed and maintained trails. The jungle is so thick it's hard to see anything through the foliage. I looked for a quetzal, a reputedly beautiful long-tailed, tropical bird, the pride of Central America. I didn't see one. What I saw were lots of howler monkeys.

The road from Monteverde to Volcan Arenal makes a big loop northwestward to get around large graceful Lake Arenal, which winds in and out around the hilly promontories. The little town of Fortuna is on the east side of the lake. I like Fortuna with its inexpensive hotel, good restaurant, fine view of the mountain, and extensive bird life. I should have spent more time there, sitting in my rocker in front of the hotel and watching the cloud patches drift across the top of Mount Arenal. The crater on the Fortuna side of the mountain is so crenellated that lava flow tracks can be seen. A hot lava flow was visible the day before I arrived. This volcano is said to be the third most active in the world. Kilauea must be one of the other two, but I don't know the third.

Along the Lake Arenal road, our busload of passengers was excited and amused when we came upon a dozen coatis frolicking in the middle of the highway. The small, raccoon-related animals gamboled about, waved their long tails in the air, and stared at the busy photographers.

When I left Flamingo Marina and sailed south, I skipped Punta Arenas, for Faido and I were there in 1982, and went into Golfito, Costa Rica's great natural harbor. It is a few miles off the direct sailing line south, and yachts often bypass it. They miss a relaxing quiet harbor and village. The marina docks are expensive, but I secured a mooring at a reasonable price.

From Golfito, I crossed the sound by ferry to visit Osa Peninsula, famous for its wildlife and poachers. Hotel Cabinas Mangalores sits in its own little private nature preserve. A stream runs through the wooded grounds. The white-faced capuchin monkeys cavort through the trees. Although they also bounced around the dining room, they were better behaved than many monkeys I've seen elsewhere. The big noisy gaudy scarlet macaws and the equally noisy, smaller green mealy parrots left me gawking. One parrot was a real showman. While I stood near him at the feeder, he showed off his vocabulary of squawks, calls, and whistles.

I hated to leave Golfito and Costa Rica.

Heading south, I reached Panamanian waters when the engine suddenly went "oomph" and stopped. The problem was easy to see: a five by ten foot heavy, plastic-weave fishing bag was wrapped around the propeller. With no wind, I could not move the boat. I drifted without power.

I put the dinghy overboard and futilely tugged at the bag. I thought of diving into the water and under the boat with a knife in my teeth, but the roll of the boat in the heavy southern swell dissuaded me. On *Idle Queen* again, using a constrictor knot, I tied a rope to the bag and threaded the rope through a winch on deck. By backing the engine by hand and exercising the winch, I painstakingly worked the bag free. The operation took four anxious hours while the boat drifted slowly toward shore. If I hadn't freed the bag, I could have been beached. I silently congratulated myself for my policy of traveling well offshore on coastwise passages.

At the Panama Canal, I needed a crew for the canal transit. I appealed to my family. In November, Carl and Dixie, and Florence and her husband, Mike, took their vacations and flew down to serve as cook and three line handlers. I hired Harper, a 72-year-old Panamanian, as the fourth line handler.

Carl, Dixie, Mike and I flew into Panama late one November night. We shared a cab--$25 per couple—to the Country Inn which overlooked the yacht harbor. Although it was 2300, Dad stood at the reception desk awaiting our arrival. We immediately adjourned to the hotel's restaurant, TGI Friday, for dinner and a drink. Afterward, Dixie and Carl went upstairs to their room.

Mike and I were staying on the boat. We followed Dad along a paved path to the yacht club where a launch motored us out to Idle Queen. *IQ was near the high Bridge of the Americas. At night the bridge lights arched in the sky like a rainbow of stars. The thundering traffic seemed constant.*

The next morning, we prepared for the transit. When Dad transited the canal twenty-two years earlier, the charge had been $13, with an $80 deposit. Now the cost is $600 for the first day, $650 if a second day is needed, with an $800 deposit. Back then, the non-commercial boats were rafted together three in a row. Today, these boats are fit in against the canal wall out of the way of the large commercial tankers or cruise ships.

Dad showed us the coiled lines, two forward and two aft, which would secure the boat to the line handlers on the canal bank. The man on the bank would throw each of us a "monkey fist," a ball wrapped in heavy rope. (The monkey fist we used in practice was the one left behind by BBC Sealand.) Dad cautioned us not to catch or get hit by this very hard ball. After we scrambled about the deck, locating and grabbing the monkey fist, it had to be quickly tied to a line that the canal handler would pull back to the bank. Our job was to tighten or slacken the line around the cleat to keep the boat straight in the locks. Sudden surges of water filling or draining from the locks, or from the large ships sharing the locks, could skew the boat and perhaps ram it into the lock wall.

Even after practice, this responsibility made me nervous. I lay in my berth that night and visualized the monkey fist dropping down. In my mind, I quickly knotted it to a line and threw the line in a figure eight around the cleat. "Quickly" is not a word usually associated with me. I feared that I would make a mistake and damage Idle Queen.

While we awaited the day of transit, we shopped for groceries and enjoyed Panama City. At the grocery store I was astonished at the number of American brands – General Mills and Smuckers – and the American merchandise, Barbie and Little Kitty. The store employed a lot of people. One worker unloaded carts; another bagged groceries. Outside, one man hailed cabs. The cab drivers were an aggressive lot. Braying horns roiled in the air as stop signs were ignored. Cabs from all directions converged in the middle of the intersection, creeping, then pushing forward in an attempt to cross first.

Downtown Panama City was another surprise, an impressive skyline of gleaming metal buildings. We spotted a casino and a Hard Rock Cafe and American banks. Burger King, McDonald's and Wendy's attested to the American presence. In the middle of the day, eight lanes of traffic, as thick as rush hour, swooped around the area. We stood in vain in a pedestrian cross walk awaiting a break in the traffic. We slowly realized the secret of crossing. We stood next to a native. When he stepped out into the curb lane, we stepped out with him.

Oncoming traffic was forced to stop. We moved with him into the second lane, forcing that lane to stop. Slowly, one lane at a time, we crossed the street.

Back at the boat, we learned that our transit was scheduled for Wednesday morning at seven, a time change from five, which made all but one of us happy.

The canal consists of six locks, three on the Atlantic side and three on the Pacific. Once in a lock, massive doors close and water spews in or is bled out to lower or raise the boat to the next level. To my utter relief, we weren't needed as line handlers. Through each lock we were rafted to a boat that was tied to the canal wall.

After three locks on the Pacific side, we motored through the Galliard Cut to the final locks. Around gentle curves, the surrounding jungle screeched with howler monkeys. Standing sentry on the shore were Titan, Goliath and Hercules, the three tallest cranes in the world.

We lagged behind the other, faster boats that shared the locks with us. Worried about our speed, the required Panamanian advisor on board hurried us off channel and through The Banana Cut, a short cut between two small islands. We emerged into Gatun Lake too late. The other boats had already entered the locks, the doors were closed, and we would not finish the transit that day.

We anchored in the lake. After our advisor was picked up, we faced a relaxing day with nothing to do. We were anchored off a resort, now closed for the season. In summer, Harper said, the resort was alive with lights and music, swimmers and swingers. Harper pointed out the swimmers' float. A large net enclosed the float all the way to the lake's bottom, Harper explained, to keep the crocodiles out. We peered uneasily into the water. We didn't go swimming.

Harper told us about his younger years when he worked on tuna and shrimp boats between Panama and Africa. Although retired, he daily walks the three miles from his home to the yacht club to pick up odd jobs, such as line handling. He and his wife, a retired government worker, put their three children through college. One daughter is a lawyer.

We remarked on the number of retired U.S. military personnel who stayed on in Panama after the canal give-away. Harper said when the United States proposed giving the canal back to Panama, the Panamanians voted on the issue. Seventy-five percent did not want the Americans to give up the canal. A lot of the economy left the country with us.

Harper told a story about the canal mules. The mules look like enclosed golf carts. Lines from large ships and tankers are attached to these vehicles which are driven along tracks at the canal's edge to help guide the ships through. Not long ago, the mule driver was a rookie, a woman who had worked for the canal for years in a supervisory position. An experienced driver was training her when the line from a tanker was violently jerked, pulling the mule off its track. As the mule fell into the canal, the trainer grabbed his co-worker and tumbled backward onto the canal path. The two workers were safe; the mule was a total loss.

As the afternoon wore on, we watched big tankers exit the canal from the Atlantic side, headed for Panama City. Tankers from Panama City began to gather. They anchored in the lake down channel from us, ready to transit the next day.

In late afternoon, we watched dark clouds approach, their black tendrils appearing like a blackout curtain obscuring the horizon. Before Idle Queen *was engulfed, Dad draped a tarp over the boom and secured it to the life lines. Rain thumped on the tarp and we retreated to the cabin for dinner.*

After dinner we contemplated the sleeping arrangements. Idle Queen *sleeps only three comfortably. Dad proposed that he and Harper sleep on deck, while the young people took the forward berth and the settee. We young people thought it ludicrous that the two oldest crewmembers would take the most uncomfortable beds. We were emphatic: Carl and Dixie took the forward berth, Harper slept on the settee, Dad slept on a cushion on the cabin floor. Mike and I, veteran tent campers, slept on the cockpit benches. We went to bed during a driving rain. The tarp, we discovered, was not wide enough to cover the entire cockpit. I awoke some time in the early hours with rain in my face. Extending an arm and a leg, I stretched the tarp so accumulated water ran off into the lake. I glanced over at Mike; he was doing the same on his side. In the morning, our pillows and clothes were soaked, but we slept surprisingly well.*

That day we waited for an Advisor to appear and guide us into the final lock. We waited through breakfast, then lunch. We watched as the big tankers, one by one, disappeared around the bend to the lock. After lunch a tour boat filled with elderly vacationers motored in and dropped anchor near us. The boat was beautiful, made of gleaming teak, and reputedly once belonged to Al Capone, circa 1920, and used for smuggling. We learned this from a woman who recognized Carl and Dixie from their hotel. They began talking and soon the vacationers heard Dad's story. They were suitably impressed. One woman said meeting Dad was the highlight of her trip. Another asked if he needed a traveling companion. Dad pretended not to hear. We were rafted to this tour boat in the remaining locks.

Exiting the final lock, we motored to Colon and docked at the yacht club. Before leaving the boat, Harper shook hands all around. He admonished us not to walk anywhere in Colon; the streets were not safe. He jumped to the pier and bent down to stuff his eighty dollar pay in his backpack. When he stood again, he held a knife with a long serrated blade. He grinned at my appalled face.

"No one will mess with me," Harper said, as he set off to walk the dangerous streets to the bus station.

That night we splurged on hotel rooms. After dinner in the hotel restaurant, Mike went out the front door to smoke on the sidewalk. A hotel employee followed and stood nearby. When Mike finished his cigarette, the employee followed him back inside and returned to his duties.

The next day, we took a cab to the bus station, a squalid place teeming with people noisily selling lottery tickets, snacks and trinkets. The bus itself was amazing. For two dollars each, we sat in the upper deck in air-conditioned comfort as an Angelina Jolie movie, in Spanish, played on a giant television screen. Back in Panama City, we spent the afternoon shopping for souvenirs and Christmas presents. We took a break to see Dad off in a taxi to the bus terminal to return to Colon and Idle Queen. *Later, I wished we had suggested he call when he made it safely to the boat. Carl pointed out that I had never worried about Dad going back and forth to strange towns. That was before I had seen Colon.*

"We should go to Balboa Yacht Club and see if Harper made it back okay," Carl said. But we were too busy shopping to worry about Harper, either.

On the plane home the next day, back to the world of paying jobs, I was grateful that Dad had included us in his adventure. I better understood his curiosity about other peoples and places. I appreciated his love of travel.

It sure beat working.

In November 2004, I sailed from Panama to Key West. One disastrous morning, 200 miles south of the western end of Cuba, the two attachments of the backstay to the hull broke simultaneously. The backstay is a vital support for the mast. I frantically replaced the broken stays with a jury-rigged rope system to keep the mast stabilized. I traveled on uneasily, aware that a heavy gust of wind could topple the mast. As a precaution, I traveled with shortened sail. Twelve days later, with great relief, I reached Oceanside Marina in Key West, the mast still standing. I had repairs made.

From Key West, my travels almost over, I made two detours before the end. The first was a sentimental journey. In 1973, Faido and I sailed across Lake Okeechobee from Florida's east coast to its west. I decided to travel the route from west to east. This time I had problems. Near Ft. Myers, I ran hard aground on a sandbar and had to be towed off. I reflected that I had sailed around the world twice, and my first grounding was back in Florida. Eventually, I reached St. Lucie on Florida's east coast and took my second detour. Instead of turning north to journey's end, I sailed nonstop south to Miami to visit Richard and Colleen Fain. Richard was Carl's roommate at Berkeley, and the Fains were interested in my travels. An outsider might find the get-together amusing: I run a 32-foot sailboat; Richard runs the Royal Caribbean Cruise Lines.

From Miami, I sailed north once again and docked at a marina in the Intracoastal Waterway east of Jacksonville. Although this was a leisurely five-day sail, the trip strained my endurance. When I docked, I could barely toss a line to the dock hand.

A few days later, fully recovered, I tied up on the waterfront at Jacksonville. I was greeted and congratulated by friends and family. The date was 4 June 2005. I was eighty-nine-years old. I had completed my second solo circumnavigation.

There would not be a third.

Epilogue

No more will he cross oceans, though the seas they still are there
The Queen, now really Idle, shows her lack of loving care
His worldwide friends, they wonder, if there is some mistake
The skipper hides his roguish smile as he looks out at the wake.
-H L Heckel, Jr., *s/v Idle Queen*

What is the significance, if any, of all this solo travel around the world by a fellow in his eighties? First, it illustrates the point that most of us retire to a sedentary life far earlier than physically or mentally necessary. I could have been working in harness for many of these years and thus lifting a grain of sand off the load that is the government pension system. My children have been amazingly supportive, but I am sure they would rather see me behind a desk than behind a compass.

Secondly, it should be noted that I did not spend much time at sea. The greater part was spent with new friends in old cultures under conditions provided only in a group of yachtsmen. My curious children, visiting me in many corners of the world, have also learned to appreciate the influence of travel on understanding the significance of what goes on in the world.

Now it's time for someone else to pull up the anchor and go looking for the known.

On June 23, 2007, in a celebration at the city park in Newport News, Virginia, Harry Heckel Jr. received the Joshua Slocum Society International's (JSSI) Golden Circle Award. Named for the first man to sail alone around the world, the award is given to documented solo circumnavigators. The Society's commodore, Ted Jones, and his wife, June, flew down from Connecticut to make the presentation. Fifty friends and relatives were on hand, including sailors Betty Root, Maryan Koehler, Capt. Kirk and Cath McGeorge, and Ann and Fabe Saxe. Other sailors sent cards and gifts. A television station aired the presentation.

Later that year, Harry nominated Captain Hoerst Kuenzel of BBC Sealand for the JSSI's Northern Light award for aiding a sailor in distress. Captain Kuenzel received his plaque in Vienna.

Now ninety-six, Harry lives with son Carl and daughter-in-law Dixie in Virginia.

In 2012, Idle Queen *was sold to a man from Massachusetts. He plans to keep the boat's name.*

Afterword

My sister Faith works in Richmond, Virginia. One Friday night she and several co-workers went out to dinner. As she walked through the restaurant's bar area, Faith overheard a man sitting on a bar stool say to his companion, "I know the oldest man to sail alone around the world."

Faith stopped. "Excuse me," she said, "but I know the oldest man to sail alone around the world."

The man swiveled around to face her. "No," he said, "I know the oldest man who sailed alone around the world."

Faith was indignant that someone else claimed that honor. "Well, I for sure know the oldest man to sail alone around the world," she retorted, "and I don't know you."

"I'm Robert Givens," the man said, "and I'm talking about my boss's father."

"And who," demanded Faith, "is your boss?"

"Harry Heckel Third."

31166669R00127

Made in the USA
Lexington, KY
01 April 2014